Hypnotherapy:
a handbook

Open University Press
Psychotherapy Handbooks Series
Series editor: Windy Dryden

Hypnotherapy: a handbook

Edited by
MICHAEL HEAP
and
WINDY DRYDEN

Open University Press
Milton Keynes · Philadelphia

Open University Press
Celtic Court
22 Ballmoor
Buckingham
MK18 1XW

and
1900 Frost Road, Suite 101
Bristol, PA 19007, USA

First published 1991
Reprinted 1993, 1995, 1998

British Library Cataloguing in Publication Data

Hypnotherapy.
   1. Hypnotherapy
   I. Heap, Michael   II. Dryden, Windy   III. Series 616.89162

   ISBN 0–335–09888–6
   ISBN 0–335–09887–8 (pbk)

Library of Congress Cataloging-in-Publication Data

Hypnotherapy: a handbook/edited by Michael Heap and Windy Dryden.
    p. cm.—(Psychotherapy handbooks series)
   Includes index.
   ISBN 0–335–09888–6. — ISBN 0–335–09887–8 (pbk.)
   1. Hypnotism—Therapeutic use.   I. Heap, Michael.   II. Dryden,
Windy.   III. Series.
RC495.H99 1991
616.89'162—dc20   90–26756
                                                           CIP

Typeset by Colset Private Limited, Singapore
Printed and bound in Great Britain by
Biddles Limited, Guildford and King's Lynn

Contents

The editors and contributors

WINDY DRYDEN is Professor of Counselling at Goldsmiths' College, University of London.

MICHAEL HEAP is a Clinical Psychologist in private practice and part-time Lecturer in Psychology at the Department of Psychiatry, University of Sheffield.

DAVID A. ALEXANDER is a Senior Lecturer in Psychology, at the Department of Mental Health, University of Aberdeen.

ASSEN ALLADIN is a Clinical Psychologist at Waterford Hospital, St John's, Newfoundland.

GIAN S. DEGUN is a Clinical Psychologist in the Elderly Speciality for South Birmingham Health Authority.

MARCIA D. DEGUN is a Clinical Psychologist at Warley Hospital, Essex.

H.B. GIBSON is a Clinical Psychologist in retirement and is an Honorary Research Fellow at the University of Hertfordshire.

BARRY B. HART is Head of Clinical Psychology Services at Scunthorpe General Hospital.

CHRISSI IOANNOU is a Clinical Psychologist at the Child and Family Unit, Lincoln.

HELLMUT W.A. KARLE is a Clinical Psychologist in retirement and was formerly at Guy's Hospital, London.

It is deeply regretted that PAULINE E. NICOLAOU formerly a dental surgeon in London, died shortly after the first printing of this book.

J.B. WILKINSON is a retired Consultant Chest Physician in London.

Preface

This book is intended for those professionals who are concerned with the management and treatment of medical and psychological disorders and the counselling of people with behavioural and emotional problems, and who wish to learn more about the applications of hypnosis to their work.

The contributors to this book are drawn from the professions of psychology, medicine and dentistry. They are all British and this reflects a recently growing trend for professional practitioners of therapeutic hypnosis in this country to publish their work in book form. The reader, however, will soon realize the indebtedness of those working in this area to the ideas and research findings of American authors, particularly in the field of experimental hypnosis.

The book assumes no prior knowledge of hypnosis on the reader's part, the first two chapters forming an introduction to the subject which will prepare the reader for the material to follow. However, detailed accounts of the history of hypnosis and the numerous theories of hypnosis have not been included; these topics are discussed in other recent publications which are mentioned in Chapter 1.

As editors, we would like to express our thanks to each contributor for his or her work in producing this volume, and to Mrs Valerie Heap and Mrs Vera Pratt for their assistance in preparing the final manuscript.

Michael Heap and Windy Dryden

Acknowledgements

The editors and contributors would like to acknowledge the authors and publishers for kind permission to reproduce the following tables.

Table 3.1 W. Heinemann publishers (Lader, M. and Marks, I., (1971)) *Clinical Anxiety*, London: W. Heinemann

Table 6.1 Dr Shirley Pearce and Dr Annabel Broome ('A review of cognitive-behavioural methods for the treatment of chronic pain' by S. Pearce in *Proceedings of the First International Conference of the Pain Interest Group*, Liverpool, 1984, Edited by A. Broome).

Table 6.2 Dr Shirley Pearce and Dr Annabel Broome ('A review of cognitive-behavioural methods for the treatment of chronic pain' by S. Pearce in *Proceedings of the First International Conference of the Pain Interest Group*, Liverpool, 1984, Edited by A. Broome).

Table 8.1 Dr P.G.F. Nixon and *The Practitioner* ('The human function curve, with special reference to cardiovascular disorders: Part I', by P.G.F. Nixon in *The Practitioner*, 1976, Vol. 217, pp. 765–70).

Introduction to hypnosis

MICHAEL HEAP

Before we can begin to understand the nature of hypnotherapy, its rationale, its aims, and the practical manner whereby these aims are realized, or at least attempted, we must first direct our attention to the nature of hypnosis itself. Hypnosis is a psychological phenomenon, not a therapy, and because it is a complex and contentious subject about which there is much misunderstanding and disagreement, it is necessary to devote a full chapter to an attempt to explain its nature and its many aspects, both theoretical and practical.

In this and the following chapter, a description of hypnosis will be put forward with the point of view and needs of the therapist in mind, rather than the theoretician or experimental psychologist. This means differences in emphasis and perhaps a more lax attitude to questions such as definition, theory and scientific evidence. If we consider the needs of those whose aim it is to help people with psychological or medical disabilities, then we may pose the question 'What ways of thinking about hypnosis are the most useful for these purposes?' We will thus arrive at a view of hypnosis which differs somewhat from that derived by asking the same question on behalf of those in search of a scientific understanding of the subject.

Now this conclusion may cause the reader some alarm in view of the continuing struggle of hypnosis to establish its scientific credentials. However, in Chapter 2 it will be argued that this difference of viewpoint is inevitable, and so long as each respects the needs of and demands placed upon the other, then there need be no great disagreement between theorist and practitioner, and their work may be mutually informative.

In the final analysis, however, it is to science and empiricism that we need to turn concerning those conjectures about hypnosis which are amenable to disproof and therefore, according to Popper (1963), legitimate matters for scientific enquiry. Thus the assertions that 'Hypnosis improves recall' and 'Hypnosis improves the clarity of one's imagery', can both be tested empirically and, as it happens, shown to be generally false (Wadden and Anderton 1982, Mingay 1988). However, when a therapist who uses hypnosis says that 'Hypnosis helps

to gain access to those sources of the patient's problems which lie in the unconscious mind', he or she is describing a model on which to base his or her
therapeutic interventions with patients. It is not so much the accuracy of the
model which is of interest to the practitioner, but whether it generates procedures
which are effective in helping the patient to change in the desired manner. This
is a complex matter and will be taken up again in Chapter 2. For the moment,
let us explore the nature of the phenomenon we call 'hypnosis'.

The nature of hypnosis

Hypnosis *as it is practised* really refers to an interaction between two people, one
of whom is identified as the hypnotist, the other as the subject. (There may, of
course, be more than one subject as in the case of group hypnosis.) The hypnotist
administers the hypnotic instructions and the subject responds to them.

Hypnosis is a complex phenomenon, the coming together of a number of
psychological processes. It involves *selective attention*: that is, the subject's attention
is focused on a limited range of stimuli, usually internal, such as feelings and
imagery. It involves *relaxation*: almost invariably for clinical purposes the subject
(unless he or she is, say, experiencing some arousing imagery) is both mentally
and physically relaxed. Hypnosis also includes the creation of *expectancy* and its
effects on the subject's experience and responding: that is, the hypnotist creates
a context in which the subject expects to feel, think, or respond in a particular
way, and by the hypnotist's building up that expectation in the subject's mind,
the suggestion is more likely to take effect. *Imagination* is very often a feature of
the hypnotic experience: the subject is absorbed in imagining some scene, usually
under the direction of the hypnotist. Generally there is a high degree of *rapport*
between the hypnotist and subject, and there is no doubt that hypnosis entails
some degree of *conformity* or *compliance* on the subject's part: that is, the subject
is motivated to conform to the wishes of the hypnotist, and it is possible that some
of his or her behaviour may be understood in those terms. For example, the hypnotist may suggest that the subject's arm is feeling so light that it will involuntarily
float into the air (the arm levitation suggestion). The subject may, however, raise
the arm because he or she would feel uneasy about not going along with the
hypnotist's instruction. *Role-playing* may be involved, the subject behaving
according to his or her beliefs about how a hypnotized person should respond.
Finally, we may invoke the concept of *attribution*: to what does the subject attribute
his or her experience? Does the subject say 'Yes, I felt hypnotized because I was
very relaxed and deeply absorbed in my imagination' or does he or she say 'No,
I didn't feel hypnotized, I was just very relaxed and deeply absorbed in my
imagination'? In fact, of relevance also are the attributions of the hypnotist. Does
the hypnotist attribute the subject's behaviour and reported experience to his or
her being hypnotized, or just very relaxed, or compliant and so on? Indeed, some
of the other above-mentioned processes may also refer to the behaviour of the
hypnotist – for example, role-playing and expectancy.

If at this point the writer were to state that the question 'What is hypnosis?'
has now been answered, the reader may justifiably conclude that 'hypnosis' is

merely a label for an interaction between two people characterized by some combination of the aforementioned psychological phenomena, rather than a special state of consciousness in its own right. Indeed, there are influential theories of hypnosis which more or less adopt this conclusion, each one emphasizing one or more of the attributes listed above. For example, it may be argued that hypnotic phenomena can be explained largely in terms of relaxation (Edmonston 1981), role-enactment (Sarbin and Coe 1972), compliance (Wagstaff 1981), imagery (Hull 1933) and various combinations of these (e.g. Barber *et al*. 1974, Spanos 1982). It is not intended here to discuss these theories at length, but we may note that they are generally referred to as 'non-state theories' as distinct from 'state theories' which do rely on the notion of an altered state of consciousness. The state v. non-state contest is the most persistent and hotly debated controversy in modern experimental hypnosis and reference will be made to it at a later stage.

If we are prepared to accept that there *is* some phenomenon with properties which warrant it being regarded as a special state, then we may include two additional and crucial ingredients, namely *suggestion* and *trance* (or the hypnotic experience). These two ingredients are related, but I shall discuss each one separately at some length.

Suggestion

A suggestion is a communication by the hypnotist to the subject and, as with any communication, it is intended to alter the recipient's feelings, thoughts and behaviour in a specified way. Provided we can agree on certain characteristics of the concept of suggestion as used in the present context, we may feel justified in speaking of 'hypnotic suggestion' as distinct from any other type of suggestion. However, in the literature on hypnosis the term is often used on its own, as will generally be the case in this discussion.

Characteristics of suggestion

1 The subject responds to the suggestion in an involuntary manner   For example, when suggestions of arm lightness and arm levitation are repeated, the subject responds by raising the arm but perceives the action as involuntary and the arm to be lifting 'all on its own'. When this happens we may say that the subject's act of moving the arm has been *dissociated* from his or her awareness so it appears to him or her that the arm moves on its own. We shall discover later when discussing the trance experience that this phenomenon of dissociation is a useful and important one for the purposes of constructing a state theory of hypnosis. Here let us note that when responding to the arm-levitation suggestion, the subject may produce the same movement entirely voluntarily, but this is not what we mean in the present context by 'responding to suggestion'. In fact, more often than not the subjective impression is a mixture of involuntary and voluntary movement (e.g. the subject may report 'Sometimes it seemed like my arm was moving all on its own, but occasionally I might have moved it deliberately'). Other suggestions which illustrate well the involuntary nature of the response are the so-called 'challenges' such as eye catalepsy ('At the count of three you will be unable to open your eyes') and the finger-lock test ('At the count of three you will be unable to separate your hands').

2 Suggestions may be explicitly augmented by suitable imagery   Indeed it may be argued that imagery of one sort or another is always involved when the subject is responding to a suggestion. For example, the arm-levitation suggestion may be accompanied by the image of a large balloon attached to a length of string which is wrapped around the subject's wrist and is tugging at the arm. Likewise, the suggestion of hand numbness may be augmented by the image of that hand being immersed in a bucket of ice and water. An image of proceeding along a bridge surrounded by mist may accompany a suggestion of regressing to a period in early childhood. Many other examples will be found throughout this book.

3 Suggestion is a multi-modal phenomenon   Arm levitation is an example of a suggestion influencing motor behaviour and as such it is designated as an *ideomotor suggestion*, the prefix 'ideo' being used to convey the notion that the subject responds to the *idea* of a movement in the arm. Another example of ideomotor suggestion is the postural-sway test of suggestibility: the experimenter stands either behind or in front of the subject and draws attention to his or her natural tendency to sway back and forth. Suggestions are given that this swaying motion is increasing and in particular that the subject is swaying more and more towards the experimenter (who is ready to stop the subject's fall should the need arise). 'Challenge' ideomotor suggestions (eye or arm catalepsy and the finger-lock test) have previously been mentioned and illustrate that suggestions may be negative as well as positive (i.e. 'You *will not* or *cannot* do or experience something' as distinct from 'You *will* do or experience something'). A negative *ideosensory* suggestion is typified by glove anaesthesia ('Your whole hand is now completely insensitive'). Ideosensory suggestions are also contained in the arm-levitation test ('Your whole arm is feeling lighter and lighter') and in instructions for relaxation ('Your whole body is feeling heavy and relaxed'). Suggestions may also be directed to the *olfactory* modality (positive: 'In a moment you will experience the most terrible smell in your nostrils'; or negative (tested by ammonia solution): 'You have completely lost your sense of smell'). Similar positive and negative suggestions can be made in the *gustatory* modality (taste).

These kinds of suggestions are often termed 'hallucinations' (positive and negative) in the literature. This is an unsatisfactory term because it also denotes certain pathological states, but the point at issue is that the subjective experience of the suggestions has a more real quality than normal imagery. This also applies to suggested 'hallucinations' in the *auditory* modality (positive: 'You can hear a fly buzzing behind your head'; negative: 'You can hear no sound at all in your left ear') and in the *visual* modality (positive: 'When you open your eyes you will see your best friend sitting in front of you'; negative: 'When you open your eyes you will not see the chair in front of you'). These kinds of suggestions are responded to successfully by only a small minority of susceptible subjects.

Some suggestions give rise to alterations in one's experience of *time* and one's *memory*. For example, suggestions may be given of time appearing to slow down

('Every second seems like a minute . . .') or speed up ('Time is going faster and faster . . .'). It may also be suggested that the subject is going back in time and vividly re-experiencing an early event in his or her life, or that the subject is moving forward to a future period in his or her life. The former experience, termed 'revivification' or, if it involves the recall of events at a radically earlier stage of development, 'age regression', may contain factually accurate recollections as well as fantasies of an entirely fictitious nature (particularly so the earlier the regression). The suggestion to move forward in time (age progression) of course evokes scenes which are pure fantasy, but these may be useful from the therapist's point of view. Suggestions of *amnesia* are generally post-hypnotic (see below). They may be global ('You will remember nothing of what has happened while you have been hypnotized') or selective ('You will not remember my giving you this suggestion'). Because of the nature of the hypnotic experience, as described below, subjects may be spontaneously amnesic for some of the events that occur during hypnosis. This is an everyday experience and is not just an example of natural forgetting but also arises from naturally occurring dissociative experiences. At such times our attention is absorbed in something of interest such as a TV programme or a daydream, while we are simultaneously engaged in some well-learned activity. A common example is the 'highway trance' when, while driving on a long car journey, one can have no recollection of part of the journey already covered, even though one was engaged in the skilful task of driving the car.

I shall examine these and similar phenomena again when I discuss the trance experience. For the moment let us note that it has been maintained that a true instance of hypnotically suggested amnesia should be reversible: that is, it should be temporary, and the forgotten material should be recalled by the subject, say when the experimenter gives a predetermined signal such as tapping on his or her desk (see Nace *et al.* 1974).

Finally, there is evidence that hypnotic suggestions can influence specific *physiological responses* – that is, bodily reactions which are mediated by the autonomic nervous system (ANS) and therefore not normally amenable to voluntary control. It is, of course, perfectly easy and natural for one person to intentionally influence the physiological responding of another by means of a verbal communication. This may be on general terms, for example, increasing the person's arousal level (increasing heart rate, sweating, respiratory rate and so on) by describing something exciting that is about to happen. However, we may be more selective in the responses which we influence. For example, we may focus on increasing salivary rate in another person by describing to him or her the experience of sucking a lemon, or we may influence his or her gastric activity by vividly relating a particularly disgusting and offensive scene which causes the listener to feel nauseous. In the hypnotic literature, of special interest are suggestions of alterations in blood flow. Typically these sorts of suggestion involve both visual imagery (e.g. 'Imagine your right hand immersed in a bucket of warm water') and direct suggestions of change (e.g. 'Your hand is becoming warmer' or even 'The circulation is flowing strongly to your hand'). Suggestions of changes in forearm blood flow have been investigated by Grabowska (1971) and of changes in gastric activity by Stacher *et al.* (1975).

Olness and her colleagues in Minnesota claim that children are particularly adept at altering their involuntary physiological functions; these include tissue oxygen, measured transcutaneously on the hands (Olness and Conroy 1985) and salivary immunoglobulin A concentrations (Olness *et al.* 1989). These studies are reported in further detail in Chapter 10 of this book.

Clearly these kinds of suggestions have an application in some areas of medicine (see Chapter 8 of this book) but it is not yet clear by how much, if at all, the physiological changes mediate recovery. This matter is discussed in Chapters 4 and 7 of Gibson and Heap (1990).

4 Suggestion is not a unitary concept   We shall see a little later that there is a relatively stable personal characteristic termed 'suggestibility' or 'susceptibility' which implies that individuals tend to be responsive to the above suggestions in varying degrees: some people not at all, some to a considerable degree, and others at points in between. However, in practice one finds that each individual varies in the types of suggestion to which he or she will respond. For example, because a person only shows a very slight response to the arm-levitation suggestion, we cannot infer that he or she will not have a profound response to, say, age regression, although there is some degree of correlation between the various types of suggestion. Eysenck and Furneaux (1945) established two factors which may be subsumed under the label 'suggestibility': *primary suggestibility* refers to suggestions of *unwilled* acts such as postural sway or blushing, and is predictive of hypnotic susceptibility, unlike *secondary suggestibility* which is a person's tendency to be compliant, credulous, and easily persuaded.

5 Suggestions may differ in style of delivery   There are a number of distinctions made with regard to style and they are of practical rather than of theoretical significance, to the extent that they have any import at all. Two will be outlined here. The first is the *authoritarian–permissive* distinction. A suggestion may be delivered as an authoritarian command ('Your arm will begin to rise in the air *now*!') or as an invitation to respond ('Just allow your hand to become as light as it wants to'). It is possible that different patients may be more comfortable with one or the other type (as indeed may therapists themselves) but Spinhoven *et al.* (1988) found little difference between their effects. The permissive type is the more favoured in recent times and has the advantage that the subject's failure to respond at all may be less of a problem than with the authoritarian type.

The second distinction is that of *direct v. indirect suggestion*. The above two suggestions are direct, even though one is in the permissive style. In the case of indirect suggestions the instruction is expressed in a covert manner which does not immediately demand that the subject behave in a prescribed way. For example, the suggestion may simply be embedded in a longer statement and the hypnotist may subtly mark it out by softening his or her voice ('You don't have to try to *relax*' or 'There may have been times when *you have lost the feeling in one of your hands*'). Another method is to *imply* that the suggested experience will take place, rather than directly state that it will (e.g. 'You will not be completely relaxed before your hand has come to rest on your lap' – implying that the subject *will* be completely relaxed once the hand has reached his or her lap). Other examples are the use of paradox ('Try not to go into hypnosis too quickly') and creating an illusion of choice ('You may go into hypnosis now or in a few minutes'). Other examples are given in Erickson *et al*. (1976).

One apparent advantage of the indirect methods is that they provide additional safeguards against the lack of any response by the subject (e.g. 'I don't know if your arm will be too heavy to begin to lift off your lap'); it is also assumed that the suggestions bypass the subject's critical faculties and therefore avoid creating resistance in some cases. Probably because of the association of indirect approaches with the late Dr Milton Erickson, who has become somewhat of a cult figure in the field of hypnotherapy since his death in 1980, these methods have received an undue amount of attention over the last ten years, despite there being little evidence of any clear advantage over direct methods (Lynn *et al*. 1987, Matthews and Mosher 1988). Nevertheless, just as with the authoritarian–permissive distinction, there may be subjects who respond better to one type of suggestion rather than the other; in Britain this possibility has recently been investigated by Hart (1990) who found that the indirect approach was no more successful than the direct approach in those patients with General Anxiety Disorder who scored low on scales of hypnotic susceptibility.

6 Suggestibility may be reliably measured As was mentioned earlier, people differ in the degree to which they respond to suggestions, and this quality of 'suggestibility', 'susceptibility', or 'hypnotic susceptibility' may be measured by means of standard scales. These scales usually consist of a number of suggestions covering the different modalities discussed earlier, and the degree to which the subject responds to each suggestion is noted – say by a rating on a scale of 0–4 points. These scores can be summed to give an overall suggestibility score. The most commonly used scales have a high degree of test–retest reliability. This is a necessary but not sufficient requirement for their validity, but because there is no agreement on the defining qualities of hypnosis, it is difficult to address the question of the validity of the scales. Encouragement comes from the finding that with some problems, such as pain and asthma (and possibly other psychosomatic ailments) a successful outcome of hypnotherapy is correlated with measured susceptibility (Wadden and Anderton 1982).

Fellows (1988) provides a review of susceptibility scales, the most widely used being the Harvard Scales derived by M.T. Orne and his colleagues and the Stanford Scales, developed by E.R. Hilgard and his colleagues. These scales consist of parallel forms for adult, individual and group assessment. There are also scales for children (e.g. London 1962). The non-state theorist and investigator, T.X. Barber, and his colleagues have developed two scales, the Barber Suggestibility Scale (BSS) and the Creative Imagination Scale (CIS) which do not have a hypnotic induction (Barber 1965, Wilson and Barber 1978). These two scales are the most extensively investigated in Britain, and Fellows (1979, 1986) has provided norms for the BSS and the CIS on a British student sample. Except for research purposes, susceptibility scales do not appear to be widely used in clinical work in Britain.

7 Hypnotic susceptibility is an individual trait which is stable over one's lifetime
However, it reaches a peak between the ages of 10 and 12 and shows a gentle
descent thereafter. Females have marginally higher susceptibility scores than
males (see e.g. Fellows 1986) but this is of no practical significance. There appears
to be no strong relationship with IQ above a certain level, and correlations with
scores on commonly used personality assessment procedures are marginal (see
Gibson 1988). There are indications, however, that people who have rich fantasy
experiences and good creative ability include a disproportionate number of highly
hypnotically susceptible subjects. These 'fantasy-prone' individuals (Rhue and
Lynn 1987) are more likely than other individuals to have suffered from sexual
or physical violence as children, and this suggests that for them a retreat into
fantasy was a means of dissociating from the harsh realities of their childhood.
People who are logical, analytical and convergent in their thinking style tend to
be lower in formally measured susceptibility, although as always there will be
many exceptions.

There have been attempts to enhance hypnotic susceptibility, for example by
biofeedback, indirect suggestion, and lately, cognitive training (Spanos *et al.*
1987). For the therapist there appears to be no easy and reliable method of
enhancing hypnotic susceptibility as a means of promoting the likelihood of
a successful therapeutic outcome. However the search continues and recently
Barabasz and Kaplan (1989) have reported on the enhancement of hypnotic
susceptibility by prolonged sensory deprivation.

8 Suggestions may differ in relation to the hypnotic induction   They may be administered without any preparation of the subject, or we may first perform a hypnotic
induction procedure and then administer the suggestions. I shall examine the
nature of the hypnotic induction in detail in Chapter 2, but first let us note that
suggestions given without their being preceded by a hypnotic induction are
termed 'waking suggestions'. For example, stage hypnotists often select their
subjects by asking the audience to participate in the finger-lock test mentioned
earlier.

We shall see in Chapter 2 that the hypnotic induction itself normally consists of a sequence of suggestions which emphasize comfort and relaxation and
which draw the subject's attention towards inner experiences such as imagery,
memories and feelings. Suggestions may then be given *following* the induction,
when the subject is described as being in a 'state of hypnosis' or 'trance'. For
example, the subject may be asked to regress to the age of 6, or it is suggested
that a part of the body is insensitive to pain. These suggestions are intended to
take effect immediately, unlike *post-hypnotic* suggestions which are intended to be
acted upon at some point after the subject has been alerted. For example, the
hypnotist may say 'At some point after you have opened your eyes I will tap on
the table and immediately you will experience an intense itchy feeling on the sole
of your right foot'. Post-hypnotic suggestion is a very commonly used technique
in hypnotherapy and examples are given in the next chapter.

The trance or hypnotic experience

When one performs a simple hypnotic induction (see Chapter 2) which emphasizes deep physical and mental relaxation and perhaps requires the subject to
engage in some pleasant imagery, and one does nothing more than this, the
subjects when re-alerted usually report that nothing particularly remarkable has
happened. They will probably say that they felt deeply relaxed and were absorbed
in the images described by the hypnotist, but they will also usually say they were
alert, certainly not unconscious or asleep, aware of where they were, aware of
the hypnotist's voice and even background sounds, and able to recall most if not
everything that happened between closing and opening their eyes. In the case
of self-hypnosis, whereby subjects are taught to go through these procedures on
their own, again the experience will probably be no more profound than that just
described.

This state of mental relaxation, absorption in inner experiences such as
imagery, memories and feelings, and the detachment from ongoing events in the
external world may be labelled 'trance'. This word may create problems for some
because of its association with spiritualism or the supernatural, but the everyday
connotations of the term convey very well what is intended by its use in the present context. We know what is meant when we say that so-and-so is 'in a trance'
or 'I must have been in trance when I did that'. Common examples occur when
we are absorbed in a daydream, but the focus of our attention may also be in
the external world – a book, a television programme, or some thrilling music.
In fact, hypnotic trances and everyday trances are very similar in their subjective
quality. In both types, the individual may experience time distortion – usually
the impression that real time has gone by much more quickly than usual, so that,
following half an hour of hypnosis, the subject, on alerting, may guess that only
10 or 15 minutes have passed by. Occasionally some spontaneous amnesia may
be present which may or may not be reversible and this may occur in everyday
trances as was described earlier in the chapter. With hypnotic inductions, as with
other relaxation methods, some subjects may also report changes in their body
image – for example, their limbs seem to extend a long way or their body seems
to have altered position.

There are in addition a number of important attributes or assumptions concerning the hypnotic trance:

1 Altered perceptions   I mentioned just now alterations in the experience of time
and the registration and recall of information. Altered perceptions, either spontaneous or suggested, may be considered the hallmark of the trance experience.
I earlier stated that hypnotic suggestions are intended to be acted upon in an
automatic and dissociated manner, and people vary in their capacity to respond
to suggestions in this way. The purpose of the induction procedure is to enhance
the subject's experience of responding to suggestions in a dissociative way to the
limit imposed by his or her hypnotic susceptibility.

The dissociative quality of the more profound perceptual alterations has been
experimentally investigated by Hilgard (1986) using the method of the 'hidden
observer'. For example, highly hypnotizable subjects were given suggestions of

analgesia of the hand and asked to immerse that hand in a bucket of ice and water. They were then asked to call out the rating of the experienced pain on a scale of 0–10. Normally these ratings would be expected to increase with the time of immersion (say 2, 4, 6, 8); however, following suggestions of hand analgesia, the spoken ratings remained at around 0–2. It was also suggested to the subjects that although they were hypnotized and their hand was insensitive to pain, there was another part of their mind – a 'hidden observer part' – which *was* aware of the experience of pain and could give, outside the subjects' awareness, a true rating of the level of pain experienced. These ratings were given using the free hand, either in writing or by pressing numbered keys, and Hilgard and his colleagues (Hilgard 1986) found that they corresponded to those given orally without the suggestion of analgesia (2, 4, 6, etc.). Similar experiments have been performed on hypnoamnesia and hypnotically suggested deafness.

Another kind of dissociation which may be demonstrated with profound alterations in perceptual experience, and therefore only in highly susceptible individuals, is that of 'trance logic' (Orne 1959, 1962). Suppose that subjects are given the hypnotic suggestion that when they open their eyes they will not see a chair in front of them. Some very susceptible subjects report not seeing the chair, yet when they are asked to get up and walk forward, they avoid the chair! Subjects who are asked only to *pretend* that they are deeply hypnotized are more likely to collide with the chair. In another experiment subjects who were able to 'hallucinate' a friend sitting in a chair opposite were also able to describe the parts of the chair which would normally be obscured by its occupant. Again, simulators were more inclined to deny being able to do this. Finally Orne (1972) describes an age-regressed subject who was only able to speak and understand German at the age to which he was regressed, yet when asked several times in English whether he understood that language (using a different phraseology each time) he replied 'Nein'.

There are criticisms of the 'hidden observer' and of 'trance logic' demonstrations both on methodological and theoretical grounds (see Wagstaff 1981, 1988). Wagstaff (1981) has suggested that these forms of dissociation are actually ways in which subjects may consciously resolve the dilemma posed by the 'hypnotist', namely to comply with the hypnotist's suggestions, and yet remain honest. Thus, via the 'hidden observer' they are truthfully describing their conscious, rather than out-of-consciousness, experiences. The interested reader may also refer to Sheehan (1986) for further discussion of this matter.

2 Altered thinking   The above examples of 'trance logic' reveal how hypnotized subjects are able, through the mechanism of dissociation, to behave in ways which are illogical and which would be recognized as such by unhypnotized subjects, even when they are instructed to pretend to be hypnotized. Thinking in the trance state, as opposed to the waking state, is regarded as being more illogical, more literal, perhaps more emotional, less verbal, less critical and less time-oriented. These characteristics of thinking have also been referred to the right hemisphere of the brain and this point is taken up by Alladin and Heap in Chapter 4 (see also Pedersen 1990).

3 Access to the unconscious Related to characteristic 2 is the assumption of greater access to unconscious material, that is memories, fantasies and emotions which have been dissociated from conscious awareness but which still exert an influence on the patient's feelings. (In the clinical context this is usually a destructive influence.) Thus, as well as facilitating the dissociation of experiences, hypnosis may facilitate the reassociation of material which is present in dissociated form. This is not to say that memory in general is enhanced by hypnosis; this is a myth and in fact memories elicited under hypnosis may be at special risk from contamination by fantasy or leading questions (Mingay 1988).

The subjective nature of the trance experience
It may have occurred to the reader from the foregoing discussion that, notwithstanding the demonstrations by Orne (see earlier) on possible *observable* differences between highly susceptible subjects and simulators, the defining characteristics of the trance experience are very much concerned with the subjective reports of the hypnotized person. Some subjects and patients are disappointed by their experience; they report nothing more profound than that they feel relaxed. I mentioned earlier the role of attribution in the subjective experience of suggestion, and also of relevance here are the subjects' expectations. Some may believe that hypnosis is a process of being 'put under' and rendered oblivious to their surroundings, in which case they will probably insist that they have not been hypnotized. Some practitioners may attempt to persuade such subjects that they *were* 'really hypnotized' but that they did not know it. This kind of exchange exposes the limitations and difficulties inherent in the terminology used to describe hypnosis. It may in fact be the case that the subject is low in susceptibility, but it may also be that he or she is having some problems experiencing hypnosis – perhaps through anxiety and an inability to 'let go'. Another possibility is that the hypnotist has not given the subject adequate opportunity to have dissociative experience. Merely relaxing may not be sufficient, and the hypnotist should allow the subject to experience his or her responses to a range of suggestions.

Trance depth
Trance depth is a rather loose idea which refers to the degree to which the subject experiences a detachment from immediate reality and an absorption in inner processes, and is responsive to suggestions requiring profound alterations in perception and experience such as age regression, amnesia and hallucinatory experiences. It is therefore useful to speak of light, medium, and deep trances; some subjects capable of very deep trances are referred to as 'somnambulistic' because they are capable of experiencing trance phenomena with their eyes open.

Trance depth is therefore related to hypnotic susceptibility but it is more concerned with subjective experience and some commonly used measures of trance depth, such as that of Tart (1970), simply consist of self-reported ratings on a numerical scale.

Conclusions and further reading

In this chapter I have surveyed the current ideas, knowledge and controversies concerning the phenomenon which we call 'hypnosis'. It was noted that there is a divergence of views concerning whether or not it is useful to conceive of a special state of consciousness which is essentially different from an everyday state of relaxation and which helps us understand better the phenomena which one observes when carrying out the procedures labelled 'hypnosis'. It was observed that 'hypnosis' as it is practised usually involves various psychological processes – relaxation, expectation, compliance, imagination, selective attention and so on – but that two pivotal and related concepts are suggestion and trance or the hypnotic experience. It was suggested that by hypnosis is meant a state of mental relaxation and restricted awareness in which subjects are usually engrossed in their inner experiences such as feelings and imagery, are less analytical and logical in their thinking, and have an enhanced capacity to respond to suggestions in an automatic and dissociated manner. It is assumed that this can be achieved or enhanced by means of the procedure termed 'hypnotic induction' (to be described in Chapter 2) the purpose of which is to relax the subject and draw his or her attention away from external realities and towards inner experiences.

This has been a condensed overview of the nature of hypnosis, intended to prepare the reader for the clinical chapters to follow. Many details and complexities have been glossed over and the reader may be interested in pursuing in greater depth some of the theoretical and research areas described. He or she may find the edited volume by Naish (1986) very useful for these purposes. Wagstaff (1981) is a wide-ranging review of research from an extreme non-state angle, but the reader may prefer a more up-to-date account such as Spanos and Chaves (1989). For a state perspective there is no better book than Hilgard (1986).

This chapter has avoided giving the historical background to hypnosis as there are several recent accounts – for example, Gauld (1988), and Chapter 2 of Gibson and Heap (1990). Rowley (1986) is a short, readable book on hypnosis and hypnotherapy, which gives the history and an overview of the different theories of hypnosis.

References

Barabasz, A.F. and Kaplan, G.M. (1989) Effects of Restricted Environmental Stimulation (REST) on hypnotizability: a test of alternative techniques, in D. Waxman, D. Pedersen, I. Wilkie and P. Mellett (eds) *Hypnosis: The Fourth European Congress at Oxford*, London: Whurr Publishers.

Barber, T.X. (1965) Measuring 'hypnotic-like' suggestibility with and without 'hypnotic induction'; psychometric properties, norms, and variables influencing response to the Barber Suggestibility Scale (BSS), *Psychological Reports* 16: 809–44.

Barber, T.X., Spanos, N.P. and Chaves, J.F. (1974) *Hypnosis, Imagination and Human Potentialities*, New York: Pergamon Press.

Edmonston, W.E. (1981) *Hypnosis and Relaxation: Modern Verification of an Old Equation,* New York and Chichester: Wiley.

Erickson, M.H., Rossi, E.L. and Rossi, S.H. (1976) *Hypnotic Realities: The Induction of Clinical Hypnosis and the Indirect Forms of Suggestion,* New York: Irvington.

Eysenck, H.J. and Furneaux, W.D. (1945) Primary and secondary suggestibility: an experimental and statistical study, *Journal of Experimental Psychology* 35: 485–503.

Fellows, B.J. (1979). British use of the Barber Suggestibility Scale: norms, psychometric properties and the effects of the sex of the subject and of the experimenter, *British Journal of Psychology* 70: 547–57.

—— (1986) The Creative Imagination Scale. Paper presented at the *Third Annual Conference of the British Society of Experimental and Clinical Hypnosis,* University of Oxford, April.

—— (1988) The use of hypnotic susceptibility scales, in M. Heap (ed.) *Hypnosis, Current Clinical, Experimental and Forensic Practices,* London: Croom Helm.

Gauld, A. (1988) History of hypnotism, in M. Heap (ed.) *Hypnosis: Current Clinical, Experimental and Forensic Practices,* London: Croom Helm.

Gibson, H.B. (1988) Correlates of hypnotic susceptibility, in M. Heap (ed.) *Hypnosis: Current Clinical, Experimental and Forensic Practices,* London: Croom Helm.

Gibson, H.B. and Heap, M. (1990) *Hypnosis in Therapy,* London: Lawrence Erlbaum.

Grabowska, M.J. (1971) The effect of hypnosis and hypnotic suggestion on the blood flow in the extremities, *Polish Medical Journal* 10: 1044–51.

Hart, B.B. (1990) The role of hypnotizability and type of suggestion in the hypnotic-assisted treatment of pervasive anxiety. Unpublished Doctoral Dissertation, Portsmouth Polytechnic.

Hilgard, E.R. (1986) *Divided Consciousness: Multiple Controls in Human Thought and Action,* 2nd edn, New York: Wiley.

Hull, C.L. (1933) *Hypnosis and Suggestibility: An Experimental Approach,* New York: Appleton Century Crofts.

London, P. (1962) *Children's Hypnotic Susceptibility Scale,* Palo Alto, Calif.: Consulting Psychologists Press.

Lynn, S.J., Neufeld, V., Matyi, C.L., Weekes, J., Dudley, K. and Weiss, F. (1987) Direct versus indirect suggestion, *Hypnos* 14: 113–20.

Matthews, W.J. and Mosher, D.L. (1988) Direct and indirect suggestion in a laboratory setting, *British Journal of Experimental and Clinical Hypnosis* 5: 63–72.

Mingay, D.J. (1988) Hypnosis and eye-witness testimony, in M. Heap (ed.) *Hypnosis: Current Clinical, Experimental and Forensic Applications,* London: Croom Helm.

Nace, E.P., Orne, M.T. and Hammer, A.G. (1974) Posthypnotic amnesia as an active psychic process: the reversibility of amnesia, *Archives of General Psychiatry* 31: 257–60.

Naish, P.L.N. (ed.) (1986) *What is Hypnosis? Current Trends and Research,* Milton Keynes: Open University Press.

Olness, K.N. and Conroy, M.M. (1985) A pilot study of voluntary control of transcutaneous PO_2 by children, *International Journal of Clinical and Experimental Hypnosis* 33: 1–5.

Olness, K.N., Culbert, T. and Uden, D. (1989) Self-regulation of salivary immunoglobulin A by children, *Pediatrics* 83: 66–71.

Orne, M.T. (1959) The nature of hypnosis: artifact and essence, *Journal of Abnormal and Social Psychology* 58: 277–99.

—— (1962) Hypnotically induced hallucinations, in L.J. West (ed.) *Hallucinations,* New York: Grune & Stratton.

—— (1972). On the simulating subject as a quasi-control in hypnosis research: what, why and how? In E. Fromm and R.E. Shor (eds) *Hypnosis: Research Developments and Perspectives,* Chicago: Aldine-Atherton.

Pedersen, D.L. (1990) Implications of cerebral specialization to hypnotherapy with an introduction to cameral analysis, *Hypnos* 17: 19–28.

Popper, K.R. (1963) *Conjectures and Refutations: The Growth of Scientific Knowledge*, London: Routledge & Kegan Paul.

Rhue, J.W. and Lynn, S.J. (1987) Fantasy proneness: the ability to hallucinate 'as real as real', *British Journal of Experimental and Clinical Hypnosis* 4: 173–80.

Rowley, D.T. (1986) *Hypnosis and Hypnotherapy*, London: Croom Helm.

Sarbin, T.R. and Coe, W.C. (1972) *Hypnosis: A Social Psychological Analysis of Influence Communication*, New York: Holt, Rinehart & Winston.

Sheehan, P.W. (1986) An individual differences account of hypnosis, in P.L.N. Naish (ed.) *What is Hypnosis? Current Theories and Research*, Milton Keynes: Open University Press.

Spanos, N.P. (1982) Hypnotic behavior: a cognitive and social psychological perspective, *Research Communications in Psychology, Psychiatry and Behavior* 7: 199–213.

Spanos, N.P. and Chaves, J.F. (1989) *Hypnosis: The Cognitive–Behavioral Perspective*, Buffalo, NY: Prometheus.

Spanos, N.P., de Gron, M. and de Groot, H. (1987) Skill training for enhancing hypnotic susceptibility and word list amnesia, *British Journal of Experimental and Clinical Hypnosis* 4: 15–24.

Spinhoven, P. (1987) Hypnosis and behaviour therapy: a review, *International Journal of Clinical and Experimental Hypnosis* 35: 8–31.

Spinhoven, P., Baak, D., van Dyck, R. and Vermeulen, P. (1988) The effectiveness of an authoritative versus permissive style of hypnotic communication, *International Journal of Clinical and Experimental Hypnosis* 36: 182–91.

Stacher, G., Berner, P., Naske, R., Schoster, P., Bauer, P., Stärker, H. and Schulze, D. (1975) Effects of hypnotic suggestions of relaxation on basal and betazole-stimulated gastric acid secretion, *Gastroenterology* 68: 656–61.

Tart, C.T. (1970) Self-report scales of hypnotic depth, *International Journal of Clinical and Experimental Hypnosis* 18: 105–25.

Wadden, T.A. and Anderton, C.H. (1982) The clinical use of hypnosis, *Psychological Bulletin* 91: 215–43.

Wagstaff, G.F. (1981) *Hypnosis, Compliance and Belief*, Brighton: Harvester Press.

—— (1988). Current theoretical and experimental issues in hypnosis: overview, in M. Heap (ed.) *Hypnosis: Current Clinical, Experimental and Forensic Practices*, London: Croom Helm.

Wilson, S.C. and Barber, T.X. (1978) The Creative Imagination Scale as a measure of hypnotic responsiveness: applications to experimental and clinical hypnosis, *American Journal of Clinical Hypnosis* 20: 235–49.

2

Role and uses of hypnosis in psychotherapy

MICHAEL HEAP

Introduction

In this chapter I will examine some general principles and considerations concerning the use of hypnosis in therapy – or for short, 'hypnotherapy'. As was
stated at the beginning of Chapter 1, hypnosis is not a therapy, but rather provides the therapist with a set of techniques which he or she may use to augment
a particular course of treatment. Thus hypnosis may be more accurately
described as an *adjunct* to therapy, although in fact we shall see that the very
experience of hypnosis is physically and mentally relaxing and that the regular
practice of self-hypnosis may have general beneficial influences in the case of
many psychological and psychosomatic problems.

Which theory of hypnosis?

One of the difficulties which the aspiring hypnotherapist must face is the fact that
not only do the experts disagree on what hypnosis is, but, as we have observed
in Chapter 1, there is a formidable school of thought which contends that hypnosis
is an outmoded and redundant concept and all the phenomena associated with
it can be explained by more mundane psychological concepts. It has even been
asserted that one reason for the delay in the abandonment of hypnosis is the
self-interest of therapists (Spanos and Chaves 1989). All this can quite naturally
undermine the confidence of therapists who use hypnosis in their work, and
dissuade others who are interested in acquiring these skills.

There are two arguments which the author feels are important to this debate.
First, some consideration should be given to the scientific nature of the theories
being offered to explain phenomena described as 'hypnotic'. In the manner
of scientific explanation, each of these theories attempts to explain hypnosis
in terms which we already understand. Now it is true that terms such as
'role-enactment', 'believed-in imaginings', 'dissociation' and 'compliance' are

familiar and understandable to us, and therefore depicting hypnosis in any of these terms may satisfy our need to have an explanation when we observe those phenomena which have been labelled 'hypnotic'. However, our understanding of these terms is largely based on our own subjective experience of them, and therefore these terms in themselves are ill-defined. Without precise objective definitions, the scientific status of a theory is compromised, since it cannot generate unambiguous predictions. Probably for this reason, much of the debate between the different theoretical schools of hypnosis has been about explaining what has been observed, rather than predicting what will be observed. Since the terms in which these explanations are framed are ill-defined, the theories, like many in psychology, inevitably drift close to being tautological. For example, Hilgard's (1986) neo-dissociation theory of hypnosis proposes that hypnotic phenomena arise through the separation of various cognitive systems by 'amnesic barriers' (see Alladin and Heap's account in Chapter 4 of this book). This raises the question of what constitutes an 'amnesic barrier' other than something we infer from a subject describing the phenomenological experience of dissociation.

Looked at in this way, the various theories of hypnosis may be judged not in terms of their validity, but in terms of how useful their way of looking at hypnosis is in a particular context. This brings us to the second consideration, namely the question concerning which of the various theories of hypnosis is the most useful for the purposes of therapy – that is, 'Which generates the most effective therapeutic procedures?' In the opinion of the author, therapists using hypnosis may find the dissociation model described in the last chapter to be the most useful of the models proposed to describe hypnosis. It is not too dissimilar from a description of everyday experiences of 'being in a trance' and it is consistent with the known high hypnotizability of people who are fantasy-prone (see Chapter 1) and who used their fantasy world to withdraw into and away from the harsh realities which beset them as children. It is consistent with the low hypnotizability of obsessive–compulsive patients (Hoogduin and de Jong 1989) and anorexic patients of the restricting type (Pettinati *et al*. 1985), both of whom need to be vigilant to and in control of their external world. It accords with the higher hypnotizability of patients who report dissociative experiences such as those who mutilate themselves, or who have multiple personalities (Hilgard 1986) or who engage in bingeing and purging in their efforts to control their weight (Pettinati *et al*. 1985), such patients often describing their behaviour in dissociative terms (e.g. 'when I am bingeing it's as though I am watching somebody else doing it'). Finally the theory will be found to generate other models and techniques which when applied for therapeutic purposes appear to be sufficiently effective to warrant their use in a wide variety of problems.

A model which describes hypnosis in terms of compliance is rather less useful to the therapist: it does not provide a convincing explanation for the above observations and does not generate models and techniques which have the same range of usefulness and effectiveness as the dissociation model. Nevertheless the dissociation model itself, like any other, has a limited range of usefulness. That is, there will be circumstances when the model does not provide a suitable description of the behaviour and experiences of the patient, and when the techniques derived from it are not appropriate (see later). At such times it may be that a model based on compliance, role-enactment, or relaxation rather than dissociation provides a more useful description of what is happening.

Theoretical disputes such as the state v. non-state controversy have drawn the criticism, especially from therapists, that they are sterile and pedantic and more concerned with semantics than with actual phenomena. Despite what has been said so far, the present author does not agree. These debates have been challenging and productive, and hypnosis has benefited from the attentions of those involved in these controversies – people of calibre and intellectual integrity, such as T.X. Barber, Hilgard, Orne, Sarbin, Spanos and Wagstaff to name but a few. In contrast, hypnotherapy and its antecedents, from the 18th century era of Mesmerism and Animal Magnetism down to the New Age therapies of the neo-Ericksonians and of Neuro-linguistic Programming (see Heap 1988) have been characterized at best by gullibility and naivety of thinking and at worst by sheer fraudulence. Hypnosis has always been a fertile seedbed for all kinds of myths and fancies and these grow and flourish as much today as they have done in the past.

The hypnotic induction in therapy

The reader who has not yet explored the modern literature on hypnosis may be surprised at the amount of attention I have given to the above theoretical controversies. This attention is important, however, because as one moves about this field, one can hardly take a step forward without encountering some fiercely contested debate, and unless one can find some way through these, one may be inclined to abandon the field altogether in a state of disenchantment and bewilderment. The matter of how a state of hypnosis is induced (or indeed whether it is induced at all) is no exception to the general picture. However, as I am now concentrating on the therapeutic application of hypnosis, the account of the induction of hypnosis will be largely practical and compatible with the dissociative viewpoint. Lengthy details of induction methods are avoided and for these the reader may consult general clinical texts such as Karle and Boys (1987) and Waxman (1989).

The importance of context

In the same way that the occurrence of any behaviour is strongly influenced by expectation, the context in which hypnotic suggestions are delivered is of great importance. A stage hypnotist's show, a health service clinic, and an experimental psychology laboratory are situations to which individuals will come with different expectations concerning the actions of the hypnotist, their own experiences and behaviour, and their relationship with the hypnotist. For example, the stage hypnotist with his or her group of willing volunteers and an excited audience expecting a hilarious performance, will find it relatively easy to elicit successfully a response to a suggestion, say, that the subjects will hop around the stage like chickens; the therapist in the clinic is unlikely to witness such a response should he or she be foolish enough to make this suggestion – it is completely out of context.

Is it not possible therefore for the hypnotist to suggest successfully to subjects that they will perform some act normally against their moral beliefs? The answer seems to be negative if we are referring to the effects of simple suggestion, but it should be remembered that the therapist or experimenter can manipulate the context in a way which may indeed result in the subjects' behaving in a manner contrary to their customary moral standards. Milgram (1963, 1974) strikingly demonstrated this, successfully persuading some members of the public to administer what they believed to be painful and even lethal electric shocks to another person (in reality a stooge subject who was experiencing no shocks at all) on the grounds that they were engaging in some important scientific research. Concerning hypnotherapy itself, Heap (1984) and Karle (Chapter 11 of this book) report instances of lay hypnotherapists whose intimate advances towards their female clients went unrepelled when it was explained that they were part of the therapy and designed to assist the clients overcome their inhibitions.

Preparing the patient for hypnosis

Regarding the legitimate therapeutic uses of hypnosis it is important, in view of the foregoing considerations, that the therapist's actions and communications be in keeping with the context, and should contribute to the creation of the appropriate expectations, thus maximizing the patient's receptivity to suggestion. A relationship of warmth, trust and mutual positive regard is essential. In some instances the patient will request hypnosis and how much this should influence the practitioner in his or her own choice of therapy will be discussed later in this chapter. In other cases, it is the therapist who will suggest hypnosis. Sometimes this decision will be made and communicated to the patient after the initial assessment but it is also possible that therapy has been in progress for some time before the practitioner gives consideration to the adjunctive use of hypnosis.

Whatever the case, whenever it is explicitly suggested to the patient that hypnosis may be a useful intervention, it is important to explore his or her reactions and expectations. For example, it is useful to ask patients if they have had any previous experience of hypnosis, either as a participant or as an observer (e.g. at a stage hypnotist's performance), and to ascertain their ideas and beliefs about the nature of hypnosis. The therapist should be alert to any misgivings and anxieties on the patient's part and allay these in a confident and reassuring manner. The most important part of the preparation is to help the patient relax mentally and physically and to draw his or her attention away from external realities and towards inner experiences – feelings, memories, images and so on. The therapist can help achieve these ends by acting and speaking in a calm and relaxed style, describing to the patient the kinds of experiences he or she will have while in the hypnotic state. It may be useful at this stage for the therapist to remind the patient of everyday trance experiences as described in Chapter 1. At some stage the patient will be asked to close his or her eyes to focus better on inner experiences, or may first be asked to stare at a point which requires elevation of the eyes, to experience the strain and heaviness in the eyes, and gradually to allow the eyes to close.

Formal induction and deepening procedures

The above suggestions mark the first stage of a sequence of manoeuvres which constitute the formal induction of hypnosis (the later stage of this sequence is usually referred to as the 'deepening' phase). There are many standardized procedures for the induction of hypnosis, but all have the aim of relaxing the patient and encouraging him or her to focus awareness inwardly. Hypnotic induction and deepening procedures have the following characteristics:

1 The focusing of the subject's attention on one stimulus or a limited range of stimuli in a particular modality – for example, visual (a spot of light), auditory (the hypnotist's voice, a metronome beat, etc.), somatosensory (feelings in the body), movement (breathing or arm levitation), imagery (a scene either described by the hypnotist or chosen by the subject) and so on. The choice of stimulus appears to be fairly arbitrary and therapists seem to develop their own preferred method.
2 Repeated suggestions of relaxation, comfort, calmness, heaviness, 'letting go', 'going deeper' and so on.
3 The coupling of 1 and 2 – for example, 'As I am counting, with each count you are going deeper and deeper relaxed', 'With each breath your body is becoming more and more relaxed', 'As your eyes are getting heavier, so your whole body is sinking deeper and deeper into the chair', and 'With each movement of your arm you are becoming more deeply hypnotized'.

It is very useful to include in the induction at least one suggestion which allows the subject, if susceptible, to experience some degree of dissociation. As was stated in Chapter 1, suggestions of relaxation and body heaviness do not necessarily evoke a sense of dissociation or non-volitional responsiveness, whereas arm levitation, arm heaviness, anaesthesia, the 'challenge' tests such as eye and limb catalepsy, and so on, do have this potential. Arm levitation is a popular method, whereas 'challenges' carry a greater risk of compromising the patient's confidence in the therapy should the suggestion fail.

In therapy one typically administers a sequence of three or four induction or deepening procedures when one hypnotizes a particular patient for the first time. This has the advantage of allowing the patient and therapist to select the most useful methods, and in later sessions the induction may be shortened considerably, some patients merely requiring a verbal cue which, when repeated several times, has the same effect as the initial, more prolonged, hypnotic induction.

Hypnotic induction procedures are a useful means of relaxation but, in the opinion of the present author, their role in hypnotherapy has been overemphasized because of too rigid an adherence to a state model which depicts the hypnotist as 'putting the subject into a hypnotic trance' (the term 'hypnotic induction' also conveys this impression). Indeed some authors such as Barber (1969) have suggested that the hypnotic induction has little more than a ceremonial function. Others, such as Hilgard (1986), regard the role of the induction as enhancing the likelihood that the subject will respond in a dissociative manner to suggestions which, in particular, require more profound alterations in perception and experience; Hilgard (1986: 226) says:

> Looked at in other ways, we find that hypnotic procedures are designed to produce a readiness for dissociative experiences by disrupting the ordinary continuities of memories and by distorting or concealing reality orientation through the power that words exert by direct suggestion, through selective attention or inattention and through stimulating the imagination appropriately.

Models and techniques in therapy

Thus far in this chapter, I have talked about theories of hypnosis or, as I prefer to call them, *models* of hypnosis, and I have paid particular attention to the model which relates the phenomena of hypnosis to the notion of dissociation. This model of hypnosis gives rise to a particular set of techniques, termed 'induction' and 'deepening', which have been described above, and I will shortly explore the models and techniques which are derived from the above ideas regarding hypnosis. First let us consider what we understand by the notion of 'technique' with regard to the conduct of the therapy. A technique in this context may be loosely defined as 'a prescribed way of responding by the therapist or, under the direction of the therapist, by the patient, which is aimed at accelerating the desired changes in behaviour, thinking, feeling and physiological functioning'.

Now all psychological therapies are aimed at bringing about changes at one or more of the above four levels. For example, a programme of behaviour therapy may be employed to help a person learn more assertive ways of interacting with others in his or her everyday life; a person with a poor self-image may come to think about himself or herself in a more realistic or positive way through a course of cognitive or psychodynamic therapy; someone suffering severe chronic pain may learn to reduce the perceived intensity of that pain by some form of cognitive-behavioural therapy; and a person with a stress-related illness may obtain benefit from learning physical relaxation procedures. Each of these therapies is associated with different kinds of techniques which reflect the theoretical model on which the therapy is based.

Hypnosis, in the form in which I have earlier described it, provides the therapist with a number of models, each one of which generates a set of techniques which the therapist may employ in the treatment of his or her patients and which have the aim of facilitating the desired changes at the various levels described above. In the last chapter I made the reasonable assumption that therapists will not be interested so much in the accuracy of the model as in the usefulness and effectiveness of the techniques which it generates.

An example may clarify this point. Consider the following model. The human mind is divided into a conscious and an unconscious part; the unconscious part of the mind contains memories, feelings, conflicts and so on which are repressed from conscious awareness. The nature of hypnosis is such that the therapist, having carried out a hypnotic induction procedure whereby the patient is 'put into a state of hypnosis', may communicate directly with the patient's unconscious mind, thereby gaining access to the repressed memories, conflicts and so on. This material may then be integrated into the patient's conscious awareness and thereby managed more effectively by the patient.

This model generates various hypnotherapeutic techniques referred to as 'exploratory', 'uncovering', or 'analytical', and I shall say more about them in due course. For the moment let us consider one such technique which uses ideomotor suggestion as described in the previous chapter. The therapist informs the patient that his or her unconscious mind can communicate by lifting different fingers, one finger indicating the message 'Yes', another finger meaning 'No', another meaning 'I don't know', and yet another meaning 'I don't want to say'. It is assumed, according to this model, that unconscious material may be accessed via these finger movements, gradually brought into the patient's conscious awareness, and interpreted and assimilated in a manner which renders the material less disruptive to the emotional life of the patient. The therapist's priority therefore is whether or not the technique works: is it useful? I will discuss this question in due course and give a cautious affirmative response. There are, however, a number of caveats which are all too often ignored. First, the technique described, like any other therapeutic manoeuvre, has a limited range of applicability: it will not be useful in many cases and often it will be found to be of no value whatsoever. Secondly, it does not follow that when the technique works effectively, the model on which it is based is thereby proved to be valid. There are many reasons why patients improve during treatment – such as placebo, spontaneous remission of symptoms, and the positive aspects of the therapist–patient relationship. Moreover, it is the author's contention that many hypnotherapeutic techniques are sufficiently complex to allow a wide range of interpretation by the patient: that is, he or she may find the techniques useful and effective for reasons other than those stipulated in the therapist's own model. In the example above, the patient may find the technique of ideomotor signalling useful, not because it enables access to unconscious material as the therapist's model supposes, but because it makes it easier for the patient to contemplate and communicate certain important and very distressing information. In other words, the act of 'putting the patient in a hypnotic state' and suggesting that the information communicated via finger movements comes from a part of the mind for which he or she is not consciously responsible may be a way of giving permission to the patient to broach material which he or she would find too embarrassing or distressing to confront in a normal face-to-face interaction with the therapist. (For a further discussion of this, see Chapter 6 of Gibson and Heap (1990).) So, in that case, the therapist's model is strictly speaking *inaccurate*, but it is not *inappropriate* in that therapeutic context.

A rather more serious error occurs when the therapist attempts to extend his or her model and techniques into areas outside their range of applicability. It seems to be the fate of all therapeutic models and the techniques derived from them, that they are extended into areas beyond those in which they have a valid application. (Indeed, the range of valid application can be very narrow or even non-existent.) This appears to be the case for contemporary medicine (both conventional and alternative), psychological therapies, and medical treatments throughout the ages and across different cultures. This, at least, is the present author's observation and I have called this phenomenon Heap's Principle (Heap 1990). For example, in the field of alternative medicine one may observe the ideomotor signalling method being used to arrive at diagnoses of illnesses and even to prescribe treatments. Likewise one comes across authors who insist that the conscious–unconscious dissociation model summarized above is at the root of *all* emotional problems (see Gibson and Heap 1990). The fact is that this model cannot be taken with any degree of seriousness as a theory of the human mind and human psychological processes, and it does not bear scrutiny by academic and experimental psychologists. Nevertheless it may be a useful, if limited, model within the context of psychotherapy.

This brings us to another consideration concerning models and techniques of therapy: because they have a limited range of usefulness it is easy for the theoreticians and experimentalists to discredit them. As the reader will have realized, the conflict between the therapist and the academic is particularly in evidence in the field of hypnosis. In fact, one may sometimes wonder if clinicians and experimentalists are actually talking about the same phenomenon. This tension could be eased if both sides recognized that the therapists' models are often only appropriate in a specific context, and that the main concern of *therapists* is whether the models generate techniques which are useful and effective *within those contexts*. Clearly the research which is most relevant to the therapist is in the form of clinical trials to establish the effectiveness of the techniques which he or she is employing. This does not give licence to therapists to ignore the findings of experimental psychologists, although it is the present author's observation that they will make every effort to do so when such research calls into question the validity and effectiveness of their therapy. Indeed it is incumbent on therapists to consider how their own ideas and speculations concerning their work require modification in the light of the findings of their academic colleagues.

Five models of hypnotherapy

There are at least five models which are important in hypnotherapy. Each model generates techniques which are presumed, and in some cases have been empirically demonstrated, to have some therapeutic degree of effectiveness. Each model has a limited range of application and, as was observed earlier, each is apt to be extended into areas beyond that range of application.

Model 1: According to their hypnotic susceptibility people have the capacity to respond automatically and in a dissociated manner to suggestions aimed at changing their feelings, perceptions, thoughts and behaviour. This capacity may be enhanced by the induction of hypnosis. This model generates techniques which are used to augment behavioural and cognitive therapy (including relaxation and anxiety management training) and to help people cope with pain, either due to illness or to some medical or dental intervention. Applications to behaviour therapy are given in a number of chapters in this book, notably in Chapters 3, 5 and 7, and Chapter 4 describes applications to cognitive therapy. Chapter 3 concerns the use of hypnosis in relaxation training and anxiety management. In these applications, one of the major sets of techniques generated by the model is the use of hypnotic suggestion and post-hypnotic suggestion, often with imaginal rehearsal, to reinforce the changes in feeling, thinking and behaviour which are the focus of the therapy. For example, in the treatment of an exhibitionist using covert aversion therapy, the following post-hypnotic suggestion may be given and rehearsed in imagination: 'As soon as you become aware of the urge to exhibit yourself, this distressing scene [previously rehearsed] will come vividly to mind and all the terrible feelings associated with it'. In the case of anxiety management training a post-hypnotic suggestion may be: 'As soon as you start to experience these anxious feelings in your stomach, you will take in a deep breath, and as you breathe out you will experience a sense of calmness and control'. Similar post-hypnotic suggestions may be used to augment cognitive changes in a course of cognitive therapy (see Chapter 4). It is assumed that the patient will respond to these post-hypnotic suggestions automatically and spontaneously without the need for deliberate conscious effort. Hypnotic procedures for managing pain and altering the experience of pain are somewhat more complex and they are described in Chapter 6 by Barry Hart.

The model and the techniques derived from it appear to be effective in the area of pain management, and support comes from the evidence that hypnotic susceptibility is related to the ability to control pain by the procedures employed (see Chapter 6). However, with the other applications there is less support. Wadden and Anderton (1982) concluded that with what they termed 'self-initiated' problems such as smoking and overeating, and in the treatment of phobias, the evidence is not clear that hypnosis is an active ingredient in the therapy, and that, contrary to what the model would predict, hypnotic susceptibility is unrelated to outcome (see also Chapter 5). Because, as was stated earlier, patients may use therapy in ways not predicted by the model, this does not mean that the techniques themselves are ineffective. However, this is an instance where it is worth re-examining the model in the light of incompatible empirical data.

One possibility which emerges from the writings of Wadden and Anderton (1982), Kihlstrom (1985) and Spinhoven (1987) is that therapists have not confined their hypnotic suggestions to discrete changes in feeling, thinking and behaviour, but have attempted to directly modify complex feelings, attitudes and habits. In the examples of post-hypnotic suggestions given earlier, the responses (and indeed the situations in which they are to occur) are clear and well defined and the patient is able to rehearse them under instruction (visualizing a particular scene or taking in and releasing a deep breath). However, it seems unlikely that a patient can respond in an automatic and involuntary fashion to suggestions such as 'You are becoming more self-confident', 'You will only eat what your body needs', 'You will no longer crave for a cigarette', 'From now on you will stand up for yourself', and so on. The patient must first be taught the skills to achieve these desirable ends, and the specific responses may then be reinforced by hypnotic suggestion and imagery (Gibson and Heap 1990).

Model 2: *Certain autonomic functions may be directly altered by appropriate suggestions and imagery to an extent which depends on the susceptibility of the subject. This process may be enhanced by the induction of hypnosis.* This model generates procedures which may be incorporated into the treatment of psychosomatic and other medical complaints. Common techniques include suggestions and imagery of recovery of the affected organ or body part, mediated by appropriate physiological changes. Examples are suggestions and imagery concerning hand-warming and peripheral vasodilation in the treatment of migraine and Reynaud's disease, reduced gastric secretions and smooth action of the intestines in the case of peptic ulceration, irritable bowel syndrome and other gastro-intestinal disorders, and improved circulation to the skin bringing nourishment and healing in the case of dermatological problems.

There is good evidence from clinical trials for the effectiveness of these techniques (see Chapter 8); hypnosis itself seems to be an active ingredient in the treatment of at least some of the above problems and hypnotic susceptibility may be related to outcome (Wadden and Anderton 1982). However, as many of the disorders treated are exacerbated by anxiety and stress, a significant component of treatment may be relaxation and anxiety and stress management techniques which are also generated by Model 1.

In the previous chapter it was stated that specific physiological responses *can* be affected by suggestion and imagery and it is a matter of scientific research to define (i) the range of involuntary responses which may be selectively modified in this manner and (ii) the extent to which recovery is mediated by these changes. With regard to the first point, in Chapter 1 we touched on peripheral blood-flow and gastric activity and, in children, tissue oxygen levels and salivary immunoglobulin A. Regarding the second point, Gibson and Heap (1990) have examined limited evidence from clinical studies and the literature on biofeedback which indicates no relationship between the degree of suggested blood-flow change and therapeutic outcome in migraine and other vascular problems. This does not support the model and suggests that it may have a limited range of valid application and that the techniques may be effective for other reasons. Nevertheless, these techniques have been widely used – for example, in the treatment of cancer by imagery of immunological change (*American Journal of Clinical Hypnosis* 1982–3).

Model 3: *Hypnosis enhances the capacity of the patient to access dissociated thoughts, feelings, memories and so on.* This model has generated some ingenious techniques generally referred to as 'exploratory' and 'uncovering' procedures, although we may also speak of 'hypnoanalytical methods'. These procedures are usually thought of as augmenting analytical or psychodynamic therapy, but there is no reason why they cannot be incorporated into behavioural or cognitive treatments.

A very popular technique – ideomotor signalling – was described earlier in this chapter. Another one is age regression, whereby it is suggested to the patient that he or she is going back in time to an event in childhood which is of significance to his or her present-day problems. It may also be suggested that the patient have a dream within the next few days which will help him or her understand the nature of the presenting problem and how to solve it (Degun and Degun

1988). Similarly, the patient may be instructed to have a dream or fantasy during hypnosis (the idea of projecting the fantasy onto a screen is sometimes useful). These techniques are alluded to in a number of chapters in the present book, but for a good overview the reader is advised to consult Karle (1988).

The range of validity and usefulness of this model and its techniques are very difficult to test empirically and we have to rely on the many individual case reports in the literature (as well as one's own clinical experience) in which the techniques appear to make a powerful contribution to the therapy.

Inappropriate application of the model is evident in the writings of some medical and lay practitioners who contend that it is always necessary to age-regress the patient 'to get to the root of the problem' – an incident or trauma which caused the presenting difficulties. The present author recalls seeing a patient with multiple sclerosis who, on consulting a lay practitioner was subjected to the ideomotor signalling procedure on the assumption that his illness was caused by a past traumatic event.

Model 4: Hypnosis is a pleasant and mood-elevating experience which involves a high degree of rapport between hypnotist and patient. These good feelings may be amplified by positive, confidence-boosting ('ego-strengthening') suggestions and imagery. The usual 'ego-strengthening', 'ego-boosting', or 'ego-enhancing' routine consists of a recitation by the therapist of a series of statements such as 'You are going to feel physically fitter and stronger in every way', 'You will become more alert, more wide awake, more energetic', 'You will no longer think nearly so much about yourself', and 'Every day your nerves will become stronger and steadier'. These examples are taken from the most widely used ego-strengthening routine, that of Hartland (1971).

At first sight it may appear that these techniques are derived from Model 1, since they are attempting to change feelings, thoughts and behaviour by suggestion. However, the reader will also notice that the suggestions are directed at complex experiences and attitudes rather than discrete and well-defined responses. Doubts were earlier raised as to whether the former kind of responses could be directly elicited by hypnotic suggestion in the same way as, say, an arm levitation or numbness of the hand.

Perhaps ego-strengthening suggestions are more associated with secondary rather than primary suggestibility (see Chapter 1). In that case their effectiveness does not depend directly on the subject's degree of hypnotic susceptibility. It seems more likely that an important factor determining their effectiveness is the degree of confidence the patient has in the therapist and the therapy being offered, the strength of the rapport, and whether indeed the patient is starting to experience some of the good feelings promised in the ego-strengthening routine. However, the temptation to overextend the model should be checked. Ego-strengthening routines cannot be relied upon as the sole therapeutic procedure with patients suffering from severe and chronic emotional and behavioural disorders. In Chapter 4 Alladin and Heap reiterate the sad experience of a depressed patient originally reported by Heap (1984) whose response to a course of ego-strengthening therapy at the hands of a lay practitioner was to make a serious suicide attempt.

Notwithstanding these caveats, there is evidence that the imaginative use of ego-strengthening routines can facilitate therapeutic change in problems concerning everyday stress and anxiety (Stanton 1990). They may also be used at any time with the idea of reinforcing the patient's progress in therapy. Both Heap (1985) and Ross (1985) have made recommendations concerning the therapeutic use of ego-strengthening.

Model 5: *This model is based on the notion that people already have the resources to overcome their problems, but these are in an unconscious part of the mind. Hypnosis provides a way of accessing these unconscious resources.* In other words, when patients come for help they are struggling to make best use of the strategies for coping which they have available to them at a conscious level; hypnosis helps them make use of other resources which are out of their conscious awareness.

This model adopts a very broad definition of hypnosis as a means of conscious–unconscious communication, and generates a number of techniques, some of them quite innovative, such as the use of metaphors and stories in which the therapist's communication to the patients covertly stimulates them to search within themselves for their own solutions. These techniques are associated in particular with the late Milton Erickson, and those who have gone on to develop his approaches. An account of metaphor and anecdotal techniques in therapy is given by Lankton and Lankton (1983), and Kirmayer (1988) gives a reasoned assessment of this aspect of Erickson's work. Some reference will also be made to these procedures in Chapter 10 of this book on applications to children.

This is a relatively untested approach so far as clinical applications are concerned although it seems to have rapidly fallen prey to Heap's Principle, judging from the deluge of books and training courses being sold on the strength of extravagant claims for the effectiveness of this form of therapy (Hammond 1988, Heap 1988). Kirmayer (1985) has also complained of the proliferation of 'fast food therapies' in North America since Erickson's death in 1980. In Britain, the author's impression is that the greatest influence has been on lay and private practitioners and amongst medical and dental practitioners who have private psychotherapy practices. The reactions of clinical psychologists and psychiatrists has been generally more sober.

Indications and contraindications for the use of hypnosis

Hypnosis is a relatively benign procedure and in the present author's opinion its 'dangers' have been oversold and confused with the risks inherent in psychological treatment generally, particularly with vulnerable and emotionally sensitive patients and those with destructive or suicidal impulses. A very good guideline is for the therapist to use hypnosis only with those patients whom he or she is competent to treat without the use of hypnosis. This means restricting one's use of hypnosis to problems which fall within one's professional training, expertise and experience. Training in hypnosis itself does not endow a person with the competence to treat problems of which he or she has hitherto no experience.

Given this caution, there are few if any problems concerning which one can say hypnosis should *never* be used to augment psychological treatment. As will be mentioned below, for some problems there *are* treatments of choice in which hypnosis does not have an obvious role, but in the main, much depends on the expertise and experience of the therapist and the characteristics of the patient and his or her problems.

Contraindications, then, are usually concerned with whether the use of hypnosis is likely to be worth the time and effort invested rather than with any adverse effects as such. One obvious consideration therefore is whether the patient is susceptible to hypnosis. Surely it is important to screen patients using hypnotic susceptibility scales and to refrain from offering hypnosis to those with very low susceptibility scores? Some practitioners would agree, but as was stated in the previous chapter, in Britain at least, susceptibility scales are not widely used in routine clinical practice. In fact, as I remarked earlier, the techniques of hypnosis may be beneficial for patients for reasons other than those predicted by the underlying model, so that they may still prove effective with some hypnotically insusceptible patients.

I myself make little use of hypnotic susceptibility scales in therapy and I never employ them with patients to whom I have introduced the idea of hypnosis (as distinct from patients who themselves ask for hypnosis). In fact I often introduce hypnosis in an informal and casual manner perhaps by suggesting at some appropriate point in the session that the patient close his or her eyes and focus on some salient experience, say an image, a feeling or his or her breathing. Even when a formal approach to hypnosis is used and the therapist has carefully explained its nature, allayed anxieties and misconceptions and so on, would it not be most unsatisfactory for him or her to spend the best part of a session measuring the patient's susceptibility, and then to inform the insusceptible patient that hypnosis is not going to be used after all? This would be especially disruptive if, as is not uncommon, the idea of using hypnosis were introduced with therapy already under way.

When patients are themselves demanding that their problem be treated by hypnosis, then I am more inclined to measure their susceptibility, even though I usually proceed with hypnotic treatment regardless of the level of hypnotic responsiveness. I find the Creative Imagination Scale of Wilson and Barber (1978) convenient for these purposes. In spite of what I have already said, susceptibility scales do provide the therapist with useful information about which kinds of suggestions and imagery a patient finds most effective. Occasionally one sees a patient who is convinced that hypnosis is the answer even though they have consulted a number of practitioners without benefit. Should hypnotherapy again prove unhelpful, it may be that the patient is low in susceptibility and this may be discussed with him or her at the end of treatment; an alternative approach may then be offered and the patient spared the search for the elusive hypnotist who can put him or her into a 'deep trance'.

When patients specifically request hypnosis I do not regard this as a definite indication for its application. Some practitioners would argue otherwise on the grounds that the patient is assuming responsibility for his or her treatment and this should be supported by the therapist. In my experience, however, the demand for hypnosis is seldom based on a rational and informed understanding of what hypnosis is and how it may help overcome the patient's problem. The patient may have merely witnessed a stage hypnotist's show or may have read a novel or seen a film in which hypnosis is misrepresented in some fundamental way. Occasionally a patient will ask for hypnosis because this is the only psychological treatment he or she has heard of and will be more than satisfied when this misconception is corrected. Whatever the case, therapists have a professional obligation to satisfy themselves that the application of hypnosis is justified on a rational assessment of their patients' problems. However, as I have indicated earlier, when a patient feels very strongly that only by his or her being hypnotized will the problem be cured, then the best plan may be to 'test reality' and proceed with hypnosis.

Conclusions

Five major models of hypnosis in therapy have been outlined, each generating a set of techniques which may be applied to a wide variety of therapies and problems. Each model is presumed to be valid within a limited context, but outside of this the techniques developed from the model may still be effective because patients may utilize them constructively in ways not intended by the model. The evidence for the validity of each model and the effectiveness of the techniques is variable across the five models but, according to Heap's Principle, there will always be a tendency for models and techniques to be extended beyond their range of useful application. It is also noteworthy that those who use hypnotic procedures in therapy often utilize more than one model and even all models, not just for different patients but also for the same patient at different stages of therapy, and even within one session of therapy. One reason for this eclecticism may be that medically and dentally qualified practitioners have played a major role in developing hypnotherapeutic methods and often they are not strongly committed to a particular school of therapy.

We may therefore see that the potential range of application of hypnosis to different therapies and problems is considerable; we must nevertheless be mindful that the range is still limited. Hypnosis itself does not offer any explanation as to how emotional and psychological disorders are acquired in the first place, unlike other methods of treatment such as behaviour therapy, cognitive therapy and psychoanalysis. As was emphasized at the beginning of this chapter, hypnosis is best construed as an adjunct to these therapies rather than as a therapy itself. Nevertheless in the treatment of psychosomatic problems, such as migraine and asthma and relatively uncomplicated cases of generalized anxiety and organic pain, the therapy may consist almost entirely of sessions of hypnosis, positive suggestions, the rehearsal of anxiety management procedures in the hypnotic state, and the regular practice of self-hypnosis in between sessions. With other problems, as will be evident from the following chapters, hypnosis may be only a small component of the treatment programme. Perhaps in the case of analytical psychotherapy or cognitive therapy the therapist may utilize hypnosis for, say, age regression or other exploratory work in only a small minority of the sessions.

There are also treatment programmes in which hypnosis does not have a particularly obvious role. For example, a programme of exposure therapy in the case of a simple phobia or agoraphobia, or a programme of response prevention in a patient with an obsessive–compulsive disorder would not necessarily benefit greatly from the time spent engaging in hypnotic procedures. Also, hypnosis is rarely used in the UK with psychotic patients and those with bipolar affective disorder. None the less, this still leaves an extensive range of possibilities for hypnosis and when used with discretion and imagination, hypnotic procedures are a valuable adjunct in any therapist's repertoire of skills.

References

American Journal of Clinical Hypnosis (1982–3) Special Issue: Hypnosis and Cancer 25: 2, 3.

Barber, T.X. (1969) *Hypnosis: A Scientific Approach*, New York: Van Nostrand.

Degun, M.D. and Degun, G. (1988) The use of hypnotic dream suggestion in psychotherapy, in M. Heap (ed.) *Hypnosis: Current Clinical, Experimental and Forensic Practices*, London: Croom Helm.

Gibson, H.B. and Heap, M. (1990) *Hypnosis in Therapy*, London: Lawrence Erlbaum.

Hammond, C.D. (1988) Will the real Milton Erickson please stand up? *International Journal of Clinical and Experimental Hypnosis* 36: 173–81.

Hartland, J. (1971) *Medical and Dental Hypnosis and its Clinical Applications*, 2nd edn, London: Baillière Tindall.

Heap, M. (1984) Four victims, *British Journal of Experimental and Clinical Hypnosis*, 2: 60–62.

—— (1985) Ego-strengthening: further considerations, *Proceedings of the Second Annual Conference of the British Society of Experimental and Clinical Hypnosis*, BSECH.

—— (1988) Born-again mesmerism? *The Psychologist* 1: 261–2.

—— (1990) Analytical applications of hypnosis. Workshop presented at the *Seventh Annual Conference of the British Society of Experimental and Clinical Hypnosis*, Sheffield University, March.

Hilgard, E.R. (1986) *Divided Consciousness: Multiple Controls in Human Thought and Action*, 2nd edn, New York: Wiley.

Hoogduin, C.A.L. and de Jong, P. (1989) Hypnotisability in obsessive compulsives, in D. Waxman, D. Pedersen, I. Wilkie and P. Mellett, *Hypnosis: The Fourth European Congress at Oxford*, London: Whurr Publishers.

Karle, H.W.A. (1988) Hypnosis in analytic psychotherapy, in M. Heap (ed.) *Hypnosis: Current Clinical, Experimental and Forensic Practices*, London: Croom Helm.

Karle, H.W.A. and Boys, J.H. (1987) *Hypnotherapy: A Practical Handbook*, London: Free Association Books.

Kihlstrom, J.F. (1985) Hypnosis, *Annual Review of Psychology* 36: 385–418.

Kirmayer, L.J. (1985) Healing and the invention of metaphor: Erickson's implicit psychology, Paper presented at the *Tenth Annual Congress of Hypnosis in Psychotherapy and Psychosomatic Medicine*, Toronto, August.

—— (1988) Word magic and the rhetoric of common sense: Erickson's metaphors for mind, *International Journal of Clinical and Experimental Hypnosis* 36: 157–72.

Lankton, S. and Lankton, C. (1983) *The Answer Within: A Clinical Framework of Ericksonian Hypnotherapy*, New York: Brunner Mazel.

Milgram, S. (1963) Behavioural study of obedience, *Journal of Abnormal and Social Psychology* 67: 371–8.

—— (1974) *Obedience to Authority*, London: Tavistock.

Pettinati, H.M., Horne, R.L. and Staats, J.M. (1985) Hypnotisability in patients with anorexia and bulimia, *Archives of General Psychiatry* 42: 1014–16.

Ross, P.J. (1985) Ego-strengthening: a critical view, *Proceedings of the Second Annual Conference of the British Society of Experimental and Clinical Hypnosis*, BSECH.

Spanos, N.P. and Chaves, J.F. (1989) *Hypnosis: The Cognitive-Behavioral Perspective*, Buffalo, NY: Prometheus.

Spinhoven, P. (1987) Hypnosis and behaviour therapy: a review, *International Journal of Clinical and Experimental Hypnosis* 35: 8–31.

Stanton, H.E. (1990) Using ego-enhancement to increase assertiveness, *British Journal of Experimental and Clinical Hypnosis* 7: 133–7.

Wadden, T.A. and Anderton, C.H. (1982) The clinical use of hypnosis, *Psychological Bulletin* 91: 215–43.

Waxman, D. (1989) *Hartland's Medical and Dental Hypnosis*, 3rd edn, London: Baillière Tindall.

Wilson, S.C. and Barber, T.X. (1978) The Creative Imagination Scale as a measure of hypnotic responsiveness: applications to clinical and experimental hypnosis, *American Journal of Clinical Hypnosis* 20: 235–49.

3

Hypnotherapy and anxiety

H.B. GIBSON

Introduction

Hypnotherapy for conditions of anxiety has a long history in Britain, but it fell out of general use at the beginning of this century although practised sporadically by some individual doctors and other professional people. Reference to the *British Medical Journal* and *The Lancet* in the first half of the century shows occasional reports of its use, mainly for anxiety-mediated conditions such as psychosomatic disorders. By the 1950s there was little use of hypnosis except by a few less orthodox psychiatrists, mainly of psychoanalytic orientation.

It is interesting to note the association between hypnotherapy and the behaviour therapy movement that was initiated at the Maudsley Hospital in London, independently of that of B.F. Skinner in the USA. The Maudsley school was very influenced by Wolpe's important book (Wolpe 1958) in which he described how he devoted the early sessions to training patients in physical relaxation and then hypnotizing them, his technique of systematic desensitization being conducted with the patient in what he referred to as 'a hypnotic trance'. He wrote: 'Patients who cannot relax will not make progress by this method. Those who cannot or will not be hypnotized but who can relax will make progress, although apparently more slowly than when hypnosis is used' (Wolpe 1958: 141).

When Wolpe's methods were taken up and adapted at the Maudsley Hospital by Eysenck and his colleagues, the question of hypnosis was quietly dropped. This was partly justified by Eysenck and Rachman who referred to some work in the USA by Lang and Lazovik who had found that in their experience hypnosis added nothing to the method of extinguishing anxiety by systematic desensitization. But there were political reasons for eschewing hypnosis at this time by therapists engaged in constructing a new form of therapy based on scientific principles, in contrast to the intuitive methods of the psychodynamic movement which had become associated with the practice of hypnotherapy. It should be remembered that up to that time there had been very little attempt to study the phenomena of hypnosis scientifically in Britain, although Eysenck himself had carried out some research on the subject and published some seminal papers, and it was he who responded to the recommendations of the 1955 report on the *Medical Use of Hypnotism* of the British Medical Association by setting up a hypnosis research unit in his department.

Rachman (1968) was later to criticize Wolpe's assumption that muscular relaxation was necessarily incompatible with anxiety. Rachman pointed out that although many workers had found that the therapeutic success of combating anxiety by systematic desensitization was greater if the preliminaries of inducing physical relaxation were observed, the matter was less simple than it appeared. Other clinicians had found that there was little correspondence between the degree of muscular relaxation manifest on physiological measuring apparatus and subjects' own reports of how mentally calm they felt. In accordance with these findings Rachman argued that what is important for therapy is not the *physical* relaxation but the degree of *mental* relaxation, that is, how calm the patient feels. It seems reasonable to suggest that only when we have induced hypnosis both by teaching the patient how to relax completely, and using imagery appropriate to the individual patient, is there a real and necessary change in the state of consciousness incompatible with anxiety. The muscular relaxation is a means to an end, inducing hypnosis, not an end in itself.

Wolpe used the hypnotic technique of Lewis Wolberg, and perhaps his early success was due to his use of hypnosis to an extent that was not fully appreciated. That some later therapists who aimed to follow Wolpe did not find hypnosis particularly useful, may be due to the nature of the hypnotic methods they used, as well as to the degree of hypnotic susceptibility of the patients with whom they were working – a factor that is often overlooked. To report that one used 'hypnosis' without actually detailing precisely what was done, and without actually assessing the degrees of hypnotic susceptibility of the patients, makes it very difficult to evaluate the merit of a study. In much of the hypnosis literature, particularly that which is published by those who are exclusively experimentalists, there is a facile assumption that by repeating a standard form of hypnotic induction, often read from a book or recorded on tape, we have 'hypnotized' the person so addressed.

What is anxiety?

Many writers advocating this or that type of therapy mention anxiety without specifying just what they mean by the word. The assumption seems to be that 'everyone knows what anxiety is' but this is by no means the case. In their dictionary of psychology English and English (1958) give six meanings for the word, and mention that in Britain we have our own meaning of the word. They caution that '*Anxiety* must be read with great vigilance for an author's meaning, or more often than not, his several meanings' (p. 35). In discussing the use of hypnotherapy in relation to anxiety it is therefore necessary first to define the meaning given to the word.

More than twenty years ago Aubrey Lewis discussed the ambiguity of the term 'anxiety', and in the present chapter I try to follow its usage by such British colleagues and students of Lewis, both psychologists and psychiatrists, as Eysenck, Gray, Lader, Marks, Mathews and Rachman who have made a distinguished contribution to its study. Anxiety is essentially a learned and anticipatory response, in contrast to fear which is to some degree innate and can be elicited by certain definable stimuli. Fear implies a response to some immediate and often visible threat (a snarling dog), whereas anxiety refers to the anticipation of some event in the future which is perhaps less clearly defined (the Inland Revenue gaining access to some undisclosed sources of income). Anxiety can be usefully conceptualized as having three main components: subjective–cognitive, motor–behavioural and physiological. In most cases of gross clinical anxiety, all three components are present together, but in some clinical cases where anxiety is important only one or two of the components are involved in the presenting symptoms. Lader and Marks (1971) have produced a very useful summary of the position which is represented in Table 3.1.

Table 3.1 Main possible patterns of anxiety responses

Component	1	2	3	4	5	6	7
Subjective–cognitive	+	+	+	–	–	–	+
Motor–behavioural	+	+	–	+	–	+	–
Physiological	+	–	–	+	+	–	+

+ indicates the component shows the response appropriate for anxiety.
– indicates the component does not show the response appropriate for anxiety.

Reproduced by kind permission from Lader and Marks (1971).

It is evident from this table that seven different combinations of the three components go to make up 'anxiety' in its many manifestations both clinically and in normal life. For instance, sufferers from most types of psychosomatic disorder have patterns similar to 1, 4, 5 and 7, and those with the pattern of 4 and 5 would probably deny that they are anxious. Pattern 6 is exemplified by a hysterical motor conversion disorder in which there is actual paralysis maintained by anxiety, but the patient presents with *la belle indifference*.

Hypnotherapeutic approaches: general principles in treating anxiety

The position that I adopt is that hypnosis is not a therapy in itself, but is a very useful tool if applied correctly in facilitating programmes of therapy that are designed according to some well-understood principle. Thus hypnosis can be used in conjunction with drugs, in the programme of antenatal training and obstetric management, in the re-education of people with speech disorders, in the treatment of people with dental phobias, in remedial therapy for children with spastic paralyses, and in the psychological treatment of patients with anxiety conditions and phobias. The six foregoing examples chosen at random show how hypnosis can be used by people who represent various professional disciplines. Thus although the term 'hypnotherapy' is useful and widely used, and will be employed in this chapter, there is no therapy that is simply 'hypnotherapy', and there is no legitimate profession of 'hypnotherapist', although many lay people adopt the name and try to make a living thereby. This matter is explained very fully by Gibson and Heap (1990).

This chapter will be concerned with hypnosis in the treatment of anxiety in conditions that are referred to psychologists, medical doctors, and other health professionals. Over the past thirty years there has been a slow but growing use of hypnosis by such professionals in Britain.

In more recent years the term 'cognitive therapy' has become fashionable, and one is frequently asked 'Is hypnotherapy a form of cognitive therapy?' In my opinion it is not. The reason some people have for regarding hypnotherapy as a form of cognitive therapy lies in the fact that, after a course of such therapy, patients will think of themselves and the world in general in a slightly different way, and perhaps alter their opinions on certain topics. It seems as though they have been 'persuaded' to think differently by the eminently reasonable arguments of the therapist. There is, of course, no harm in trying to persuade patients, by rational argument, to give up irrational beliefs about themselves and their environment. But it can be argued (as does Marks 1987) that disordered thinking associated with states of anxiety does not necessarily stem from false cognitive processes. The woman who is phobic for moths and butterflies does not really think that they are 'dangerous, ugly and dirty' though she may say that this is how they *appear* to her. Her anxiety with regard to them stems from processes outside the realm of cognition, namely, processes of emotional conditioning.

Hypnosis owes its special virtue in appealing more to that part of the brain represented by the hypothalamus and the limbic system than the cerebral cortex! Isaac Marks (1987) demonstrates that although behaviour therapy is concerned directly with the emotions of the patient and does not attempt any deliberate cognitive restructuring, after therapy is complete the patient will think differently about objects and topics that were relevant to the neurotic disorder. Some people tend to put the cart before the horse and think of the changes as having been effected by cognitive means. Marks states 'We have to distinguish cognitions that are epiphenomenal from cognitions that cause action'. He uses the post-hypnotic suggestion as the paradigm for people unwittingly executing actions and giving plausible but erroneous reasons for acting thus. Dryden makes the following distinction that is relevant to the different sorts of standpoint that therapists take:

> *Cognitive–affective* Cognitive theories are the so-called ego theories which see man as essentially rational, with the emotions subserving the intellect. Conversely, affective theories see man as operating on an emotional basis, and with the intellect at the service of the emotions.
>
> (Dryden 1984: 296)

Hypnotherapy is definitely based on the latter presumption. It is unique in that in therapy there is a deliberate attempt by the therapist to get the patient to put aside the ordinary mode of rational thinking and adopt an uncritical, dream-like state of mind in which fantasy and imagery predominate. In such a state the level of anxiety can be controlled and patients are induced to think calmly about topics and objects that are normally too distressing to be faced in ordinary waking life. A reprogramming of attitudes can then be effected. This may be a slow process, and normally patients are expected to learn to practise self-hypnosis at home, and as cassette tape-recorders are now so common, home sessions can take place daily, the therapist's recorded voice substituting for his or her actual presence.

In his chapter on 'Anxiety Control' Anthony Humphreys (1988) uses much the same tripartite division as that of Lader and Marks (1971) that was discussed earlier, and he makes the point that early in treatment the therapist should address the immediate problem of the extremely distressing somatic symptoms that make it so difficult for the patient to come to grips with his or her disorder. This is not always the case, as in categories of anxiety represented in 2, 3 and 6 in Table 3.1, but it is generally so, and Humphreys writes:

> The more serious block to clients reducing their fear responses is the somatic sensations (component three). Clients dread that these will re-occur, that friends, colleagues etc, will notice and that they (the clients) will lose control. These severe somatic manifestations of anxiety need to be brought under control by measures aimed directly at the disabling experiences. Therefore, one of the initial uses of hypnosis with anxious persons is to employ it as a means of teaching the client deep relaxation with a view to self-control of the distressing somatic sensations.
>
> (Humphreys 1988: 109)

I do not agree that it is simply deep relaxation that is involved, for patients with anxiety problems can be taught by hypnosis and repeated post-hypnotic suggestions to control the anxiety and its distressing somatic symptoms in situations in which they are physically active and certainly not deeply relaxed, as in the case of agoraphobics who need to control their anxiety while out shopping. Again we must refer to Rachman's criticism of Wolpe's early conceptualization of muscular relaxation being incompatible with anxiety.

In hypnotherapy we do not seek only to reduce the level of current anxiety; it may be necessary deliberately to provoke a certain degree of anxiety later in therapy to give the patient practice in coping with distressing situations, at first in imagery and later in real life if possible, such as going with a patient on a trip along the motorway in the course of treating a phobia for driving.

Another example of the therapist using hypnosis as a means whereby anxiety can be used constructively is the deliberate provocation of abreaction. This is usually in cases where patients find it difficult to express their emotions, or admit to themselves that they feel both anxiety and anger. Feelings of guilt may make them unable to express anger towards certain institutions and people in their lives, but it may be necessary to express their anger, and to experience the consequent anxiety, before a resolution of their problems may be attempted. Again, it has been recognized since the time of Aristotle that one may 'purge the soul through pity and terror', and this was alleged by him to be one of the functions of the Greek tragedies. From time to time this idea has been made use of in therapy, as in the 'crises' provoked in Mesmer's salon, the abreactions of

Breuer's and Freud's patients, the abreactive treatment of soldiers with battle neuroses, 'flooding' in behaviour therapy, and the technique of inducing anxiety first advocated by Sipprelle, and later developed by Meichenbaum (1977) into a technique of 'stress inoculation' in which the patient is taught to come to terms with anxiety and cope with it.

Some therapists use hypnotherapy as a means of investigating anxiety-producing incidents that are alleged to, or are suspected of, producing trauma that is operative in contributing to a current disorder. The usual way of doing this is to age-regress the patient to a time at which the incidents are supposed to have taken place. This is characteristic of therapists who practise 'analytic psychotherapy' (see Chapter 2) and raises some highly controversial questions. Critics have pointed out the danger of therapists foisting on to their patients false memories of events that never happened, which is not difficult in hypnosis, and of formulating their own theories of the patient's present dilemmas which, if eventually accepted by the patient, are regarded as the latter gaining 'insight'. Modern analytic psychotherapists such as Hellmut Karle (1988) are aware of all the criticisms that have been levelled against this sort of practice, and at least admit that 'uncovering is not in itself a treatment', and that what the patient apparently remembers may be the product of fantasy. But despite this sop to their critics, by the use of the word 'uncovering' they imply that what is spoken of was really there to be 'uncovered', rather than being the joint creation of the therapist and patient. A more cautious and less controversial use of age-regression in hypnosis is the technique of the 'affect bridge' described by Watkins (1971) and discussed by Gibson and Heap (1990, Chapter 6). This technique enables the therapist to explore the circumstances, both past and present, that are associated with the patient's experience of anxiety, in a way that might not have been possible by the patient simply trying to give a descriptive account of his or her troubles.

In this section of the chapter I have dealt with the general principles of the treatment by hypnotherapy of anxiety as it appears in strictly clinical cases. However, anxiety also occurs very extensively in normal life, and is, in some measure, essential to normal functioning. Some degree of appropriate anxiety is necessary in order that people shall drive safely, study for examinations efficiently, perform well in sports contests, and maximize their potential in various other fields of human activity. Trouble arises when the level of anxiety rises too high and inhibits rather than potentiates good performance. I shall deal later with how hypnotic techniques for controlling anxiety may help in promoting maximum performance in situations that do not involve actual psychopathology, but the principles of its application are the same.

Specific applications

1 Hypnotherapy for anxiety in psychological problems

It is rather artificial to divide problems between the psychological and the psycho-somatic, but this is a traditional division which springs from the age-old division between mind and body that we have all grown up with. The experience of anxiety is relevant to the generation and maintenance of most, if not all, neurotic psychological problems, such as anxiety states and specific phobias, addictive disorders, insomnia, feelings of inadequacy, sexual problems and obsessional neuroses. The disorder that presents is often a mechanism that the patient has evolved as a means of fending off anxiety, as in the case of compulsive obsessional rituals, and the complex system of avoidances that the phobic patient observes in order not to be faced with an anxiety-generating situation. States of free-floating anxiety are less easily understood, and lead to a consideration of 'anxiety about anxiety'.

Anxiety-depression
It may be objected that one large class of neurotic disorders, the depressions, do not always present the symptoms of anxiety, although many do. This is true, and we are here in the controversial area of debate concerning the extent to which different types of depression are generated by biochemical factors. Some therapists argue that depressive disorders should not be treated by hypnotherapy, while others claim to use it effectively; probably it is most useful in those states known as anxiety-depression (see Chapter 4).

In general, depressive states that are of a clearly endogenous nature, that is, in which some biochemical disorder is thought to be largely responsible, do not yield to purely psychological therapy, and so hypnosis is not appropriate. However, in cases of reactive depression, the therapist's task is often to focus on the state of anxiety that is causing the depression. The depression is often the most obvious symptom of the disorder, but underlying it there is frequently a state of generalized anxiety of an agoraphobic variety. Treatment may usefully employ hypnotic suggestion to assist ego-strengthening after the model of Hartland (1971), to alter the patient's perception of his or her situation, to overcome concomitant distressful symptoms such as insomnia, and to implement programmes of behaviour therapy appropriate to the individual case. On the cognitive side, hypnosis may be used to assist patients realistically to face issues which they tend to avoid thinking about because they are too emotionally distressing (see Chapter 4).

Emmelkamp and Kuipers (1979) treated a group of depressed patients by focusing on the modification of their agoraphobic anxiety. They wrote: 'the amelioration of depression as *a consequence* of behavioral treatment for phobias is particularly noteworthy when seen in the light of the frequently mentioned connection between them' (p. 354).

Phobic disorders
Apart from phobic conditions of a vague and agoraphobic nature, as discussed above, therapists are frequently confronted with highly specific phobias which can exist in the lives of people who may be otherwise reasonably well adjusted. Therapists of different theoretical orientations naturally employ different methods in their treatment of psychological disorders, but all must be concerned with the control of anxiety in its various manifestations. The work of Wolpe in his original formulation of behaviour therapy has already been discussed, and it is significant that the early behaviour therapists were concerned chiefly with

conditions in which phobic anxiety played a large part. Hypnotherapy has an obvious role to play in the treatment of phobic disorders and Lazarus (1973) has described the various ways in which hypnotherapy can be integrated with behavioural treatments. It would be redundant to repeat here the details of Lazarus's early but very adequate review. The subject has been greatly expanded in the 1970s and 1980s, and Clarke and Jackson (1983) have devoted a substantial book to the treatment of anxiety and phobias not *by* hypnosis, but using hypnotic techniques to facilitate processes that are traditionally known as behaviour therapy, often with a more modern attempt to implicate cognitive processes.

Addictive disorders
These include alcoholism, drug abuse, compulsive use of tobacco, and over-eating. Contrary to popular belief, hypnotherapy is not specially effective in treating such addictions when it is applied with the intention of direct symptom removal (see Chapter 5). There is good evidence that such habits are acquired in different ways by different individuals, but they all serve the function of allaying the anxiety that builds up if the customary 'prop' is withdrawn. Treatments, which need to be highly individualized, concentrate on changing the patients' life-style and enabling them to deal with anxiety-provoking situations by alternative means, and it is in this way that hypnotherapy can be a useful adjunct, rather than by employing it in direct suggestion aimed to break the habit.

Insomnia
This is one of the commonest results of daytime anxiety. Paradoxically, during the daytime the patient may not be conscious of being particularly anxious: it is when all the distractions of the working day are over that the patient is seized by anxious ruminations that either prevent the normal onset of sleep, or act as an awakening stimulus in the small hours of the morning. There is a large literature on the treatment of insomnia, and one form of treatment consists of teaching the patient self-hypnosis and supplying a tape which ends by inducing natural sleep. It needs to be stated that commercial tapes that are supposed to do this are of doubtful value, for what suits one patient does not suit another. Each tape should be tailored to the patient's individual requirements, and supply the imagery appropriate for the person concerned.

Many people believe that they need far more sleep than is really necessary, and individual differences in sleep requirements are very great. Patients should be reassured about this as they may worry unnecessarily if their natural requirement for sleep is considerably less than most people's. Worry about sleep will, of course, set up a vicious circle of insomnia. Idiopathic insomnia is treated fairly easily by the patient learning self-hypnosis, with, as described above, the assistance of an audiotape which has been individually prepared. However, insomnia may be the presenting symptom of more serious neurotic or psychotic disorders. If the insomniac condition does not clear up after several weeks of treatment, which may incorporate all the usual features of behaviour therapy in addition to self-hypnosis (see Bootzin and Nicassio 1976), then more intensive diagnostic investigation of the patient's condition is indicated.

Personal inadequacy

Feelings of personal inadequacy are entirely subjective, and may severely cripple the lives of people who may not be perceived as inadequate by others. It is thought that repeated traumatic events that provoke anxiety in interpersonal situations combine to produce in such people this negative view of themselves. The so-called 'ego-strengthening' routine in hypnosis that was devised by Hartland (1971) has been found very useful (see Chapter 2). It consists of giving the hypnotized patient suggestions that the future will be brighter and that he or she will recover confidence, health, and energy, and the suggestions involve a substantial reappraisal of the self, the therapist's authority vouching for the validity of the new self-image that is to be built up. As the patient's existing self-image in such a condition is quite unrealistically poor, the therapist does not have to depart from reality in suggesting a much more positive image. Reassurance has to be given repeatedly and confidently, and the process can be conceptualized in terms of reconditioning, giving repeated rewards to counter the effect of all the punishing events that have been experienced in the past. This, in conjunction with other therapeutic measures such as assertiveness training, works towards eliminating the anxiety that has made social interaction so difficult.

No simple outline of a remedial programme can be given here. Each case may present unique features, and the therapist must tackle the individual problems that present. Again the reader is referred to Lader and Marks's formulation of the complexities of anxiety set out in Table 3.1 and decide what patterns of anxiety have caused the individual patient to feel personally inadequate.

Sexual problems

All therapists who have studied and treated problems of functional sexual inadequacy are agreed that the main barrier to successful performance and enjoyment is simply anxiety. The sexual response is entirely dependent on a correct balance in the autonomic nervous system, and a condition of anxiety is absolutely antipathetic to such a state. Sex therapies normally include a programme of simple instruction about the relevant physiology and anatomy, but successful therapy depends upon the re-education of the patient's responses so that the stimuli which should normally arouse pleasant erotic feelings, no longer arouse an anxiety response. Hypnosis has proved an excellent medium whereby such re-education may take place, and in Britain, Prem Misra (1985) has initiated some valuable programmes of treatment by hypnotherapy (see Chapter 7).

As yet little is published in the UK concerning the use of hypnotic techniques in sex therapy, and we must look to the American literature on the subject which is more advanced (e.g. Araoz 1982). In the most recent publication about sex therapy in Britain (Cole and Dryden 1988) there is no mention of hypnotherapy, although an innovative therapist could adapt some of the techniques described therein to make an imaginative use of hypnosis.

Obsessional neurosis

This is a condition in which certain mental and behavioural rituals have to be performed in order to ward off the onset of anxiety, and in its most severe manifestation it presents as a general neurotic disorder that can be crippling for the whole personality. All that we know about the correlates of hypnotic susceptibility indicates that the obsessional personality is generally most resistant to experiencing hypnosis, and in fact Hoogduin and de Jong (1989) have recently reported much lower than average hypnotizability scores in a sample of 94 patients with obsessive–compulsive neurosis.

With this serious caveat, it should be mentioned that there are disorders of a compulsive nature that some people refer to as 'obsessional' because the sufferers have an obsession with some irrational behaviour. Thus Snaith (1981) refers to sexual exhibitionism as an 'obsessional neurosis', and describes how he treats it with a form of behaviour therapy involving hypnotically induced imagery that he calls 'Anxiety Control Training'. However, he admits that in this therapy there will only be a successful outcome in 'the absence of other major psychopathology'. This certainly restricts its use, and permits us to observe that in most states of obsessional neurosis, hypnotherapy is contraindicated. Expertise in the clinical applications of hypnosis involves knowing when not to attempt to use it. The properly qualified clinician will be able to employ his or her professional skills without the aid of hypnosis, and it is a waste of time and effort to persist with hypnosis with patients who prove to be very insusceptible.

2 Psychosomatic disorders

This section must inevitably overlap to some extent with Chapter 8 on Hypnosis in Medicine. Reference is made to some of the conditions dealt with at length in that chapter to emphasize the extent to which anxiety is involved in their aetiology and maintenance, and how they can be alleviated by the lowering of the level of anxiety by hypnotic techniques. There are two approaches to the treatment of psychosomatic disorders by hypnotherapy: giving suggestions directed at the function of the organ or area of the body implicated, and giving suggestions and implementing programmes of behavioural treatment that will lower the patient's general level of anxiety.

Gastrointestinal disorders

The whole of the intestinal tract is very much affected by emotional factors, and it is not surprising that anxiety affects the digestive and eliminative function both temporarily, as in sickness or diarrhoea precipitated by sudden fear, or in the long term when a continued anxiety state disrupts the physiological functions and sometimes causes organic changes. Because emotional factors are involved, various psychological techniques including hypnotherapy are ideally suited to be included in therapeutic programmes. Of the many gastrointestinal disorders in which anxiety plays a part in the aetiology and maintenance, the two that are dealt with in Chapter 8, the irritable bowel syndrome (IBS) and ulceration of the duodenum, will be briefly discussed.

The IBS generally includes not only the physical disorder, but a certain degree of pervasive anxiety and sometimes depression. It is commonly treated by dietary control and by drugs, but the rate of cure, as established by follow-up after a year, is not high; Holdsworth and DuCann (1986) estimate it at only 20%. The study by Whorwell *et al.* (1984), which is described in Chapter 8, demonstrates the use of direct suggestions concerning the affected organs as well as a programme of hypnotherapy designed to lower the patients' general level of anxiety. The patients in the control group who received placebo medication also received psychotherapy in which symptoms were discussed and their emotional problems and stressful life-events were reviewed, but they did not improve to the same degree. This indicates that it is important to treat *organ-specific* anxiety, and hypnosis is a very suitable medium for doing this.

There have been a number of small studies reporting the beneficial results of hypnotherapy in the case of peptic ulceration, but, as described in Chapter 8, Colgan *et al.* (1988) carried out a controlled study using hypnotherapy with a reasonably large number of patients and found that after a year 53% of the hypnotherapy group had relapsed as compared with 100% relapse of the unhypnotized group.

It is evident that in the successful treatment of the two conditions discussed above, it is not wholly the generalized anxiety as such that is being meliorated. Neither condition is produced and maintained by anxiety alone: both are multi-factorial in origin. But in all such conditions where anxiety is involved there is a vicious circle, anxiety exacerbating the disease process and the disorder making the sufferer increasingly and chronically anxious. It may be suggested that the role of the hypnotherapy is dual: to make the patient less anxious in general, and hence aid the natural healing process, and to attack *organ-specific* anxiety, restoring the patients' control over their bowel movements or lessening the gastric secretion.

Asthma

This disorder is examined at length in Chapter 8. In considering hypnotherapy for asthma we may ask, what exactly does the 'hypnosis' consist of? Are direct suggestions being made about the patients' experience of the physical symptoms, or is the suggestive therapy being directed to the alleviation of the anxiety that is maintaining the disorder? It may surprise some that Wilkinson specifically warns against giving suggestions for the actual symptom removal. Details of the actual procedures are given in the later chapter, the main purpose of hypnotherapy for asthmatic patients being to reduce their general level of anxiety and to build up their confidence by ego-strengthening suggestions.

Skin disorders

There are many types of skin disorders, and it is generally agreed that psychological factors often contribute to their aetiology, maintenance and cure. Among disorders for which hypnosis has been found to be useful in treatment, Rowley (1986) lists eczema, psoriasis, acne, pruritus, herpes and warts. He states, they 'are often triggered and made worse by psychological states such as anxiety'. Several good reviews have been published relating to the treatment of one or other type of skin disorder by hypnotherapy (see Gibson and Heap 1990). It is suggested here that where hypnotherapy is successful in the alleviation and cure of skin disorders it is through its action as a medium lowering the anxiety status of the patient, and, as with the gastrointestinal disorders, attacking the organ-specific anxiety. This is in contrast to the view that skin disorders are improved simply by direct suggestion, either under hypnosis or in the waking state, patients being able somehow to improve their skin by the power of thought. There is now much evidence that such disorders are partly due to the low immunological status of the body, anxiety playing its part in reducing the efficiency of the immunological system (Bunney 1982). It is only in recent years that the full part that the immune system plays in the maintenance of the health of the skin has been acknowledged, many new insights in immunology having been gained through transplant surgery.

In suggesting that it is the anxiety-reducing aspect of hypnotherapy that is the main effective factor in the treatment of skin disorders, I am partly in agreement with Bowers and Kelly (1979) when they write:

> The healing aspect of communications that are suggestions can vary on a dimension of specificity. For example, the simple suggestion to relax and become hypnotized seems to have the nonspecific effect of lowering the amount of circulating corticosteroids . . . As we have seen, corticosteroids have a negative impact on the ability of the immune system to protect the body from various foreign agents. So hypnotic relaxation may be capable of increasing the body's resistance to disease.
>
> (p. 495)

I would point out that these observations should not be taken as supporting the idea, sometimes promoted by lay hypnotherapists, that whatever may be wrong with patients one has only to hypnotize them and tell them to get better, and all will be well. The view expressed in this present chapter is that when patients are taken into treatment there is a deliberate effort to build up their general sense of esteem and self-control and to combat their anxiety, sometimes with the 'ego-strengthening suggestions' referred to earlier. This aspect of the therapy is not always fully described in clinical reports which focus on the particular disorder in question, such as a warty skin.

Hypnotherapy for cutaneous warts will be discussed as an example of treatment of a skin disease, and the emphasis here is rather different from that placed on suggestion by Wilkinson in Chapter 8. In discussing hypnotherapy for warts it is not suggested that there should be a widespread use of this relatively time-consuming form of treatment. However, some cases of warts are remarkably resistant to the more routine forms of treatment, and hypnotherapy remains one possibility that should be kept in mind. Reports of the treatment of warts by psychological means may be divided into those dealing with 'charming' or waking suggestibility, and those concerned with treatment by hypnosis. A good review of both areas is given by Bunney (1982). Although lay people, and many professionals are firmly convinced that warts can be 'charmed' away, there is very little hard evidence for this belief.

A few words should be said here about 'spontaneous remission' in medicine and psychology. It does not mean that cure has taken place without any reason, but merely that we do not know the reason. Rachman (1973) writes:

We can begin by dismissing those simple-minded views that suggest that the term spontaneous means 'uncaused'. It has been pointed out in previous publications that it is not the mere passage of time that produces an improvement in neurotic disorders . . . Events such as promotion, financial windfalls, successful love affairs may all be therapeutic but, regrettably perhaps, they cannot be considered as forms of psychological treatment.

(p. 813)

It is of interest to observe that two-thirds of minor states of anxiety left untreated remit after about two years (Rachman 1973) and the mean rate of 'spontaneous remission' of warts is reliably estimated at about the same period.

One of the early observations about the treatment of warts by hypnotherapy was that a relatively high rate of success was obtained when patients were good hypnotic subjects, and a relatively poor improvement characterized patients who lacked much hypnotic ability. Various studies that are reviewed by Wadden and Anderton (1982) support this finding on the whole. Unfortunately many clinicians are adverse to assessing the degree of hypnotic susceptibility of their patients, and may go on hopefully trying to hypnotize patients who are very little affected. All this has contributed to the confusion in the area. The factor of differential susceptibility to hypnosis in the treatment of skin diseases is obviously important, but it does not decide the issue either way as to whether it is specific suggestions for improvement of the skin condition, or general suggestions that lower the anxiety of the patient, that are the more important.

Until quite recent times clinicians have been very unsure how the therapy for warts and other skin diseases works. For instance, it is well documented that blood-flow and peripheral dilation can be affected by hypnotic suggestion (Dubin and Shapiro 1974), and so many therapists have assumed that this is what they were manipulating in hypnosis. Unfortunately there is no agreement as to whether the blood-flow should be *increased* (Ewin 1974), or *decreased* (Clawson and Swade 1975) by suggestion, some therapists giving exactly the *opposite* suggestions, and claiming equal success. In Chapter 8 Wilkinson prefers the latter theory.

It is now generally agreed that a viral infection is involved, and it is known that when patients have been on immunosuppressive drugs there is a raised probability of the pappiloma virus producing cutaneous warts. One therapy is to administer interferon, but this has dangerous side-effects. As the immune reaction in the skin is cell-mediated, it is not clear whether increasing or decreasing the blood-flow within normal limits is particularly relevant. It may be that hypnotherapy for warts and other skin diseases may have nothing to do with either increasing or decreasing the blood supply to the afflicted area but, where successful, it operates on the anxiety level of the patient, even though the therapist is trying to implement some theory he or she has about the aetiology and maintenance of the disorder, and gives specific suggestions about what the 'subconscious mind' should do to the skin.

It is not argued here that people with warts or other skin disorders are perpetually in a state of high anxiety. What seems more probable is that they suffer from some degree of deficiency in the immune system, and that at different times in their lives their level of anxiety may be raised to a degree sufficient to impair the efficiency of the system so that invading viral or bacterial agents cause the observable disorders. Lowering the general level of anxiety by hypnotherapy or by other means is one way in which a reasonable degree of efficiency may be restored to the immune system.

Proposing that the patients' level of anxiety should be considered in therapy does not necessarily present an either/or hypothesis. It is quite likely that in many cases giving direct hypnotic suggestions concerning the condition of the skin will have some effect. The skin, like the gastrointestinal tract, responds to transient and long-term psychological stimuli. A person with a skin complaint in one part of the body will naturally be anxious about that particular area, and hypnotic suggestions which focus on that area will tend to calm the organ-specific anxiety.

Migraine
A chronic predisposition to suffer from severe headaches involves the borderline between the psychosomatic and the more purely somatic disorders. Some people make a distinction between tension headaches and migraine headaches, but there is controversy about distinguishing between the two as there is a great overlap between these categories. The physiological response to anxiety is a constriction of the cranial arteries followed by dilation, and normally the arteries return to their usual width. However, in some people subjected to repeated and chronic stress there is first overconstriction followed by overdilation, and this is accompanied by severe pain and sometimes nausea. As in the treatment of warts by hypnotherapy, some therapists have concentrated on suggesting that the excess blood will drain away from the brain and others have suggested the opposite, and success has been claimed in both cases. In Chapter 8 Wilkinson describes and discusses the important work of Alladin (1984) in the treatment of migraine. It is possible that the suggestions for warmth, relaxation and so on have little direct effect on the blood-flow, but where the treatment does good it is because the patient is made less anxious by the hypnotherapy and there is a general improvement in his or her emotional state. It should be noted that in Alladin's study, as all patients were selected as being highly susceptible to hypnosis, whatever the form of treatment that was given to them it is likely that some degree of self-hypnosis was involved and had a therapeutic benefit.

Conclusion regarding anxiety in psychosomatic disorders
There is literature reporting the hypnotic treatment of other psychosomatic disorders, but the four types discussed above serve to illustrate the main ways in which hypnotherapy has been used in their treatment, and the suggestion is offered that the main effect brought about is the lowering of the patients' general level of anxiety, as well as anxiety specifically concerned with the disorder itself, although therapists are not always clear just what they are doing when they engage in 'hypnotherapy', and do not always report fully all that they did in the therapeutic sessions.

3 Maximizing human potential

For normal people to exert themselves fully in the pursuit of various goals it is necessary for them to experience some degree of anxiety. Athletes find that they can exert themselves to peak performance only when there is the anxiety generated by the strong incentive of a competitive test, and students know that a certain amount of anxiety is necessary to get them to study hard and perform well in examination conditions. However, each individual has an optimal level of anxiety for a given situation, and if anxiety rises too high it inhibits rather than aids performance. Hypnosis used in training programmes to modulate the level of anxiety has been found to be useful in a number of areas with both adults and children.

Mairs (1988) gives an extensive review of hypnotherapy applied to sports training, and discusses her own work in Britain applied to archery. Such hypnotic training is not wholly concerned with the optimal level of anxiety required, but this is an integral part of it. Essential in the hypnotic training for athletic performance is the fine adjustment of mental set. Shone (1984) suggests that there are five basic aspects to consider:

1 The environment can engender a degree of anxiety that will inhibit a performer from operating at peak efficiency, but rehearsal in hypnosis can minimize such unwanted influences by careful visualizing of the environmental situation, and ego-boosting by the hypnotist–trainer.
2 Faults in technique can occur when the athlete is under stress and fatigued in training sessions, and such faults can be learnt and further exacerbated. Mental practice and rehearsal with anxiety controlled under hypnosis can lay down a blueprint of near-perfect performance in the mind in a manner not possible in the stress-producing practice situation.
3 Athletes are naturally anxious about their performance, and tend to set mental limits on themselves through fear of failure. In hypnosis the individual's confidence can be built up and these limits extended; this is an aspect of the ego-boosting that is part of the hypnotic training.
4 Anxiety tends to limit performance because it produces too great a degree of muscular tension, and interferes with the proper control of breathing. Hypnotic training is therefore directed to teaching the athlete how to attain deep muscular relaxation and control of breathing. Mairs (1988) points out that the ideal is to find the right balance between mental relaxation and tension for each individual and his or her own sport because being too relaxed may lead to poor performance.
5 Competitive attitudes depend on the correct balance between personal aggressiveness and co-operativeness according to the sport, and the 'psyching-up' process involves attaining the correct emotional and mental set appropriate to the activity. The hypnotic training is directed to attaining this requisite emotional and mental attitude.

Davies (1988) describes his use of hypnotherapy in the management of examination anxiety, and this is certainly a more complex procedure than many people think. It requires a more sophisticated knowledge of the problems involved than is possessed by some people who regard themselves as 'hypnotherapists' on the basis, say, of some work in dentistry. Readers must be reminded that 'anxiety' is by no means a simple condition, as analysed in Table 3.1, and those undertaking the treatment of students with examination anxiety will be confronted with a variety of disparate problems, some students having suffered from two little anxiety in the past, leading them to neglect their studies until they find themselves ill-prepared when the examinations are pending. No adequate description of the forms of hypnotherapy appropriate to the complex range of problems posed under the general rubric of 'examination anxiety' can be attempted in this section, and readers are referred to Davies's paper mentioned above.

Hypnotherapy is also being used by educational psychologists in some areas of Britain to help children and adolescents attain their full potential at school, and this requires a proper understanding of the role of anxiety in learning. Four chapters are devoted to this subject in Section 6 of Heap (1988).

Research developments and the future

This book is concerned with hypnotherapy in Britain, and therefore I refrain from too much reference to work carried out in other countries although, of course, we in Britain follow developments abroad. It may be noted that in the sections devoted to 'Specific Applications' some space is devoted to the treatment of psychosomatic disorders as well as to psychological disorders and maximizing human potential, although the matter is again discussed in Chapter 8. In this country there has been more published about work in hypnotherapy that is in a clearly assessable form in the area of the treatment of anxiety in relation to psychosomatic medicine than in other areas. Often studies of treatment of anxiety in more purely psychological disorders are not easy to assess as to value and significance, because they are in the form of reports of one-case studies or where there has been no attempt at experimental control. Reasons of space have necessitated that I have given only a few examples of well-controlled clinical trials, and readers are referred to the paper by Wadden and Anderton (1982) for a useful review of the details of much that has been mentioned in this brief chapter.

Some people will not agree with me in the emphasis I put on the role of anxiety in the aetiology and maintenance of psychosomatic disorders and will prefer alternative explanations. That is a matter for discussion. As I see it, the future development of hypnosis as a valuable tool in the service of the health professions in Britain stands in some danger of hypnosis becoming too popular with a fringe of untrained and marginally trained people who have little appreciation of the nature of scientific procedures. They do not understand how such procedures have contributed to the great strides in health care that have been accomplished in this century. We still lack an adequate appreciation of the various meanings of that ambiguous term 'anxiety' in much of the published literature. I have already mentioned how the early work of Wolpe that was so influential with a group of Maudsley psychologists and psychiatrists, and has now had a world-wide influence in the behaviour therapy movement, suffered a pruning of one of its most interesting aspects, the induction of hypnosis. There was an understandable reluctance of behaviourally oriented scientists to become associated in any way with hypnotherapy because of its unfortunate reputation at that time. Things have now changed in Britain, and despite the continued publication of much cultist trash about hypnotherapy, it is up to serious health professionals to sift the grain from the chaff and take up the challenge that is offered by this promising technique.

References

Alladin, A.A. (1984) Hypnosis in the treatment of head pain, in M. Heap (ed.), *Proceedings of the First Annual Conference of the British Society of Experimental and Clinical Hypnosis*, BSECH.

Araoz, D.L. (1982) *Hypnosis and Sex Therapy*, New York: Brunner/Mazel.

Bootzin, R.R. and Nicassio, P.M. (1976) Behavioral treatment for insomnia, in M. Herson, R.M. Eisler and P.M. Mitler (eds) *Progress in Behavior Modification*, Vol. 6, New York: Academic Press.

Bowers, K.S. and Kelly, P. (1979) Stress, disease, psychotherapy and hypnosis, *Journal of Abnormal Psychology* 88: 490–503.

Bunney, M.H. (1982) *Viral Warts: Their Biology and Treatment*, Oxford: Oxford University Press.

Clarke, J.C. and Jackson, J.A. (1983) *Hypnosis and Behavior Therapy*, New York: Springer.

Clawson, T.A. and Swade, R.H. (1975) The hypnotic control of blood flow and pain: the cure of warts and the potential for the use of hypnosis in the treatment of cancer, *American Journal of Clinical Hypnosis* 17: 160–69.

Cole, M. and Dryden, W. (eds) (1988) *Sex Therapy in Britain*, Milton Keynes: Open University Press.

Colgan, S.M., Faragher, E.B. and Whorwell, P.J. (1988) Controlled trial of hypnotherapy in relapse prevention of duodenal ulceration, *The Lancet* 2(i): 1299–1300.

Davies, P. (1988) The use of hypnosis in the management of examination anxiety, *British Journal of Experimental and Clinical Hypnosis* 5: 105–6.

Dryden, W. (1984) Individual therapies: a comparative analysis, in W. Dryden (ed.) *Individual Therapy in Britain*, London: Harper & Row.

Dubin, L.L. and Shapiro, S.S. (1974) Use of hypnosis to facilitate dental extraction and hemostasis in a classic hemophiliac with a high antibody titer to factor VIII, *American Journal of Clinical Hypnosis* 17: 79–83.

Emmelkamp, P.M.G. and Kuipers, A.C.M. (1979) Agoraphobia: a follow-up study four years after treatment, *British Journal of Psychiatry* 134: 352–5.

English, H.B. and English, A.C. (1958) *A Comprehensive Dictionary of Psychological and Psychoanalytical Terms*, London: Longman.

Ewin, D.M. (1974) Condyloma acuminatum: successful treatment of four cases by hypnosis, *American Journal of Clinical Hypnosis* 17: 73–8.

Gibson, H.B. and Heap, M. (1990) *Hypnosis in Therapy*, London: Lawrence Erlbaum.

Hartland, J. (1971) *Medical and Dental Hypnosis and its Clinical Applications*, 2nd edn, London: Baillière Tindall.

Heap, M. (1988) *Hypnosis: Current Clinical, Experimental and Forensic Practices*, London: Croom Helm.

Holdsworth, C.D. and DuCann, P.A. (1986) Irritable bowel syndrome, *Medicine International* 25: 1018–83.

Hoogduin, C.A.L. and de Jong, P. (1989) Hypnotizability in obsessive–compulsives, in

D. Waxman, D. Pedersen, I. Wilkie and P. Mellett (eds) *Hypnosis: The Fourth European Congress at Oxford*, London: Whurr Publishers.

Humphreys, A. (1988) Applications of hypnosis to anxiety control, in M. Heap (ed.) *Hypnosis: Current Clinical, Experimental and Forensic Practices*, London: Croom Helm.

Karle, H.W.A. (1988) Hypnosis in analytic psychotherapy, in M. Heap (ed.) *Hypnosis: Current Clinical, Experimental and Forensic Practices*, London: Croom Helm.

Lader, M. and Marks, I. (1971) *Clinical Anxiety*, London: Heinemann.

Lazarus, A. (1973) 'Hypnosis' as a facilitator in behavior therapy, *International Journal of Clinical and Experimental Hypnosis* 21: 25–31.

Mairs, D.A.E. (1988) Hypnosis in sport, in M. Heap (ed.) *Hypnosis: Current Clinical, Experimental and Forensic Practices*, London: Croom Helm.

Marks, I.M. (1987) Comment on S. Lloyd Williams' 'On anxiety and phobia', *Journal of Anxiety Disorders* 1: 181–96.

Meichenbaum, D. (1977) *Cognitive-Behavior Modification: An Integrative Approach*, New York: Plenum Press.

Misra, P.C. (1985) Hypnosis and Sexual Disorders, in D. Waxman, P.C. Misra, M. Gibson and M.A. Basker (eds) *Modern Trends in Hypnosis*, New York: Plenum Press.

Rachman, S. (1968) The role of muscular relaxation in behaviour therapy, *Behaviour Research and Therapy* 6: 159–66.

—— (1973) The effects of psychological treatment, in H.J. Eysenck (ed.) *Handbook of Abnormal Psychology*, London: Pitman.

Rowley, D.T. (1986) *Hypnosis and Hypnotherapy*, London: Croom Helm.

Shone, R. (1984) *Creative Visualization*, Wellingborough: Thorsons.

Snaith, R.P. (1981) *Clinical Neurosis*, Oxford: Oxford University Press.

Wadden, T.A. and Anderton, C.H. (1982) The clinical use of hypnosis, *Psychological Bulletin* 91: 215–43.

Watkins, J.G. (1971) The affect bridge: a hypnoanalytic technique, *International Journal of Clinical and Experimental Hypnosis* 19: 21–7.

Whorwell, P.J., Prior, A. and Faragher, E.B. (1984) Controlled trial of hypnotherapy in the treatment of severe refractory irritable bowel syndrome, *The Lancet* 2: 1232–4.

Wolpe, J. (1958) *Psychotherapy by Reciprocal Inhibition*, Stanford, Calif.: Stanford University Press.

4

Hypnosis and depression

ASSEN ALLADIN AND MICHAEL HEAP

Introduction

In the previous chapter the applications of hypnosis to anxiety were discussed. It is evident that the treatment of anxiety covers an extensive range of problems including generalized anxiety disorder, traumatic stress responses, phobias, obsessive–compulsive disorders and psychosomatic complaints. In fact it is very common for patients referred for psychological treatment to be described by the referring person as 'anxious'.

Another very common description of patients referred for therapy is 'depressed' and in the everyday usage of the term it usually suits its purpose very well. However, in the present chapter we will be concerned with the application of hypnosis to patients who have been diagnosed as suffering from clinical depression rather than as being merely unhappy about their circumstances. This is an important point because clinical depression poses special problems for the therapist: it is difficult to treat from a psychological standpoint and it is essential that the practitioner has a rigorous understanding and knowledge of the nature of the disorder.

Definition and description

Stern and Mendels (1980) define clinical depression as 'a condition characterized by a persistent and abnormal lowering of mood (feeling sad, blue, unhappy) and/or a loss of interest in usual activities, accompanied by a variety of characteristic signs and symptoms' (p. 205). These include changes in five areas:

Negative affect: low mood, anhedonia, guilt, nervousness, irritability, boredom;
Negative cognitions: negative view of the self, the world and the future; indecisiveness, self-blame, and feelings of worthlessness and hopelessness;
Negative motivations: loss of interest, suicidal ideation, social withdrawal, neglect of appearance;

Behavioural changes: reduction in behavioural activities, agitation or psychomotor retardation;

Vegetative changes: insomnia, loss of appetite and weight, reduced libido, vague aches and pains.

The revised third edition of the *Diagnostic and Statistical Manual* (DSM-III-R) published by the American Psychiatric Association (1987) has replaced depressive or affective disorders by the term 'mood' disorders. DSM-III-R divides mood disorders into *bipolar* and *depressive* disorders. Bipolar disorders are characterized by the presence of one or more episodes of *mania* (elevated mood, increased activity, and expansive and self-important ideas) or *hypomania* (mild mania) and are subdivided into *bipolar disorder*, in which there is one or more manic episodes, and *cyclothymia*, in which there are numerous periods of hypomania and depressive symptoms.

Unipolar depressive disorders are characterized by one or more periods of depression, without a history of manic or hypomanic episodes. Depressive disorders are separated into *major depression* and *dysthymia* (or depressive neurosis). The essential feature of major depression is one or more episodes of depressed mood or loss of interest or pleasure in all, or almost all activities, and associated symptoms for a period of at least two weeks. Current major depression can be specified as either *melancholic type* (severe form of major depressive episode, responsive to somatic therapies; often referred to as endogenous or biological depression) or *chronic* (current episode lasting over two years).

Dysthymia or depressive neurosis (often referred to as reactive, non-endogenous, or exogenous depression) is a chronic, mild-to-moderate form of clinical depression, occurring for at least two years. Dysthymia does not seem to respond to chemotherapy but is responsive to psychotherapy (Kaplan and Sadock 1981), particularly to cognitive therapy.

The present chapter is confined to unipolar depressive disorders (major depression and dysthymia); therefore the terms depression, affective disorder, mood disorder and unipolar depression are used interchangeably to denote non-bipolar depression. Although reference is made to endogenous and non-endogenous depressions, the terms are largely descriptive; they provide a pragmatic approach to treatment but do not allow inferences be made concerning aetiology.

Prevalence and course

Depression is the most common emotional disorder accounting for approximately one-half of all psychiatric admissions (Gallant and Simpson 1976). Both American and British statistics suggest that the lifetime expectancy of developing unipolar depression is approximately 20% in women and 10% in men, and is greater in the lower socio-economic group, the divorced and the separated (Boyd and Weissman 1982). Estimates of the percentages of severely depressed patients receiving treatment range from 20% to 33% world-wide (Kaplan and Sadock 1981).

Over 50% of depressives have their first episode of depression before the age of 40 (American Psychiatric Association 1987). An untreated episode of depression may last 6 to 13 months, while most treated episodes last about 3 months. Approximately 50–85% of patients have a second depressive episode within the next 4 to 6 months. The risk of recurrence is increased by coexisting dysthymia, alcohol or drug abuse, anxiety symptoms, older age at onset, and a history of more than one previous depressive episode (Mollica 1989). Approximately half of all patients recover completely but in 20% to 35% of cases there is a chronic course, with considerable residual symptomatic and social impairment (American Psychiatric Association 1987). About 15% of patients suffering from primary affective disorder ultimately take their own lives (Motto 1975).

Theories of depression

The causes of depression are not known. Given the many forms of depression, it is probable that a number of factors may be involved. Moreover, these factors can interact with each other. Some of the well-known theories of depression will now be briefly and selectively reviewed to underline the limitation of searching for a single causative factor. The cognitive theory is described in greater detail as it forms part of the integrated model (Dissociative Model of Depression) described later.

Biochemical theories of depression

Several biochemical theories of depression have been proposed, including the hypotheses that (1) there is a deficiency of important neurotransmitters (such as noradrenalin and serotonin) in certain areas of the brain; (2) there is an abnormality in the functioning of the brain systems (e.g. the diencephalon) that regulate hormonal secretion and other important biological activities; and (3) nerve cell function is disturbed owing to an alteration in the distribution of certain positively charged ions (such as potassium and sodium) across the nerve cell membrane, which leads to a state of unstable hyperexcitability of the central nervous system (Stern and Mendels 1980).

Although there is some support for these hypotheses, they do not account for all the symptoms occurring in depression. Moreover, erratic regulation of the neurotransmitters may occur in response to exogenous factors, such as psychosocial stresses (e.g. bereavement or losing one's job). However, this should not obscure the advances made in biochemical research over the past 30 years, which have led to considerable progress in somatic treatments of the depressive disorders.

Psychodynamic theories of depression

In psychodynamic theories a sense of *loss* is regarded as the chief component of depression. Abraham (1911) suggested that the depressive person redirects his or her feelings of hostility previously felt towards the lost person (parent, spouse, or close friend) and channels them inwardly. Abraham's conceptualization was further developed by Freud (1917), who emphasized the importance of symbolic loss (i.e. not necessarily the actual loss of a loved object) in depression. Freud suggested that the withdrawal of love and support by a significant person (usually a parent) during the oral stage of development predisposes an individual to depression in later life.

Psychodynamic theories of depression are lacking because (1) the above formulations are not applicable to all types of depression; (2) there is no evidence that low self-esteem is more common in people who develop depression than those who do not; (3) in some depressives anger is directed towards people other than the self; and (4) some studies have found that depression is not associated with parental death, divorce, broken engagements and similar losses of a significant relationship (Malmquist 1970, Watts and Nicoli 1979).

The learned helplessness theory of depression

Drawing on data from animal studies, Seligman (1975) proposed the 'learned helplessness' theory of depression. This model views depression as the product of a history of faulty learnings regarding personal locus of control. Seligman suggested that when one is subjected to negative events perceived as outside of one's control, one becomes hopeless, passive and depressed.

Since most of the human studies on learned helplessness have relied on the experimental induction of depression in normal or mildly depressed subjects, the findings cannot be generalized to clinical depression. The model also fails to distinguish adequately between the symptoms of depression and the syndrome of depressive disorder.

The cognitive theory of depression

Traditionally, cognitive changes in depression are viewed as secondary to a primary disturbance of mood. Beck (1967, 1976), however, has suggested that 'depressive cognitions' or 'cognitive dysfunction' may be the primary disorder, or at least powerful factors in aggravating and perpetuating the disorder. Beck has identified three major features of cognition which are relevant to the experience of depression: (1) the 'cognitive triad', (2) faulty information processing or cognitive errors, and (3) schemas.

1 The cognitive triad   This consists of negative cognitions regarding oneself, the world, and one's future. First is a negative belief that one is defective, inadequate, undesirable, worthless and deprived. Second is the tendency to view the world as negative, defeating, and so demanding that one is bound to fail and experience hardship and punishment. Third is an expectation of continued hardship, deprivation, failure and suffering.

2 Faulty information processing or cognitive errors   These are distorted interpretations of events that maintain the cognitive triad. Burns (1980) has listed ten types of distortions in thinking, or cognitive errors, including all-or-nothing thinking, over-generalizations, mental filter, disqualifying the positive, jumping to conclusions, magnification (catastrophizing) or minimization, emotional reasoning, 'should' statements, labelling and mislabelling, and personalization. These thinking errors or *negative self-talk* gradually become autonomous, plausible, repetitive and idiosyncratic. The concept of *negative self-hypnosis* (NSH), described later, resembles this cognitive process.

3 Schemas   These are hypothetical cognitive structures that influence the screening, coding and organization of incoming stimuli. Negative or depressogenic schemas can be learned during childhood. The child learns to construct reality through his or her early experiences with the environment, especially with significant others. Sometimes these early experiences can shape maladaptive attitudes and beliefs in the child. Beck believes negative schemas predispose depressed patients to distort events in a characteristic fashion (cognitive distortions or faulty information processing) leading to the maintenance of the cognitive triad. Negative schemas are usually out of awareness and may remain dormant until an undesirable life-event stimulates the schema. Once a particular schema is activated (e.g. sense of failure), the patient categorizes, selects and encodes information in such a way that the failure schema is maintained.

Although clear evidence for cognitive factors in the aetiology and pathogenesis of depression is lacking, most studies support the role of cognitive dysfunction in clinical depression. For example, Norman *et al.* (1983) reported cognitive dysfunction in 50–60% of depressives and the level of dysfunction was correlated with the severity and chronicity of depression. However, only a few clinical studies (Teasdale and Dent 1987, Parry and Brewin 1988) have provided evidence for the primacy of cognition in mood disorders. Moreover, the model cannot explain the evolution of all depressive subtypes and Beck has not satisfactorily explained the process by which cognitive distortions lead to clinical depression. Nevertheless, Beck's model does provide a framework for understanding the psychological process in depressives.

Current treatments: summary

Just as there are many theories of depression, so there are many approaches to treatment, although none of the approaches is effective with every depressed patient. The main therapeutic approach is pharmacotherapy, specifically the use of various antidepressants (e.g. tricyclics, tetracyclics, and monoamine oxidase inhibitors). With severe or psychotic depressives, electroconvulsive therapy (ECT) is usually used. Over 20% of the patients do not seem to respond to any of these treatments (e.g. Medical Research Council 1965) and 12–32% relapse in a period of 6 months to 2 years after discontinuation of medication (Quitkin *et al.* 1976).

The most effective and widely used psychological treatment for depression is cognitive therapy. Cognitive therapy appears to be as efficacious (Murphy *et al.* 1984) or superior (Rush *et al.* 1977, Kovacs *et al.* 1981) to antidepressant medication in terms of outcome and relapse rate. Cognitive therapy, however, is not generally effective with severe depression and not all types of depression respond to it. Therefore it would appear that a substantial proportion of depressed patients do not respond to the current forms of treatment.

Hypnotherapeutic approaches: general principles

Clinical depression has traditionally occupied a low ranking in the list of disorders for which hypnosis is recommended as an effective adjunct to treatment. Influential texts on hypnotherapy, such as Hartland (1971) and Kroger (1977) scarcely mention the topic. In fact the former author and more recently Burrows (1980) counsel against using hypnosis with those clinically depressed patients who have suicidal tendencies, on the grounds that any temporary elevation in mood due to hypnosis may sufficiently mobilize them into making a suicide bid.

The potentially suicidal patient does indeed require and deserve the most careful and sensitive handling but the present authors are not convinced that the patient's experience of a hypnotic induction may in itself increase the likelihood of a suicide attempt. It seems more likely that when the patient does not discern any immediate benefits from his or her being hypnotized, then thoughts of suicide may become stronger. This may be particularly so if, as is not uncommonly the case, the patient is seeking hypnosis 'as a last resort' and discovers that the experience is not the profound or dramatic one that he or she was hoping for. We shall illustrate this with a case in due course. One can also imagine the risks to the depressed patient of uncovering and reliving distressing memories when a hypnoanalytical approach is being employed, particularly if the patient leaves the session to return to an unsympathetic and unsupportive spouse or family.

As well as the necessary vigilance concerning suicide risk, other matters complicate the psychological treatment of the clinically depressed patient. The ongoing mental and physical characteristics of the disorder – poor memory and concentration, feelings of helplessness, lack of energy, agitation and so on – make engagement in psychological therapy difficult for the patient; and hypnosis *does* require the active participation of the patient. At the same time, hypnosis traditionally involves physical and mental relaxation and there is something counterintuitive about doing relaxation with patients who are often lethargic and who may spend long periods in a state of immobility. (Perhaps the value of the active, 'alert' type of hypnotic induction and imagery, described by Gibbons (1979) amongst others, could be explored with depressed patients.) Yet the restless, agitated, 'churning' feelings which depressed people often report, especially on wakening, are not in our experience easy to alleviate by standard physical relaxation procedures.

As we shall note later, in the treatment of depression the more therapeutic techniques and procedures that the therapist uses (with due competence, of course) the better the chance of a successful outcome. It follows, therefore, that therapists should be flexible and open to ideas and methods derived from schools of thought other than the one to which they themselves hold allegiance. Fortunately, as was noted in Chapter 2, hypnosis provides the therapist with a set of techniques which can be adapted to a wide range of therapeutic approaches including the analytical, the behavioural and the cognitive. Nevertheless, it is paramount that the therapist use these procedures only within a carefully structured and comprehensive programme of therapy which is grounded in the scientific understanding of the nature of depression and the needs of the depressed patient. Thus, the course of therapy should be able to stand on its own, *without* the use of hypnosis; hypnotic techniques are introduced as a means of adding power to the therapy.

With the above caveats in mind, let us examine some hypnotherapeutic procedures which may be incorporated into a programme of therapy for the depressed patient.

1 Hypnosis as a relaxation procedure

The habitual practice of self-hypnosis purely as a means of relaxation may benefit some depressed patients, although, as we have noted above, the severe states of agitation which many depressed patients experience are not, in the authors' opinion, effectively addressed by simple relaxation methods.

2 Hypnotic suggestion as means of influencing behaviour, thoughts and feelings

This application of hypnosis may be used to augment behavioural and cognitive procedures employed in the treatment of depression. An illustration of this is the simple use of post-hypnotic suggestion to reinforce cognitive or behavioural changes. For example, after working with a patient on disputing negative cognitions in a particular situation and substituting these with rational thoughts, the post-hypnotic suggestion may be given that 'Each and every time you find yourself in this situation, the following thoughts will come immediately and vividly to mind . . .'. This suggestion may be further augmented by (i) re-running in imagination one or more previous occasions when the patient felt distressed in that situation, this time using the rational thoughts and (ii) rehearsing, in a similar way, future encounters with that same type of situation. These instructions may be put on tape for practice at home.

In the above work the use of cues or anchors may further strengthen the suggestion. For example, positive thoughts and feelings may be anchored to a pleasant image or memory, and the suggestion given that the patient may alleviate depressive feelings by vividly bringing to mind the image and the positive feelings associated with it. The beneficial use of this kind of procedure in the treatment of depressed patients has been reported by Matheson (1979).

A commonly used anchor is the clenched fist. Stein (1963) described a popular procedure which anchors, using positive imagery, good feelings to the dominant hand and likewise bad feelings to the non-preferred hand. The bad feelings can be anchored by clenching the left fist and dispelled by releasing it, whilst simultaneously (or consecutively) clenching the right fist to facilitate the bringing to mind of the positive feelings and resources. Again, imaginal rehearsal of this method in problem situations may strengthen its effectiveness.

An illustration of the use of a cue word to augment a post-hypnotic suggestion is in the treatment of a mildly depressed patient who recognized that his dysphoric episodes often resulted from his responding passively to problems which could be solved by his taking appropriate action. For example, he became depressed when a friend he was expecting to telephone did not do so, and on another occasion when a friend had not returned something he had lent him and which he needed urgently. Both of these problems could have been solved by simply telephoning the friend, but in neither case did he even think of this course of action. 'Passivity' was his choice of cue word to bring to mind whenever he began to experience depressive feelings in situations such as these, and this would remind him to consider what action he might take to forestall what he termed a 'downer'.

3 Analytical methods

Although hypnotic procedures such as exploratory and uncovering techniques (see Chapter 2) which have traditionally been employed in an analytical frame-work, may be adapted to behavioural and cognitive therapies, we shall first consider them from the analytical standpoint. Here we invoke the notion of dissociation and interpret hypnoanalytical methods as having the purpose, among others, of accessing and resolving dissociated feelings, memories, fantasies, conflicts and so on. Such work usually, though not always, involves regression to early memories, the assimilation, if necessary, into consciousness of the contents of those memories and the feelings associated with them, and the satisfactory resolution or re-evaluation of those memories so that they no longer trouble the patient.

The reader will find many case illustrations of this kind of work in the literature. Karle (1988) reports some good examples from his casework. For example, a depressed man was regressed to the moment when, as an infant, he learned he was adopted. Previously unacknowledged negative feelings surrounding this were uncovered and integrated into conscious awareness. Similar analytical procedures are reported by the same author with patients who have been sexually abused as children and those who have experienced early traumatic hospitalizations.

These approaches are consistent with psychoanalytical theories of depression, expressed in terms of loss, rejection and anger turned inwards (see earlier). The uncovering, expression and conscious assimilation of the feelings, such as sadness and anger, are therefore the aim of these hypnoanalytical procedures. Nevertheless, they have been criticized as insufficient in themselves to make a lasting impact on the depressive experience. For example, cognitive therapists such as Beck *et al.* (1979) and Burns (1980) acknowledge the value of releasing pent-up feelings such as anger and sadness, but insist that any relief is likely to be short-lived because the patient's depressive cognitive schemas remain unaffected.

We should like to make three points regarding this issue and how it pertains to hypnotherapy. First, Gibson and Heap (1990) have drawn attention to the fact that there is a myth which is taken seriously by many lay hypnotherapists and some medical practitioners that all psychological problems and disorders are associated with some repressed trauma, the memory of which must be relived along with any attendant emotions. Consequently, a 'good abreaction' is regarded as a significant therapeutic event (just as in many of the active psycho-therapies such as bioenergetics and gestalt therapy, a high premium is placed on the patient's giving vent to his or her feelings).

There are in fact occasional case reports in the literature where a patient's problem appears to have responded rapidly to regression to a traumatic incident (see, for example, Degun and Degun (1977) and Hart (1984)). However, these have tended to be fairly well circumscribed problems such as phobias, as opposed to a chronic and disabling condition such as clinical depression. From what we know of the latter, it seems unlikely that a single cathartic release of emotion is going to make the same lasting impact on the patient's condition.

The second point we wish to make, however, is that the expression of a strong emotion which has been held in check can, with sensitive support by the therapist, lead to significant cognitive change. Say, for example, that one important contribution to a patient's depressive mood is a lack of assertiveness and a fear of expressing anger. This problem may be understood in cognitive terms (e.g. catastrophic thoughts and beliefs about the consequences of disagreeing with somebody). Suppose also that during the course of a hypnotic age-regression the patient gives vent to considerable anger against his or her mother, feelings that the patient has hitherto been unable to acknowledge. Now, through the therapist's non-judgemental acceptance of the expression of these feelings, the patient may come to adopt a more rational attitude to his or her anger and assertiveness. Moreover, a change in self-image may occur: that is, the patient's self-perception may change from 'someone who cannot express anger' to 'someone who can'.

This leads us to our third point, namely that exploratory and uncovering procedures also require that the memories elicited be re-evaluated by the patient in some way so that they cease to have a destructive influence on his or her present well-being. Karle (1988) describes a variety of manoeuvres. For example, after a patient relived the childhood trauma of his parents leaving him in hospital, he was instructed to bring immediately and vividly to mind the scene of his parents returning to collect him and to re-experience the good feelings he had at the time. Karle describes this method as 'telescoping trauma and too-late comfort'.

Another procedure uses the notion of ego states. The patient is directed to relive a past traumatic experience, then to imagine returning to that scene in the adult state and providing the child self with all the comfort, support, reassurance and strength that he or she needs to feel better in that situation. This process can lead directly to cognitive restructuring of the way the patient construes his or her *present* circumstances. For example, a depressed patient seen by one of the authors was, as a child, repeatedly belittled and compared unfavourably to others by his father. The patient was regressed to such an incident and taken through the 'ego state' procedure described above. In the next session he reported that that week, whenever he had been worried about how he compared with other people, he found he was counselling himself and reassuring himself that he did not need to be like other people, and that it was better for him just to be himself. He was able to do this without any guidance from the therapist in cognitive restructuring.

A final example of the use of a 'hypnoanalytical' technique in a cognitive framework is that provided by Degun and Degun (1980, 1988) who have developed the use of dream suggestion as an augmentative procedure in cognitive-behavioural therapy for depressed patients. The patient is hypnotized and the following suggestion given: 'Listen carefully to what I say. You *will* be able to solve your problem when you understand what is causing it. A thought or a dream will come into your mind which will throw light on the cause of your problem. It may come at any time during the day or night, but *you will remember it to tell me*' (Degun and Degun 1980: 18).

In the ensuing session the patient is again hypnotized and then taken through the dream. No attempt is made by the therapist to interpret the dream; the patient is encouraged to provide his or her own understanding of the dream and how it pertains to his or her problems and their possible resolution in terms of cognitive and behavioural change. The case presented by Degun and Degun (1980) responded very rapidly; this may not be typical but the procedure may be a useful adjunct in enhancing the effectiveness of cognitive-behavioural therapy for depression as well as other psychological disorders.

4 Ego-strengthening

In Chapter 2 ego-strengthening was described as a way of exploiting the positive experience of hypnosis and the therapist–patient relationship to develop feelings of confidence and optimism and an improved self-image. Consequently ego-strengthening may be an augmentative procedure in the cognitive–behavioural treatment of depression and, as will be described below in the account of Alladin's cognitive hypnotherapy programme, the hypnotic induction and ego-strengthening routine may be taped and listened to daily by the patient. The therapist may use a script such as that provided by Hartland (1971) or may take the advice of Heap (1985) and Ross (1985) and tailor the ego-strengthening routine to the needs and characteristics of the individual patient, make use of his or her imaginative capabilities and perhaps use some of the procedures described in Section 2 above.

Note that ego-strengthening is used to amplify positive feelings; therefore there must be positive feelings already present! The reader may imagine the reaction of a depressed patient, who in desperation, seeks hypnosis 'as a last resort' and is subjected to a hypnotic induction procedure and a rendering of Hartland's (1971) ego-strengthening routine. 'This isn't working . . .', 'Nothing's going to work . . .' etc. may well be his or her thoughts as the therapist drones on. This was precisely the response of a patient described by Heap (1984) who consulted a Mr M in Harley Street (a 'hypnotherapist' whose authenticity was bolstered by his advertising his services in a quality Sunday newspaper). After eleven sessions of the aforementioned treatment (purchased at no mean cost by concerned relatives), so disheartened and desperate was the patient that, declining Mr M's suggestion that he appeal to his family to fund a further twelve sessions of the same ordeal, he made a serious attempt to take his own life.

Again, the moral is that we have here a useful procedure which may augment a carefully constructed programme of therapy, but it is not the therapy itself and if it is used as such then disappointment and even disaster may ensue. With this in mind, we shall now present such a structured programme of therapy which has recently been devised by Alladin, and uses hypnotherapeutic methods alongside orthodox cognitive and behavioural procedures.

Specific application of hypnosis to cognitive therapy for depression

An example of a structured multi-modal approach to the treatment of depression in which hypnosis is an important integral component is that recently developed by Alladin (1987, 1989) and is based on his dissociative model of depression which will be outlined first.

The Dissociative Model of Depression

Returning to our earlier discussion of the nature of depression we may readily acknowledge that it is a complicated disorder involving multiple factors. Therefore it is unlikely that a single causative factor, either biological or psychological, will be found. Similarly any single intervention is unlikely to be effective with every depressed patient. Williams (1984), in his comprehensive review of the psychological therapies for depression, concluded that the more techniques that are used, the more effective is the treatment. This suggests that the more techniques a therapist chooses from, the greater is the likelihood that a maximally suitable treatment combination will be found for a particular patient.

Guided by the above finding, Alladin (1987, 1989) has developed a working model of clinical depression which combines hypnotic and cognitive paradigms and has implications for multiple intervention. The model is referred to as the 'Dissociative Model of Depression' because (1) it encompasses the *dissociative theory* of hypnosis and (2) it is proposed that non-endogenous unipolar depression is a form of *negative self-hypnosis* (a concept to be explained later) which leads to the dissociation of depressive affect.

Depression as dissociation

Hilgard (1986) describes hypnosis and other related phenomena such as fugues, possession states and multiple personality, in terms of *dissociation* or *divided consciousness*. Dissociation or hypnotic involvement is seen as a cognitive process on a continuum ranging from minor to profound. The theory also takes the concept of 'self' and 'will' into consideration and maintains that hypnosis and other dissociative experiences all involve some degree of loss of voluntary control or there is division of control between conscious and unconscious processes. A hierarchical model is proposed with a central control structure (executive ego) and various subordinate control structures each with its own input and output connections with the world. Though the central structure is normally in control, the other structures can take over as a result of hypnotic suggestions or other similar procedures or situations. Now, without reference to hypnosis or dissociation, Beck *et al.* (1979) have noted that the depressed patient's constant stereotypic preoccupation with his or her alleged negative personal attributes is likely to strengthen subordinate cognitive structures or schemas. Once these subordinate systems have been established, they develop a certain degree of autonomy: the activity which they control passes out of voluntary control (partly or completely) and the associated experiences may be registered outside of normal awareness (i.e. dissociated from the executive ego).

Further support for this link between hypnosis and depression may be derived from Tart's (1975) ideas on states of consciousness. He makes a distinction between *discrete states of consciousness*, *discrete altered states of consciousness*, and *baseline states of consciousness*. A discrete state of consciousness is a 'unique, dynamic pattern of configuration of psychological structures' such as ordinary waking state, sleep and dreaming. A discrete altered state of consciousness (d-ASC) refers to a state that is different from some baseline consciousness and has properties that have been generated as a restructuring of consciousness or reality. In other words, dissociation or a d-ASC results from repatterning of existing resources or cognitions. This view can be easily extended to cognitive processing in depression. In response to some external or internal stimulus, the existing cognitions (negative schemas) are repatterned (restructured or distorted), resulting in depressive affect (d-ASC). The severity of the symptoms will depend on the continuation and the extent of the repatterning of the existing schemas.

Negative self-hypnosis
It is not unreasonable, then, to assume that similar cognitive processes are involved in both the depressive state and the hypnotic state. However, there is a fundamental difference in the cognitive contents of the two experiences. Hypnosis may involve either negative or positive cognitions (negative or positive experience), whereas depression invariably involves negative cognitions (usually a negative experience). Moreover, hypnosis is a transitory state, either self-induced or other-induced, and it is easily terminated (i.e. the subject easily returns to a baseline state of consciousness). Depression is *negative self-hypnosis* (NSH) and not easily terminated. Araoz (1981) regards NSH to be the common denominator of all psychogenic problems. According to Araoz, NSH consists of non-conscious (automatic) negative statements and defeatist mental images that the person indulges in, encourages, and often works hard at fostering, while at the same time consciously wanting to get better. He calls this NSH because it consists of three hypnotic elements: (1) non-critical thinking which becomes a negative activation of subconscious processes, (2) active negative imagery, and (3) powerful post-hypnotic suggestions in the form of negative affirmations. Since NSH is very active in depressives, the depressed state is not easily terminated. Additionally, as depressives tend to have vivid negative images, they easily *lose control* over emotional images (see Horowitz 1972). Through such loss of control, distortion, delusion and errors can take place, leading to dissociation of affect and the maintenance of the depressive reality.

Neuropsychological comparisons
Although the two cerebral hemispheres interact with each other, there is lateralized specialization in terms of information processing. The left or dominant hemisphere excels in verbal, sequential and analytical perception and cognition, whereas the right or non-dominant hemisphere is skilled in non-verbal, emotional

and holistic apprehension of information (Tucker and Frederick 1989). The right hemisphere tends to process information in a more negative way (Galin 1974, Diamond *et al.* 1976) and registers information more intensely (Tucker and Frederick 1989). The content of the left-hemisphere representations are in their fundamental form verbal – that is, an internal code (semantics) is substituted for sensory experience – whereas the mental representations in the right hemisphere are analogical (affective or syncretic representation) – that is, a continuous and direct mirroring of the qualities of sensation.

Neuropsychological and neurophysiological studies of both hypnosis (e.g. Frumkin *et al.* 1978, Gruzelier *et al.* 1984, Gruzelier and Brow 1985) and depression (e.g. Flor-Henry 1976, Wexler 1980) have suggested that they are both associated with a redistribution of cerebral activity in favour of greater right-hemisphere (or diminished left-hemisphere) involvement. Thus there is a neuropsychological correlate of dissociation/hypnosis and the depressed reality, namely the right hemisphere. The shift to right-brain function dominance during hypnosis and depression, and hence the unavailability of analytic and reasoning language, may explain the subjective experience of both hypnosis and depression.

The Circular Feedback Model of Depression

The notions of dissociation and negative self-hypnosis may also be incorporated into the Circular Feedback Model of Depression (CFMD) of Beck (1967), later elaborated by Schultz (1978). The CFMD maintains that there is a mutually reinforcing interaction between cognition and affect so that thoughts not only influence feelings but feelings can influence thought content. An event (a feeling, a thought, a goal, a situation, etc.) can trigger a negative schema, which is cognitively rehearsed (automatic cognitive distortion, i.e. NSH is induced), leading to dissociation. Since depressives find it difficult to redirect thinking and negative imagery from negative life-concerns because of NSH, they lose control over emotional imagery and this permits continual reinforcement of the depressive mood (Schultz 1976), thus establishing their belief in the depressive reality (negative affirmations, or in terms of the dissociation model, post-hypnotic suggestions). Hence depressives become very sensitive to negative and emotional stimuli: they have a low threshold of information processing to emotional and negative stimuli and tend to focus mainly on affectively relevant events (related to self-schema). Such focusing leads to a poor construction of reality and thus helps to maintain the depressive state.

Clinical implications: Cognitive Hypnotherapy for Depression

The Dissociative Model of Depression outlined above provides the grounding for an approach to treatment which combines both hypnotic and cognitive procedures as well as behavioural techniques which are appropriate to the needs of depressed patients. This therapy, termed 'Cognitive Hypnotherapy for Depression', normally consists of twelve weekly sessions with follow-ups and booster sessions. The first four involve history-taking, assessment, explanation of the cognitive model and cognitive therapy, and training in monitoring and disputing dysfunctional and depressogenic thinking (cognitive restructuring). The patient is also introduced to a set of techniques adapted from Overlade (1986) and described as 'first aid for depression', being first encouraged to ventilate his or her emotions and then trained in the use of posture, imagery and key words to combat acute depressive moods. A formal hypnotic induction is introduced in the fifth session and ego-strengthening suggestions (Hartland 1971) are administered. The hypnotic session is recorded on tape for daily use. In subsequent sessions cognitive restructuring is carried out using scenes imagined by the patient. There are three additional therapeutic procedures involving hypnosis or imagery and these will now be described in detail.

1 Expansion of awareness

Tosi and Baisden (1984) argue that rather than the mind being bifurcated into the conscious and the unconscious, human experiences can be conceptualized along the dimensions of time and awareness. Time ranges from the distant past to the projected future, and awareness from what is least consciously known to what is fully conscious (Figure 4.1). Therefore behaviour may not be a response to the immediate situation, but may also be functionally related to the past and the future. To the extent that an experience is related to the past or future projections, it can be placed along a time continuum. However, a person may not be fully aware of this relationship, and even within the present moment may not be fully aware of the whole range of cognitive, affective and physiological responses that he or she is making; thus the experience can also be placed along an awareness continuum (Figure 4.1). Taking such a view of experience implies any element of the event–cognitions–feelings sequence can occur within any quadrant of the time and awareness continua. It also implies that some cognitive processes (e.g. distortions) may be operating below the threshold of awareness.

Hypnosis provides a vehicle whereby cognitive distortions below the level of awareness can be explored and expanded. This is achieved by directing the patient's attention to the psychological content occurring in each quadrant of the time and awareness continua. The patient is guided to focus attention on a specific area of concern where dysfunctional cognitions are present, or is instructed to move within any of the two dimensions (time and awareness) until such an area is established. Next the patient is encouraged to dispute the cognitions as in the early stages of therapy, and then attend to the emotional consequences of engaging in these disputations. Other hypnotic uncovering or restructuring procedures such as age-regression and -progression and dream induction can be used to explore and restructure non-conscious negative schemas. Patients are usually given post-hypnotic suggestions regarding 'positive focusing' and they are encouraged to practise such focusing (i.e. imagining disputing negative cognitions and feeling the positive consequences) as often as possible.

2 Attention-switching and positive mood induction

Depressed patients are often preoccupied with thoughts and images of suicide, inability to cope, never being right again, self-blame and so on. Such ruminations

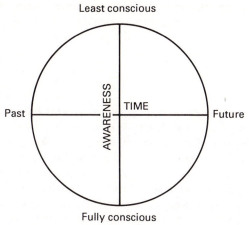

Least conscious

Past — AWARENESS — TIME — Future

Fully conscious

Figure 4.1 The time and awareness continua in human experience

can become obsessional in nature and are likely to impede therapeutic progress. To help the obsessional depressive break the ruminative cycle and replace negative thoughts by positive experience he or she is advised to make a list of 10 to 15 pleasant life-experiences and to 'practise holding each experience in your mind for about 30 seconds'. The patient is encouraged (1) to practise with the list about four to five times a day, and (2) to switch negative or 'undesirable' experiences (whenever the patient dwells on these) 'out of your mind and replace them by one of the pleasant items from your list'.

3 Active-interactive training
This technique attempts to break dissociative habits and encourage 'associations' with the relevant environment. When interacting with their internal or external environment, depressive patients, like neurotic patients, tend to *passively dissociate* rather than *actively interact* with the presented information. By 'active-interactive' is meant being alert and 'in tune' with the incoming information, whereas passive-dissociation is the tendency to anchor to 'inner reality' (negative schemas and experiences). Through passive-dissociation a person constructs an autonomous system (divided consciousness) which does not relate to conceptual reality and often this leads to social rejection since the person cannot 'tune in' to social interactions.

In order to prevent passive-dissociation a person must (1) become aware of such a process occurring and (2) actively attempt to inhibit it. Once a patient becomes aware of this process, he or she is advised to (a) switch attention away from 'bad anchors' and (b) actively attend to relevant cues. In other words, the patient learns to actively engage the left hemisphere by becoming analytical, logical, realistic and syntactical.

Other procedures
One session may be devoted to social skills and assertiveness training, and the patient is also instructed, using hypnosis, in the setting of relevant and realistic

goals and planning appropriate strategies for achieving them. He or she is also encouraged to take up some form of daily exercise such as jogging, walking, or weight-training.

Recent research

There is a vast learned literature on depression. This literature describes the nature of depression, the various methods of classifying the disorder, epidemiological findings, theories of the origins and causes of depression, and methods of treatment. It is the last area we are interested in, but whereas there are plenty of individual case reports and descriptions of therapeutic strategies (and we may include here the psychoanalytical literature) we find that when it comes to controlled clinical trials of psychological treatments, there has until recently been very little published work. It has been very encouraging, therefore, to read of the positive outcome reported for cognitive therapy in well-conducted clinical trials with depressed patients, its favourable comparison with pharmacological treatment, particularly in terms of relapse rate, and the fact that the therapy is complementary to and not in competition with antidepressant medication (Rush *et al.* 1977, Blackburn *et al.* 1981, Kovacs *et al.* 1981). This work should spur those using hypnotherapeutic methods to investigate the efficacy of their procedures with depressed patients, but we have yet to see any serious and substantial research in this field, in contrast, say, to work on the hypnotic treatment for psychosomatic ailments (see Chapters 2 and 8).

The cognitive–hypnotherapy approach described above has so far been compared with Beck's cognitive therapy informally in a sample of 20 patients by Alladin (1989). The results so far suggest that there are no differences between the two therapies in reducing depressive moods. However, cognitive hypnotherapy appears to achieve a more rapid improvement, lead to a greater reduction in measured anxiety, and promote greater self-confidence than the cognitive therapy alone.

Future directions

For a number of reasons the hypnotherapy literature is of varying quality and there is too heavy a reliance on the single-case illustration. Nevertheless, the value of single-case illustrations is that they do provide the reader with ideas about the kinds of techniques he or she may use when encountering similar cases in his or her own clinical practice. In Chapter 2 a technique was defined as a procedure deliberately aimed at accelerating the desired changes in the patient.

The assumption that hypnotherapeutic techniques – such as self-hypnosis, ego-strengthening and methods of resolving traumatic memories – often accelerate desired change needs to be the focus of further experimental investigation. Ideally we should compare a therapy, such as a course of cognitive therapy, with and without a particular hypnotherapeutic technique, such as ego-strengthening or dream suggestion. A difference in outcome favouring the inclusion of the technique will give therapists the confidence to incorporate that technique into their therapeutic programme. This kind of comparison has been undertaken informally by Alladin (see above) with some favourable results for hypnotherapeutic methods, although in this case several techniques were used in parallel and one can say little about the contribution of each one in isolation.

Clearly, results gleaned from clinical trials comparing different treatments in the above manner only accumulate over a long period of time and clinical research itself does not always give clear-cut answers. One difficulty arises if a particular technique – say dream suggestion – accelerates change for some patients but has a negative influence for others. Group statistics will show no effect due to that intervention. Hence the question to ask is 'For which patients and under what circumstances is this procedure efficacious?' Here the use of robust assessment procedures with patients is called for.

One may also investigate a hypnotic technique by observing the effect on the patient's rate of improvement of delaying its implementation. Thus one could introduce dream suggestion early or late in the programme of therapy. Although there are logical problems in interpreting the results, no difference in rates of improvement would call into question the usefulness of this procedure.

The hypnotherapy literature would also benefit from greater use of the single-case experiment, although not all techniques are suitable for this kind of investigation. The impact of daily exposure to an auto-hypnosis tape with ego-strengthening instructions could be investigated by periodically asking the patient to surrender the tape for a while, then to resume its use. Again, logical problems abound, but if no measurable change occurs, then the usefulness of this procedure, at least for some patients, would be in doubt.

Through these kinds of investigations, both group trials and single-case experiments, we will gradually derive a clearer idea of the effectiveness of the hypnotherapeutic methods described above as augmentative procedures in the psychological treatment of depressed patients.

References

Abraham, K. (1911) Notes on the psychoanalytic investigation and treatment of manic-depressive insanity and allied conditions, in K. Abraham (ed.) *Selected Papers on Psycho-analysis*, London: Hogarth Press.

Alladin, A. (1987) Cognitive-hypnotherapy: an integrated approach to the treatment of depression. Unpublished manuscript.

—— (1989) Cognitive-hypnotherapy for depression, in D. Waxman, D. Pedersen, I. Wilkie and P. Mellett (eds) *Hypnosis: The 4th European Congress at Oxford*, London: Whurr Publishers.

American Psychiatric Association (1987) *Diagnostic and Statistical Manual of Mental Disorders*, 3rd edn (revised), Washington, DC: American Psychiatric Association.

Araoz, D.L. (1981) Negative self-hypnosis, *Journal of Contemporary Psychotherapy* 12: 45–52.

Beck, A.T. (1967) *Depression: Clinical, Experimental and Theoretical Aspects*, New York: Hoeber.

—— (1976) *Cognitive Therapy and the Emotional Disorders*, New York: International University Press.

Beck, A.T., Rush, A.J., Shaw, B.F. and Emery, G. (1979) *Cognitive Therapy of Depression*, New York: Guilford Press.

Blackburn, I., Bishop, S., Glen, M., Whalley, L.J. and Christie, J. (1981) The efficacy of cognitive therapy in depression: a treatment trial using cognitive therapy and pharmacotherapy, each alone and in combination, *British Journal of Psychiatry* 139: 181–9.

Boyd, J.H. and Weissman, M.M. (1982) Epidemiology, in E.S. Paykel (ed.) *Handbook of Affective Disorders*, New York: Guilford Press.

Burns, D.D. (1980) *Feeling Good: The New Mood Therapy*, New York: William Morrow.

Burrows, G.D. (1980) Affective disorders and hypnosis, in G.D. Burrows and L. Dennerstein (eds) *Handbook of Hypnosis and Psychosomatic Medicine*, New York: Elsevier Press.

Degun, G.S. and Degun, M.D. (1977) Hypnotic abreaction: a case of an agoraphobic and claustrophobic patient, *Bulletin of the British Society of Experimental and Clinical Hypnosis* 1: 5–6.

Degun, M.D. and Degun, G.S. (1980). Hypnosis: An effective treatment for depression. *Bulletin of the British Society of Experimental and Clinical Hypnosis* 3, 18–19.

—— (1988) The use of hypnotic dream suggestion in psychotherapy, in M. Heap (ed.) *Hypnosis: Current Clinical, Experimental and Forensic Practices*, London: Croom Helm.

Diamond, S.J., Farrington, L. and Johnson, P. (1976) Differing emotional response from right to left hemisphere, *Nature* 261: 690–92.

Flor-Henry, P. (1976) Lateralized temporal-limbic dysfunction and psychopathology, *Annals of New York Academy of Science* 280: 777–95.

Freud, S. (1917) Mourning and melancholia, in *The Standard Edition of the Complete Psychological Works, Vol. 14*, London: Hogarth Press.

Frumkin, L.R., Ripley, H.S. and Cox, G.B. (1978) Changes in cerebral hemispheric lateralisation with hypnosis, *Biological Psychiatry* 13: 741.

Galin, D. (1974) Implications for psychiatry of left and right cerebral specialization, *Archives of General Psychiatry* 31: 572–83.

Gallant, D.M. and Simpson, G.M. (eds) (1976) *Depression: Behavioral, Biochemical, Diagnostic and Treatment Concepts*, New York: Spectrum.

Gibbons, D.E. (1979) *Applied Hypnosis and Hyperempiria*, New York: Plenum Press.

Gibson, H.B. and Heap, M. (1990) *Hypnosis in Therapy*, London: Lawrence Erlbaum.

Gruzelier, J.H. and Brow, T.D. (1985) Psychophysiological evidence for a state theory of hypnosis and susceptibility, *Journal of Psychosomatic Research* 29: 287–302.

Gruzelier, J.H., Brow, T., Perry, A., Rhonder, J. and Thomas, M. (1984) Hypnotic susceptibility: a lateral predisposition and altered cerebral asymmetry under hypnosis, *International Journal of Psychophysiology* 2: 131–9.

Hart, B.B. (1984). Hypnotic age regression of longstanding phobias: two case studies, *Proceedings of the British Society of Experimental and Clinical Hypnosis*, BSECH.

Hartland, J. (1971) *Medical and Dental Hypnosis and its Clinical Applications*, 2nd edn, London: Baillière Tindall.

Heap, M. (1984) Four victims, *British Journal of Experimental and Clinical Hypnosis* 3: 25–7.

—— (1985) Ego-strengthening: further considerations, *Proceedings of the Second Annual Conference of the British Society of Experimental and Clinical Hypnosis*, BSECH.

Hilgard, E.R. (1986) *Divided Consciousness: Multiple Controls in Human Thought and Action*, 2nd edn, New York: Wiley.

Horowitz, M.J. (1972) Image formation: clinical observation and a cognitive model, in P.W. Sheehan (ed.) *The Function and Nature of Imagery*, New York: Academic Press.

Kaplan, H.I. and Sadock, B.J. (1981) *Modern Synopsis of Comprehensive Textbook of Psychiatry*, 3rd edn, Baltimore: Williams & Wilkins.

Karle, H.W.A. (1988) Hypnosis in analytical psychotherapy, in M. Heap (ed.) *Hypnosis: Current Clinical, Experimental and Forensic Practices*, London: Croom Helm.

Kovacs, M., Rush, A.J., Beck, A.T. and Hollon, S.D. (1981) Depressed outpatients treated with cognitive therapy or pharmacotherapy: a one-year follow-up, *Archives of General Psychiatry* 38: 33–9.

Kroger, W.S. (1977) *Clinical and Experimental Hypnosis in Medicine, Dentistry and Psychology*, Philadelphia: J.B. Lippincott.

Malmquist, C.P. (1970) Depression and object loss in psychiatric admissions, *American Journal of Psychiatry* 126: 1782–7.

Matheson, G. (1979) Modification of depressive symptoms through post-hypnotic suggestion, *American Journal of Clinical Hypnosis* 22: 61–4.

Medical Research Council (1965) Clinical trial of the treatment of depressive illness, *British Medical Journal* 1: 881–6.

Mollica, R.R. (1989) Mood disorders: Epidemiology, in H.I. Kaplan and B.J. Sadock (eds) *Comprehensive Textbook of Psychiatry*, 5th edn, Baltimore: Williams & Wilkins.

Motto, J.A. (1975) The recognition and management of the suicidal patient, in F.F. Flach and S.C. Draghi (eds) *The Nature and Treatment of Depression*, New York: Wiley.

Murphy, G.E., Simons, A.D., Wetzel, R.D. and Lustman, P.J. (1984) Cognitive therapy and pharmacotherapy, *Archives of General Psychiatry* 41: 33–41.

Norman, W., Miller, I.W. and Klee, S. (1983) Assessment of cognitive distortion in a clinically depressed population, *Cognitive Therapy and Research* 7: 133–40.

Overlade, D.C. (1986) First aid for depression, in E.T. Dowd and J.M. Healy (eds) *Case Studies in Hypnotherapy*, New York: Guilford Press.

Parry, G. and Brewin, C.R. (1988) Cognitive style and depression: symptom-related, event-related or independent provoking factor? *British Journal of Clinical Psychology* 27: 23–5.

Quitkin, F., Rifkin, R. and Klein, D. (1976) Prophylaxis of affective disorders, *Archives of General Psychiatry* 33: 337–41.

Ross, P.J. (1985) Ego-strengthening: a critical view, *Proceedings of the Second Annual Conference of the British Society of Experimental and Clinical Hypnosis*, BSECH.

Rush, A.J., Beck, A.T., Kovac, M. and Hollons, S. (1977) Comparative efficacy of cognitive therapy and imipramine in the treatment of depressed outpatients, *Cognitive Therapy and Research* 1: 17–37.

Schultz, K.D. (1976) Fantasy stimulation in depression: direct intervention and correlational studies. Unpublished Doctoral Dissertation, Yale University.

—— (1978) Imagery and the control of depression, in J.L. Singer and K.S. Pope (eds) *The Power of Human Imagination: New Methods in Psychotherapy*, New York: Plenum Press.

Seligman, M.E.P. (1975) *Helplessness: On Depression, Development and Death*, San Francisco: Freeman.

Stein, C. (1963) The clenched fist technique as a hypnotic procedure in clinical psychotherapy, *American Journal of Clinical Hypnosis* 6: 113–9.

Stern, S.L. and Mendels, J. (1980) Affective disorders, in A.E. Kazdin, A.S. Bellack and M. Hersen (eds) *New Perspectives in Abnormal Psychology*, New York: Oxford University Press.

Tart, C. (1975) *States of Consciousness*, New York: Dutton.

Teasdale, J.D. and Dent, J. (1987) Cognitive vulnerability to depression – an investigation of two hypotheses, *British Journal of Clinical Psychology* 26: 113–26.

Tosi, D.J. and Baisden, B.S. (1984) Cognitive–experiential therapy and hypnosis, in W.C. Wester and A.H. Smith (eds) *Clinical Hypnosis: A Multidisciplinary Approach*, Philadephia: Lippincott.

Tucker, D.M. and Frederick, S.L. (1989) Emotion and brain lateralization, in H. Wagner and A. Manstead (eds) *Handbook of Social Psychophysiology*, New York: Wiley.

Watts, N.F. and Nicoli, A.M. (1979) Early death of a parent as an etiological factor in schizophrenia, *American Journal of Orthopsychiatry* 49: 465–73.

Wexler, B.E. (1980) Cerebral laterality and psychiatry: a review of the literature, *American Journal of Psychiatry* 137: 279–91.

Williams, J.M.G. (1984) *The Psychological Treatment of Depression*, London: Croom Helm.

5

Hypnosis and habit disorders

DAVID A. ALEXANDER

Introduction

Although it appears in neither the psychiatric classification used in the UK (ICD9) nor that used in the USA (DSM-III-R), the term 'habit disorder' is commonly employed to describe a certain group of conditions which involve an 'unhealthy repetitive behavior that phenomenologically speaking is out of the person's control' (Citrenbaum *et al.* 1985: xi). Such behaviour includes hair pulling (trichotillomania), nail biting, thumb sucking and the excessive use of food, alcohol and tobacco. This chapter will be concerned with the last group because they constitute some of the most common reasons for individuals seeking help.

It is striking that the British professional literature contains few references to the use of hypnosis for these conditions, in contrast to the situation in the USA where clinicians and researchers regularly present their findings. The reason for this difference is however beyond the scope of the present chapter. It has five aims: (1) to describe some of the features of these three habit disorders and how they are treated by non-hypnotic means, (2) to outline some of the general principles of the hypnotic procedures most commonly used, (3) to describe some of their specific applications, (4) to give an overview of recent research findings in this field, and (5) to suggest some directions in which subsequent research and clinical work might develop.

The remainder of the present section will therefore consider current views on these three habit disorders in terms of their aetiology, presentation and (non-hypnotic) treatment.

Overeating

Most commonly, overeating is seen as a problem because of its alleged association with obesity. Generally, in our culture, being overweight is not favourably viewed, but our highly ambivalent attitude to food is represented by the fact that, on the one hand, there are many inducements through the media and advertisements to eat high-calorie foods but, on the other hand, the social, medical and sexual virtues of slimness are extolled. The complex role of food in our society is also shown by the fact that it can be used, for instance, as a reward, a source of pleasure and a means of displaying one's wealth or social status.

Despite much research the relationship between eating and obesity has defied an easy description. Some investigators have emphasized the role of physical factors, such as the distribution of fat cells and metabolic rate. Others have drawn attention to the role of psychological and social factors, suggesting (without much evidence) that, compared to those of normal weight, obese individuals eat more, eat too quickly, and eat not just when they are hungry but when they are angry, anxious, or depressed.

The emerging conclusion regarding the aetiology of obesity appears to involve a compromise, for obesity is probably multi-determined. Genetic predisposition certainly plays a part and, therefore, it is an inaccurate and unfair allegation that fat people are merely 'weak-willed gluttons'. Non-physical factors also exert an influence, but as yet there is no evidence that any particular personality trait is associated with overeating and obesity.

In view of the unclear picture of causation, it is not surprising that a range of treatments has been proposed. For a while, medication (especially amphetamine-based products) was popular but its long-term value is not proven, and it can be a source of iatrogenic problems such as dependence. Surgery (wiring of the jaws and jejuno-ileal bypass) has had its supporters, but generally these rather drastic steps are reserved for extreme cases, where there are strong medical grounds for their use. Simple psychological methods such as keeping a diary of food consumed and group support have been tried with some success, as has the use of fines if the patient fails to meet a certain target weight. With the advent of behaviour therapy, more elaborate methods have been tried. A common one is stimulus control which is based on the belief that excessive eating is often associated with certain environmental cues (e.g. seeing the food cupboard or watching TV). Consequently, patients are encouraged to eat only at specific times and in specific places. Cue cards containing messages reminding patients of their need to stop overeating may also be displayed at strategic places. Collectively falling under the heading of cognitive therapy, other methods have been devised to alter patients' thoughts and attitudes. Commonly, obese patients entertain negative and self-defeating attitudes: 'I'm a fat slob; nobody could like me like this; I'll never lose weight'. Cognitive methods help patients to test out these negative assumptions and acquire a more realistic view of themselves, their world and their future.

Modern treatment methods also display an awareness of the social dimension to the problems of overeating and weight control. Perhaps only inadvertently, spouses and others sometimes sabotage the patients' efforts (e.g. by saying to them, 'one little biscuit won't do any harm'). Because of this, patients are often required to keep a record of social exchanges involving food to identify such influences.

Exercise has frequently been regarded as the solution to obesity. However, there is no evidence that one can just 'burn off the fat' and, in any case, compliance with exercise regimes is generally poor. On the other hand, exercise may be helpful by increasing the patients' metabolic rate and by preventing the loss of healthy lean tissue.

Alcohol

Alcohol has been used for religious purposes, as a food, and for its anaesthetic qualities, but its most common and controversial use is as an intoxicating psychoactive drug. What constitutes 'alcohol abuse' has, however, long been disputed, and the imprecise term 'alcoholism' has become sullied by various negative connotations. 'Problem drinker' is now a term more commonly employed to identify a person whose drinking gives rise to alcohol-related disability but who has not reached the stage of alcohol dependence. Also, the Royal Colleges of Physicians and Psychiatrists have offered some guidelines indicating the risks associated with different levels of consumption in terms of 'units' of alcohol. (By one 'unit' is meant one half-pint of beer or lager, or a standard measure of spirits, wine, or fortified wine.) The Colleges propose that 21 units or less per week for men, and 14 units for non-pregnant women, carry a low risk of harm. The potential for harm increases greatly above 50 units per week for men and 35 units for women (i.e. 'high risk'). Consumption between these two cut-off points is defined as 'intermediate risk'. We should not assume, however, that only certain individuals are at risk: there are no absolutely safe levels, and the impact of alcohol varies greatly with age, sex, general health and other factors.

Increasing concerns about the consequences of alcohol abuse have fostered much interest in which measures might be effective in curbing this abuse. One obvious way would be to limit alcohol use throughout the whole community rather than targeting those deemed at risk. There appears to be a fixed relation between average and excessive consumption of alcohol: an association often referred to as the Ledermann hypothesis (Kendell 1979). It implies that as average consumption increases the number of excessive drinkers will rise even more. Modifying drinking habits in the community is not, however, an easy challenge.

At the vanguard of providing help for problem drinkers have been the voluntary agencies, Alcoholics Anonymous (AA) in particular and its less well-known offshoots Al-Anon and Al-Alteen for the spouses and teenage children of such individuals respectively. The National Council on Alcoholism and its local branches also do much to help. Once having acknowledged they have a problem many individuals, without specialized assistance, respond well to support, advice and information, particularly if early intervention is available.

Specialist units are now quite common and utilize many methods, including supportive psychotherapy and group psychotherapy, to help individuals with day-to-day living, to provide an accepting climate, and to provide models of how to cope without alcohol. A variety of behavioural methods have also been tried, but no single method has a claim to superiority over the others. For a while, there was a preference for aversive methods, such as electric shocks, but this has given way to a move towards methods which emphasize the positive gains for the patient of reducing his or her use of alcohol. One variant of the aversive approach is the use of Antabuse (disulphiram), which patients take on a daily basis: if they consume alcohol on top of this a violent reaction occurs, with tachycardia, flushing, dyspnoea and nausea, due to the blocking of the oxidation of alcohol leading to an accumulation of acetaldehyde in the body. Although critics of this method point to the physical risks it carries, as an adjunct to other methods it can help patients to achieve a period of abstinence, thereby allowing them to experience the physical, social and emotional benefits of a life without alcohol, as well as making them more amenable to other therapies.

One question which remains unanswered is whether the therapeutic goal should be complete abstinence or controlled drinking (i.e. drinking within certain prescribed limits). Whatever the goal, it is clear that achieving enduring change in drinking habits defies any simple, single approach and (as has been found with eating disorders) biological, social and psychological factors are implicated.

Smoking

Nicotine, the effective ingredient in tobacco, is a highly toxic and addictive drug which is now recognized to have powerful stimulating effects on the central nervous system. Various reasons have been proposed for people continuing to smoke in full knowledge of the fact that it is strongly linked with major disorders, including cardiovascular and respiratory ones. The so-called addiction model suggests smoking is merely a means of maintaining a certain concentration of nicotine in the blood to prevent the occurrence of withdrawal effects (Russell *et al.* 1980). An alternative view is that smoking allows individuals to alter their own psychological state, including their level of arousal. Other proposed psychological reasons include sexual sublimation, peer pressure and an unconscious wish for self-destruction.

As with the other habit disorders, aversive methods initially proved to be attractive, but such approaches (including requiring the patient to 'chain-smoke' for up to 20 hours!) have been questioned not only on health grounds but because of their doubtful long-term value. Other methods, such as systematic desensitization, are used to help smokers feel more comfortable and relaxed in settings in which previously they would have resorted to cigarettes. Alternatively, cue cards can be carried by smokers to remind them of reasons for curbing the habit, and 'programmed smoking' can be used to restrict their smoking to certain times or places. 'Contracts' can also be made with friends or family whereby a set of financial or other sanctions are agreed upon as rewards or punishments for desirable and undesirable changes in smoking habits respectively.

Pharmacological methods have also been devised. Substances, such as lobeline, which mimic many of the effects of nicotine without its serious side-effects, have been popular but they have achieved limited success. More recently, Nicorette (nicotine in a resin complex) has been used to help combat the withdrawal effects whilst giving up the habit. Unfortunately, it is not particularly pleasant to chew and should not be used by patients suffering from gastric or duodenal ulceration.

In general, no single method, even those used in specialist clinics, has proved to be outstandingly successful. Moreover, as is the case with alcohol reduction, it is not clear whether total and sudden abstinence is necessarily more effective than a gradual weaning off, although some argue that the latter merely prolongs the agony. (A factor to take into account is that smokers are adept at altering their inhalation patterns to maintain their optimum blood/nicotine concentration.)

Conclusions

There is one common theme which links all attempts to modify these habits, and that is the need to avoid relapse. Most measures are effective in the short term, a finding encapsulated in Mark Twain's alleged remark: 'Giving up smoking is easy. I've done it hundreds of times.' Many reasons have been put forward to account for the high relapse rates. The Abstinence Violation Effect has been invoked and refers to the fact that, if the individual breaches his or her rule of abstinence even once, the rule is generally completely abandoned. Other factors which appear to contribute to relapse are: (1) the individuals' inability to tolerate the unpleasant effects of reduced consumption; (2) having initially unrealistic expectations of treatment; (3) little confidence in their ability to cope with the pressures of living without the aid of food, alcohol, or cigarettes; (4) the powerful social and environmental influences to continue their consumption; (5) adverse affective states (anxiety, depression and anger), and (6) possible biological limits to the extent to which improvements can be readily attained. (In relation to weight the Set Point hypothesis proposes that our weight is biologically predetermined within certain limits, and will seek to reassert itself whatever efforts we use to reduce it.)

Hypnotherapeutic approaches: general principles

This section will focus on the main hypnotic methods used with habit disorders. However, before considering these it will be helpful first to outline recommendations widely supported in relation to the use of these methods in this field.

1   As has been emphasized by the British practitioner, Elliott (1988), a full history should be taken of the patient's habit and its role in his or her life, including its influence on significant others. The motives for change, the likely consequences of change, and those factors which trigger or are associated with the habit should also be explored.
2   Patients need to be disabused of their misconceptions and anxieties about hypnosis. More specifically, they must appreciate that hypnosis is not a magical tool which will relieve them of their habit without effort on their part. For this reason some authorities teach a skills model of hypnosis, emphasizing that it is essentially a method of self-control and involves a set of cognitive skills to be used actively by the patient.
3   A contract should be agreed between patient and therapist in which the following are outlined: (a) realistic short-term and long-term goals (short-term ones help to maintain motivation by providing early successes); (b) mutually agreed

sanctions for failure to comply, or prerequisites of treatment (such as a period of pre-treatment abstinence), and (c) a clear definition of the respective roles and responsibilities of the patient and therapist.

4 Because preventing relapse is critical, and yet difficult to achieve, in addition to any specific hypnotic techniques used, patients need much support and encouragement.

It is not possible to describe every specific technique used in this field as they are too numerous; however, underlying this variety one can identify three basic themes which will be described below.

Habit change through direct suggestion

One of the most simple methods is to suggest directly to patients that they will stop smoking, eating, or drinking. This may involve the use of vivid imagery, including aversive images of vomit and of foul tastes and smells. Miller (1976), a well-known proponent of aversive methods, claims they can be particularly effective when other methods have failed. Generally, however, there is a stronger preference for the use of positive suggestions, emphasizing the positive gains, for example, clean breath, financial saving and better health. Elliott (1988) has also pointed out that it might be better to emphasize the positive emotional gains, such as increased self-esteem, because they are more immediately evident than are the physical gains. (The key point is that one must know the patient well enough to be aware of what will serve as a reward or positive reinforcement.)

There are three factors which may make methods using aversive suggestions less attractive than other methods: (1) they might be injurious to the patient's health (e.g. repeated suggestions of vomiting), (2) the proposed unpleasant consequences are often contrary to the patient's own experiences of the pleasure the habit brings, and (3) focusing on the aversive aspects alone may not create a particularly favourable relationship between therapist and patient.

Other suggestions which can be put to those who overeat are that they will eat like gourmets rather than gourmands and that they will relish every mouthful, thereby enhancing the sensory experience rather than the one of consumption. More imaginative methods include altering the patient's perception of time to shorten the time intervals between meals. Intensifying the desire might be used with smokers by suggesting they put a cigarette in their mouth but refrain from lighting it, and then asking them to throw it away. 'Symptom substitution' may be used by suggesting to hypnotized patients that each time they crave for an alcoholic drink they will instead eat a malted milk tablet which they will find pleasurable and relaxing. Altering the patients' physiological state has also been tried. To alleviate unpleasant withdrawal effects in patients who overeat the therapist may induce first glove anaesthesia under hypnosis and then suggest to the patients the transfer of the anaesthesia to the stomach to prevent 'hunger pangs'. Similarly, they can be taught to become more discriminating about their emotional states of anger, anxiety and hunger, and to narrow the range of experiences and sensations to which they respond by overeating.

One of the criticisms levelled against these methods is that they evoke resistance from the patient. For this reason, Erickson (1964) has devised ingenious methods to circumvent this opposition, using metaphors and highly symbolic stories containing hidden messages for the patient and indirect references to the habit disorder without confronting it directly. The reader is advised to read such examples to obtain an understanding of this unusual approach.

Ego-enhancement and cognitive methods

The methods described here are more concerned with changes in the patient and only aim at habit change indirectly.

One such method involves 'ego-enhancing' or ego-strengthening procedures, whereby the patients are given under hypnosis a series of suggestions to reinforce their feelings of self-worth and confidence and to relieve them of anxieties and emotions which may underlie the habit. (See Chapter 2.) Building up the patients' coping resources in this way also helps to ameliorate the transition period whilst the habits undergo change. Suggestions used under self-hypnosis can also be employed in this way. Following the success in the 1960s and 1970s of the cognitive approach to the treatment of depression and other symptoms, behaviour therapists in particular have extended their view of hypnosis to include it as a means of inculcating more realistic styles of thinking and attitudes. Too often patients with habit disorders engage in inaccurate observations and thoughts: for instance, 'I'm just a fat slob, nobody could love me, I'll never change' or 'I'm just a drunk, I could never manage a day's work without a drink'. Saddled with such thoughts the patients' problems are self-perpetuating. A related method is that of age-progression whereby patients are required under hypnosis to envisage themselves coping in situations (especially high-risk ones), which previously would have resulted in their eating, smoking, or drinking. Patients may also be encouraged to rehearse under hypnosis their new role as non-drinkers or whatever, in order that they can foresee and learn how to deal in advance with any problems which emerge (e.g. being offered a drink at a party). It is important to remember that the social world offers many blandishments and temptations to those who have problems with smoking, eating, or drinking.

The uncovering approach

Freud himself developed this use of hypnosis after he became disenchanted with hypnosis as a means of suggesting away troublesome symptoms. His view was that, unless you dealt with the unconscious urges or conflicts which led to the development of the patient's problem, treatment would not be successful in the long term. Either the problem would persist or other symptoms would replace it (symptom substitution); in fact, the evidence for the latter occurring is scant. Motives underlying alcohol abuse, for example, might be a strong but unrecognized self-destructive tendency or, in the case of obesity, excessive layers of adipose tissue might be the patient's defence against physical intimacy.

It is argued, therefore, that age-regression exposes unconscious events, experiences, or motives which underlie the habit disorder. By this means, under hypnosis, patients are asked to retrace their steps in life, identifying critical stages or incidents and re-experiencing the associated emotions. This offers not only an opportunity for catharsis but also for reappraising the event or experience.

Schoen (1985) proposes that under hypnosis it is also helpful to ask patients what motives they themselves may have for sabotaging efforts to modify their habits. There is also an interesting paradoxical element in this approach because the patients are encouraged to think consciously about their urges to continue the habit. This is contrary to the more repressive methods which try to inhibit the patients' needs to think about their habit. This paradox might have a hidden benefit in that it gives patients permission to think about the 'forbidden' substance in a new way, a way which lets patients feel in control of the urges rather than the other way round. In terms of self-control it is important for patients to learn that they can think about, for instance, food without it necessarily leading to overindulgence.

Derived partly from Erickson's methods and partly from Neuro-linguistic Programming techniques (Bandler and Grinder 1982), an alternative version of the uncovering method has been described by Citrenbaum *et al.* (1985). These authors emphasize the need to explore under hypnosis the patients' reasons for their habit disorder, and to establish to what circumstances or situations they are 'anchored' (i.e. what they are doing when they drink, eat, or smoke). It is necessary these authors claim, to identify the secondary gain derived from the habit (a point overlooked by many investigators and clinicians). Does the habit, for instance, gain sympathy or attention for the patient which ordinarily does not accrue? By their method of 'reframing', Citrenbaum and his colleagues ensure that whatever needs were satisfied by the habit in the past are also satisfied by new means. They make the important point, however, that these new ways of coping have to be compatible with the patient's personality, life-style and so on. To establish this, an 'ecological check' can be conducted under hypnosis in which patients are asked to see themselves behaving in new ways to see if these are acceptable to themselves.

It is evident that there are many ways of classifying the various (and at times idiosyncratic) hypnotic methods used to treat habit disorders: the present is but one way. Moreover, it should be recognized that, as will be seen shortly, modern practitioners are becoming more keen to use hypnosis as an adjunct within a treatment package (to be used for individual patients or in a group setting), rather than as a treatment in its own right.

Specific applications

In this section there will be a description of some of the specific techniques used to treat habit disorders associated with eating, smoking and drinking.

Short-term treatment methods

For a number of reasons, including economy of effort, the value of single hypnotic sessions has frequently been emphasized (e.g. Spiegel 1970, Rabkin *et al.* 1984). Although there are many variations, including the use of tape-recorded versions, the following sample is fairly standard. Patients would first be introduced to the principles of hypnosis, and their doubts and ignorance dispelled. They would then be given various instructions which would include:

> Now, look at me. As you hold your head in that position, I am going to count to three. One, look up toward your eyebrows. Try to look up still more and as you continue to look up, two, close your eyelids slowly. Keep your eyes rolled upward, and take a deep breath. Hold. Now, three, exhale, let your eyes relax. Keep your eyes closed and let your body float.
>
> (Spiegel 1970: 239)

Whilst in the hypnotic state, the patient is then given the following injunctions: 'One: For your body, not for you, for your body smoking is a poison. Two: You need your body to live. Three: You owe your body this respect and protection' (Spiegel 1970: 241).

There is an interesting theoretical point in relation to the three strategic injunctions described above. In contrast to the usual behavioural approach of emphasizing behaviour-change itself, patients are being challenged to exercise their right of choice as to how to conduct their lives and relate to their bodies. For those who dislike the more authoritarian style of hypnotic injunction (e.g. 'You will not smoke again'), this approach may have more appeal because it gives the patient rather than the therapist the responsibility for change.

Crasilneck and Hall (1985) have developed their own variation. Patients would first be screened for major psychiatric illness and then informed about the nature of hypnosis. Prior to being seen for four hypnotic sessions, patients would be shown how to induce under hypnosis glove anaesthesia and arm catalepsy. Achieving these states, it is claimed, demonstrates to patients the extent of the control they can exert over their bodies, and helps to persuade them that they have the ability to control their habit disorder. Under hypnosis smokers, for example, would be given a range of suggestions including:

> You will block the craving for tobacco – a habit that is causing your heart and lungs to work much harder than necessary . . . You will not be hungry or eat excessively . . . As you permit your body to rid itself of this undesired burden of smoking, your lungs will again become efficient, your red blood cells will carry more oxygen to all your vital organs, you will feel more alert and alive . . . Your craving for tobacco will be minimal and will rapidly decline to a zero level at a rapid pace.
>
> (pp. 225–6)

They claim there is no real contradiction between referring to a complete absence as well as a decline of the craving, because it is important to acknowledge that some patients will experience continued craving which should not be seen as evidence that the suggestions are ineffective. Subjects need to maintain their faith in these suggestions even in the presence of a craving.

They also prescribe a precise organization for sessions. The first three are given on consecutive days, then there is a gap of a month between the penultimate and last sessions. In addition, patients are advised to telephone in daily for the first week, twice in the second week and once in the week before the final hypnotic session. The aim of these contacts is to reinforce the post-hypnotic suggestions and the patients' desire to give up smoking. Daily exercise is also advocated, as is a cigarette substitute (such as a cinnamon stick) if patients re-experience the urge to smoke.

Aversive methods

One aversive method, 'conditioned reflex reinforcement', involves giving patients a drink of alcohol followed by an emetic thereby causing them to feel sick. This builds up a conditioned association between alcohol and feeling unwell: an association which can be reinforced by post-hypnotic suggestions which encourage patients to recollect these unpleasant tastes, smells and other sensations if the urge to take alcohol reappears. An alternative aversive procedure is to give patients an alcoholic drink from a newly opened bottle and ask them to hold a mouthful for a few moments until the full tingling sensation is experienced. They are told, however, under hypnosis that the contents were not alcohol but something bitter and unpleasant such as ammonia, lemon juice, or vinegar. Post-hypnotic suggestions are then given that each time the patients think of taking a drink or are offered one they will experience the same horrible, bitter taste which will make them feel sick.

It can be seen how such methods can be modified for other habit disorders. For example, post-hypnotic suggestions can be given to curb the consumption of high-calorie foods: patients can be told under hypnosis that each time they eat sugary foods they will develop a horrible taste, and that there will be a horrible smell like rotten eggs which makes them want to be sick. In conjunction with this kind of approach it is also common to give suggestions to confirm the patients' belief in their ability to cope, and to propose ways of redirecting (sublimating) needs which underlie the habit by, for example, taking up a healthy sport, activity, or interest.

Currently, aversive methods are less commonly favoured than those which involve emphasizing the positive gains to be made from changing habits. Commonly, these are linked with suggestions enhancing the patient's self-esteem and resolution to achieve habit change. For instance, patients may be told (either live or by tape-recording) that whenever they find themselves able to stop taking a drink they will feel very pleased with themselves and their confidence will grow. Alternatively, obese patients may be asked under hypnosis to imagine themselves at their target weight, and visualize themselves stepping on to scales registering this weight, to the acclaim and admiring comments of their friends and families.

Additional treatment procedures

As has been stated earlier, patients with habit disorders are frequently the victims of their own self-defeating negative expectations and pessimism following the repeated failure of previous treatments (although sometimes failure can also be due to their own unrealistic expectations of a successful outcome). For this reason, some therapists advocate avoiding total prohibitions because any relapse, however small, becomes magnified and further disillusionment may be the result. Other methods to ensure patients' motivation include inviting the obese patients to buy clothes for their ideal size and have these displayed in a prominent place, and describing to the patients previous successful treatments carried out with other patients (Wadden and Flaxman 1981).

There has also been a move towards more personalized treatments which are based specifically on the patient's own individual motives for stopping the habit and reasons for having begun it in the first place. An example of this approach has been described in detail by Cochrane (1987). An abbreviated version of one of his cases will give an idea of what is involved. The patient was a 46-year-old nurse whose pre-treatment weight was 195 pounds. Her background had been punctuated by family disharmony, but in her own marriage and job she was happy. Hypnosis was used to explore some of the pertinent family conflicts and dynamics which underlay her eating difficulties. As she became more aware of their relevance she became more emotionally vulnerable and, consequently, ego-enhancing suggestions were used to increase her sense of self-worth and confidence. Whilst attending to these matters, she was also required to adhere to an appropriate diet and exercise programme: an audiotape was made by herself to supplement her efforts at this stage. A key feature was that her weight reduction was extended over a fairly lengthy period: sudden and rapid weight loss was not aimed for.

In summary, therefore, the patient was required to take much responsibility for her own treatment, having gained some insight into the factors which contributed to her problem. Food was no longer to be the medium through which she dealt with her difficulties.

Obviously the reader should consult some of the original texts to obtain fuller details of how hypnosis is used, but it is appropriate now to turn to evaluative literature concerned with the efficacy of such methods.

Research developments

Assessing the significance of findings in this field is difficult because of the methodological shortcomings (such as the lack of control groups, heterogeneous patient samples and inadequate outcome measures) to be found in many studies. Even the definition of 'successful' outcome varies. In some studies success is defined in terms of the percentage of patients who were abstinent at the end of the trial, excluding those who dropped out or could not be contacted. This method will obviously give a more favourable picture than if successes were calculated on the basis of the total number who entered the trial. The length of the follow-up period is also important because early achievements may not be sustained. Matters such as these probably contribute to the inconsistent findings reported by earlier reviews. For instance, Holroyd (1980), reviewing the use of hypnosis for smoking control, found success rates to vary from 4% to 88% at six-month follow-up.

Smoking

In a study of 300 patients, Barabasz *et al.* (1986) compared six different treatment methods, including a novel hypnotic treatment condition in which patients were subjected to sensory deprivation (Restricted Environmental Stimulation Therapy). At six-month follow-up, 47% of patients in this condition had stopped smoking, confirming the authors' view that sensory deprivation enhances the individual's responsiveness to hypnotic suggestion. Two further factors which may have contributed to a good outcome were having 'booster' sessions and having experienced therapists. Positive features of this study are the fact that length of treatment time and experience of the therapist were controlled between treatment conditions. Unfortunately, however, patients were not randomly assigned to these different conditions.

In another study (Rabkin *et al.* 1984) patients were randomly allocated to single-session hypnosis, a health education group, a behaviour modification group, or a control group. In addition to daily self-report, the level of serum thiocyanate in the blood was used as an objective measure (the level of thiocyanate, a metabolite of cyanide, rises in the plasma after smoking). At six-month follow-up there was no difference between the patients in the different treatment groups. Neither socio-economic status nor the presence of a smoker in the patient's family had a bearing on outcome. These results, however, have to be seen against three features of the study: namely, small numbers, only one method of hypnosis (Spiegel's) was used, and the control group was only a delayed treatment group and not an attention placebo group. (An attention placebo controls for the amount of time the patient has with a therapist. During the sessions, however, the therapist does not actively conduct any formal treatment.)

A more thorough assessment of hypnosis has, however, been provided by Hyman *et al.* (1986) who compared Spiegel's single-session approach with an attention placebo, a waiting-list control, and 'focused smoking' (in which patients smoked at their normal rate, but at the same time had to think of the aversive aspects of the habit). Assessed by self-report, self-monitoring and chemical analysis, patients in the two active treatment groups did better at six months than those in the placebo and control groups, but hypnosis did not show itself to be superior to the other active treatment. However, a more favourable outcome was achieved by Williams and Hall (1988) using an extended version of Spiegel's approach (patients were taught relaxation and deep breathing exercises, were given ego-enhancing instructions, and were told to drink a glass of water if they felt the urge to smoke). At 48 weeks about half of the patients were abstinent, but no patient in either the attention placebo group or waiting-list control group achieved abstinence. (The fact that the subjects' employers sponsored the treatment, however, may have added to their motivation to attend and succeed because of their wish to please their employers.)

Although single-session therapy has attracted much attention because of the ease of administration and compliance, the role of hypnosis as an adjunct to more extensive treatment programmes has also been researched. Frank *et al.* (1986) randomly assigned patients to one of three treatment conditions in which hypnosis was used with and without booster sessions and with and without behavioural procedures (such as environmental management and stimulus control). Outcome was assessed at three months and six months using self-report and blood levels of serum thiocyanate levels as an objective measure of smoking, but no differences were found between the groups (approximately 20% of patients in each group stopped smoking). The data did suggest, however, that the value of giving the patient several hypnotic sessions close together should be explored further. Jeffrey *et al.* (1985) also investigated the value of extending the number of sessions and of combining hypnotic techniques with cognitive and behavioural ones. Used in a group setting, this approach achieved an abstinence rate of 31% at three months but no patient in the control group stopped smoking. Encouraged by these initial results the treatment package was repeated (Jeffrey and Jeffrey 1988) but with an additional feature: patients had to be abstinent for 48 hours before being given the second of five treatment sessions, in the belief that confronting this issue early and giving the patients a chance to experience mastery over their habit would be helpful. This 'exclusion therapy' did not, however, lead to higher abstinence levels assessed at three months: 24 patients in the exclusion group were abstinent three months after treatment, and 20 in the non-exclusive group were also abstinent.

In conclusion, there is certainly evidence to confirm the effectiveness of hypnosis in achieving abstinence, with relatively few sessions, but the problem is how to maintain this change (a challenge hypnosis shares with other approaches). Various relevant factors have been proposed. For instance, some have investigated the role of hypnotizability and, although the results have been conflicting, it would appear that low hypnotizability is a poor prognostic indicator of long-term abstinence; but beyond this contribution, hypnotizability probably has little bearing on outcome (Wadden and Anderton 1982). Other factors which appear to facilitate sustained abstinence are less pleasure experienced from the habit, use of self-hypnosis, 'live' hypnosis rather than recorded packages, group support, booster sessions, extended sessions, and hypnotic suggestions tailored to the needs of the individual.

Obesity and overeating

Obviously there is overlap between the problems of smoking and those of overeating but there is one difference: one does have to eat, nobody has to smoke. Consequently, with regard to eating, abstinence cannot be an aim, only a reduction in consumption. None the less, many of the earliest hypnotherapeutic efforts are similar to those used for smoking cessation. In particular, investigators tried to foster a positive attitude towards the gains to be made from losing weight instead of focusing directly on weight loss *per se* (Spiegel and Spiegel 1978).

Stanton (1976) used a more elaborate method which included ego-enhancing suggestions that the subjects' efforts at weight loss would be successful. In particular, however, he found that those who paid fees were more successful in losing weight than non-fee-paying patients. Similarly, Miller (1976) found aversive techniques, using suggestions of nausea and vomiting in relation to high-calorie foods, allowed half of his patients to maintain at least 50% of their weight loss over one year.

Confronted by such a complex problem, however, it is not surprising that combined approaches have been tried. Cochrane and Friesen (1986), for example, emphasize the need to attend to behavioural, dietary and psychosocial issues at different phases of treatment. Using hypnosis to uncover reasons for overeating as well as to promote ego-enhancement and self-control they found that at six month follow-up patients in the treatment group achieved a mean weight loss of about 18 pounds, whereas those in the control group managed only about 2 pounds. This study also showed that hypnosis used principally as a self-control technique can be effective, and it was noted that those who were willing to take personal responsibility for changes in their weight did better than those who blamed the treatment rather than themselves when they failed to lose weight. An interesting point advanced by the investigators, however, was that one should aim for modest weight losses which can be sustained rather than dramatic ones which cannot, because the latter lead to a sense of failure for the patient. Although the numbers involved were small, Wadden and Flaxman (1981) compared hypnosis with covert modelling and relaxation. In the first two conditions the patients were asked to imagine themselves showing appropriate eating habits and enjoying the benefits thereof. No reference to hypnosis was made, however, to those in the modelling group. In the relaxation-attention control group patients were taught progressive relaxation, and asked to imagine themselves in a peaceful setting (thereby controlling for the use of imagery). In each condition patients were encouraged to have positive expectations of outcome. At the end of the 7-week course all groups showed significant weight loss but there was no difference between the groups; this remained true at 16-week follow-up. These investigators suggest that non-specific factors, such as expectancy and motivation, may account for the success of hypnosis. The validity of this claim may be challenged because of the small numbers involved and the short follow-up period, but the question these investigators raise is an important one.

Alcohol

The earliest attempts to use hypnosis typically involved simple suggestions that the patients' need for alcohol would diminish or that they would find alcohol unpleasant. Aversive methods used by Miller (1976) were claimed to be particularly effective, with success rates of over 60% being reported at one-year follow-up. However, less faith has been shown in the long-term value of aversive methods, and in those relying solely on direct suggestion. Because of this, a more comprehensive strategy for problem drinkers has been advocated. Gabrynowicz's (1977) programme reflected this shift in the role of hypnotic methods. Patients initially attended weekly therapy sessions for the first six weeks, followed by monthly meetings and, finally, 6-monthly meetings for the remainder of the year. Hypnosis was used to relieve anxiety, and to facilitate the development of more effective methods of coping with life's problems than resorting to alcohol. Unfortunately, because of a variable follow-up period, the small number of patients involved (25), and the lack of a control group, it is difficult to know how significant was Gabrynowicz's report of a 76% abstinence rate.

In their review of experimental findings, Wadden and Penrod (1981) took a careful look at such claims and emphasized the need to look critically at the methods used in such studies before placing too much reliance on claims of successful abstinence. Well-designed studies have not always cast hypnosis in such a favourable light. Edwards (1966) randomly assigned 40 patients to two treatment conditions, each involving individual psychotherapy, attendance at AA meetings and chemotherapy. The only difference between the conditions was that in only one was hypnosis used to encourage the patients' compliance with treatment and to heighten their aversion to alcohol. The groups were matched for age, years of alcohol addiction, intelligence and personality. No differences were found on follow-up, leading Edwards to the conclusion that hypnosis offered no special advantages as a treatment procedure – a conclusion also reached by Jacobson and Silfverskiold (1973) using an even more extensive evaluation of drinking behaviour and outcome. However, possible shortcomings of these studies are that they used relatively short follow-up periods and that the issue of hypnotizability was not considered.

As was the case with smoking and overeating, the challenge is to achieve a sustained change in behaviour and attitudes to prevent relapse. At this stage in our knowledge, it seems likely that factors which are related to a more favourable long-term outcome are: a genuine wish to achieve abstinence, at least moderate responsiveness to hypnosis, realistic therapeutic goals, and a focus on the advantages of abstinence or change as well as preparation for the difficulties to which they may give rise.

Future developments

As a therapeutic agent, hypnosis has led a chequered career: it has been heralded as a panacea but, at other times in its history, it has been ridiculed and dismissed as nonsense and deception. However, even when its reputation has been at its lowest, hypnosis has shown a remarkable resilience. Moreover, because of the increasing willingness of many of its practitioners to subject their ideas and endeavours to systematic empirical scrutiny, a more realistic picture of its therapeutic potential has begun to emerge. In the previous section, evidence has been presented which demonstrates that hypnosis can be an effective method of altering an individual's behaviour in relation to alcohol, tobacco and food. However, this leaves many questions unanswered about the nature of hypnosis itself. Even the notion of 'trance' is poorly understood because, at present, there is no objective, independent correlate of this state (if, indeed, there is a special mental state). Similarly, we do not know the nature of the relationship between hypnosis and suggestion.

In relation to the specific contribution of hypnosis to the management of habit disorders there are also a number of important issues which have to be addressed to enhance the scientific and clinical standing of hypnosis in this field, and to counter some of the dramatic and at times outrageous claims reported in the media and by some practitioners.

1 Although the move towards comprehensive treatment packages, incorporating hypnosis in different ways, is justifiable in view of their success in dealing with habit disorders, we still do not know what is the specific value of hypnosis in relation to attitude and behaviour change. Not only do we need to know what are the factors specific to hypnosis which are effective, we also need to know what is the contribution of non-specific factors (such as motivation and expectation), as well as the role of particular therapist variables, such as perceived experience and competence.

2 We need to know more about the relevance of patient characteristics and those pertaining to the disorder being treated. Clearly, not all individuals with, for example, an alcohol problem respond to the same treatment in the same way, but why this should be so is far from clear. Moreover, in the case of obesity, for instance, there are reasons for believing that there are different kinds of obesity (Cooper and Cooper 1988): that which begins in childhood and that which starts in adulthood may involve different aetiological factors and, therefore, combining them in a treatment trial is likely to result in confusing findings.

3 Still a relatively uncharted field of study is the role of underlying psychodynamics and psychopathology in the development and maintenance of habit disorders, and how these are influenced by the use of hypnosis.

4 Each of these issues is related to another major need, and that is to explore what are the factors related to a lack of favourable outcome. It should not be assumed that patients who fail to respond to a hypnotic approach will constitute a homogeneous group. For instance, there may be something distinctive about those who fail to respond to hypnotic suggestions regarding weight loss at an early stage in treatment, compared to those who display a favourable response initially but relapse later.

5 Practitioners in this field will also have to continue their efforts to link their therapeutic interventions with their theoretical ideas about the development and maintenance of habit disorders. Schoen (1985) has pointed out one direction in which further study must be conducted, by emphasizing the need to recognize different phases of the recovery process. He argues that different treatment efforts are required at these different phases. It may be, for instance, that hypnotically induced relaxation may help during the withdrawal stages, whereas ego-enhancing hypnotic suggestions might have a greater role to play in helping to maintain abstinence thereafter.

6 Certain assumptions underlying the use of hypnotic suggestions need to be questioned. For instance, can it be assumed that suggestions given by the therapist are received passively by patients who then act on them as they were given? It is most unlikely that this is what happens in the hypnotic setting, because perception is an active process. Yet we do not know how subjects

interpret and modify the suggestions put to them, and whether their doing so has any bearing on outcome. Sheehan (1986) is justified, therefore, in proposing that we consider individual differences in cognitive style in responding to suggestions.

To answer some of these and other important questions, improved methodologies are required. The task is certainly a difficult one, particularly in the clinical setting where it is much harder than it is in the laboratory to control the influence of extraneous variables. Definitions of the phenomena being studied must be explicitly stated. To describe a patient as obese or overweight tells us very little about the magnitude or nature of the problem. Similarly, methods of hypnotic induction and the precise nature of the procedures used must be clearly stated in order that replication is possible. More reliable and valid measures of behaviour and attitude change, in relation to habit disorders, must continue to be developed. Although self-report by the patient is a convenient and widely used measure, it can be a misleading one for a variety of reasons. Hence, objective measures should be used whenever possible.

Definitions of what constitutes success and failure are also important issues. Total abstinence from alcohol and tobacco is a clearly defined achievement, but in the case of food, since abstinence is not possible, other criteria have to be agreed upon. It is also worth noting that there are degrees of success which should not be discounted. For instance, reducing alcohol or tobacco intake by 90% is still better than no change, and achieving total abstinence for even 6 months is better than never having achieved abstinence.

There is a need for more studies in which patients, matched on various criteria such as severity of their disorder, are randomly assigned to different treatment conditions and to waiting-list and attention placebo controls. Long-term follow-up is also necessary because of the regular finding that many interventions are effective over a matter of weeks or a few months, with relapse rates becoming marked after a year. What investigators need to do is to devise methods of preventing relapse and maintaining positive change.

Many of these developments and others will be facilitated by a closer affiliation between those who practise medicine and those in the field of behavioural medicine. As behaviour therapists develop a broader view of the role of hypnosis there is likely to be more collaboration and cross-fertilization of ideas. Hypnosis may prove to be a clinical tool which can be used to enhance a variety of treatment methods, rather than a treatment in its own right (Spinhoven 1987), but even in this more limited role hypnotic phenomena are worthy of scientific and clinical scrutiny. Habit disorders have proved to be formidable adversaries to all forms of treatment; any method which appears to have some therapeutic value is worthy of our careful attention.

References

Bandler, R. and Grinder, J. (1982) *Reframing: Neuro-linguistic Programming and the Transformation of Meaning*, Moab, Utah: Real People Press.

Barabasz, A.F., Baer, L., Sheehan, D.V. and Barabasz, M. (1986) A three-year follow-up of hypnosis and restricted environmental stimulation therapy for smoking, *International Journal of Clinical and Experimental Hypnosis* 34: 169–81.

Citrenbaum, C.M., King, M.E. and Cohen, W.I. (1985) *Modern Clinical Hypnosis for Habit Control*, London: Norton.

Cochrane, G.J. (1987) Hypnotherapy in weight-loss treatment: case illustrations, *American Journal of Clinical Hypnosis* 30: 20–7.

Cochrane, G.J. and Friesen, J. (1986) Hypnotherapy in weight loss, *Journal of Consulting and Clinical Psychology* 54: 489–92.

Cooper, P.J. and Cooper, Z. (1988) Eating disorders, in E. Miller and P.J. Cooper (eds), *Adult Abnormal Psychology*, Edinburgh: Churchill Livingstone.

Crasilneck, H.B. and Hall, J.A. (1985) *Clinical Hypnosis: Principles and Applications*, 2nd edn, New York: Grune & Stratton.

Edwards, G. (1966) Hypnosis in treatment of alcohol addiction: controlled trial, with analysis of factors affecting outcome, *Quarterly Journal of Studies of Alcohol* 27: 221–41.

Elliott, J. (1988) Hypnotherapy for compulsive smokers, *Hypnos* 15: 87–92.

Erickson, M.H. (1964) An hypnotic technique for resistant patients: the patient, the technique and its rationale and field experiments, *American Journal of Clinical Hypnosis* 7: 8–32.

Frank, R.G., Umlauf, R.L., Wonderlich, S.A. and Ashkanazi, G.S. (1986) Hypnosis and behavioral treatment in a worksite smoking cessation project, *Addictive Behaviors* 11: 59–62.

Gabrynowicz, J. (1977) Hypnosis in a treatment programme for alcoholism, *Medical Journal of Australia* 64: 643–56.

Holroyd, J. (1980) Hypnosis treatment for smoking: an evaluative review, *International Journal of Clinical and Experimental Hypnosis* 28: 341–57.

Hyman, G.J., Stanley, R.O., Burrows, G.D. and Horne, D.J. (1986) Treatment effectiveness of hypnosis and behaviour therapy in smoking cessation: a methodological refinement, *Addictive Behaviors* 11: 355–65.

Jacobson, D.D. and Silfverskiold, N.P. (1973) A controlled study of hypnotic method in the treatment of alcoholism, with the evaluation by objective criteria, *British Journal of Addiction* 68: 25–31.

Jeffrey, L.K. and Jeffrey, T.B. (1988) Exclusion therapy in smoking cessation: a brief communication, *International Journal of Clinical and Experimental Hypnosis* 36: 70–4.

Jeffrey, T.B., Jeffrey, L.K., Greuling, J.W. and Gentry, W.R. (1985) Evaluation of a brief group treatment package including hypnotic induction for maintenance of smoking cessation: a brief communication, *International Journal of Clinical and Experimental Hypnosis* 23: 95–8.

Kendell, R.E. (1979) Alcoholism: a medical or a political problem? *British Medical Journal* 1: 367–71.

Miller, M.M. (1976) Hypno-aversion treatment in alcoholism, nicotinism and weight control, *Journal of the National Medical Association* 68: 129–30.

Rabkin, S.W., Boyko, E., Shane, F. and Kaufret, J. (1984) A randomized trial comparing smoking cessation programs utilizing behavior modification, health education or hypnosis, *Addictive Behaviors* 9: 157–73.

Russell, M.A.H., Raw, M. and Jarvis, M.J. (1980) Clinical use of nicotine chewing gum, *British Medical Journal* 280: 1599–1602.

Schoen, M. (1985) A conceptual framework and treatment strategy for the alcoholic urge to drink utilizing hypnosis, *International Journal of the Addictions* 20: 403–15.

Sheehan, P.W. (1986) An individual difference account of hypnosis, in P.L.N. Naish (ed.) *What is Hypnosis? Current Theories and Research*, Milton Keynes: Open University Press.

Spiegel, H. (1970) A single treatment method to stop smoking using ancillary self-hypnosis, *International Journal of Clinical and Experimental Hypnosis* 18: 235–50.

Spiegel, H. and Spiegel, D. (1978) *Trance and Treatment. Clinical Uses of Hypnosis*, Washington, DC: American Psychiatric Press.

Spinhoven, P. (1987) Hypnosis and behavior therapy: a review, *International Journal of Clinical and Experimental Hypnosis* 35: 8–31.

Stanton, H.E. (1976) Fee-paying and weight loss: evidence for an interesting interaction, *American Journal of Clinical Hypnosis* 19: 47–9.

Wadden, T.A. and Anderton, C.H. (1982) The clinical use of hypnosis, *Psychological Bulletin* 91: 215–43.

Wadden, T.A. and Flaxman. J. (1981) Hypnosis and weight loss: a preliminary study, *International Journal of Clinical and Experimental Hypnosis* 24: 162–73.

Wadden, T.A. and Penrod, J.H. (1981) Hypnosis in the treatment of alcoholism: a review and appraisal, *American Journal of Clinical Hypnosis* 24: 41–7.

Williams, J.M. and Hall, D.W. (1988) Use of single session hypnosis for smoking cessation, *Addictive Behaviors* 13: 205–8.

6

Hypnosis and pain

BARRY B. HART

Introduction

Pain is a ubiquitous human experience, attracting an enormous amount of human resources, money and energy in an attempt to understand it and gain control over the suffering it produces. The disproportionate amount of time that physicians spend on the alleviation of pain would logically point to its being a focus of medical school training when, in fact, it is the diagnosis and treatment of organic pathology that is emphasized (Galvin and Thompson 1984). Thus, front-line medical practitioners often still labour under the outmoded and misleading specificity model which presents the experience of pain as being a simple linear function of the number of peripheral pain receptors stimulated. Without the appreciation of the central mediation and modulation of pain accounted for by Melzack and Wall's (1965) Gate Control Theory, the medical community often still continues to practise surgery and multiple-drug treatments for chronic pain conditions despite the lack of supporting evidence for this mode of therapy. Fortunately, social and psychological influences on pain perception have been recognized by more informed pain specialists who have come to acknowledge the need for 'multiple convergent therapy' (i.e. the convergence of different treatment approaches) in chronic pain (Melzack and Wall 1982). It was the lack of a clear relationship between painful stimuli and the subjective experience of pain (i.e. the 'puzzle of pain') that led Melzack and Wall to propose the revolutionary Gate Control Theory in 1965, giving credence to psychological interventions. Very briefly, this proposes that input from the pain receptors passes through a gating mechanism in the spinal cord. This gate may be open or closed depending on the distribution of activity in ascending and descending nerve fibres. Thus the gate may be influenced by both the peripheral response to a painful stimulus and higher brain activity such as cognition and emotion.

For our purposes, pain will be considered to be a multi-dimensional psychobiosocial experience including real sensory input, emotional factors (e.g. suffering, fear, expectation, mood, anxiety, tension, suggestion, memory and motivation), and social components (e.g. culture and environmental consequences). Hypnosis is defined here as an altered state of consciousness characterized by distortion in sensation, perception and memory involving behaviour experienced as non-volitional and allowing greater access to unconscious processes.

This chapter will review psychological treatment practices (hypnotic and non-hypnotic) for acute and chronic pain disorders. Although cognitive–behavioural methods will be presented, the emphasis will be on hypnotic approaches as practised in Britain. Reference will be made to American work, however, as it has been so influential on practices overseas. A 1989 survey of 350 members of the British Society of Experimental and Clinical Hypnosis has revealed that while a number of clinicians in this country are using hypnosis for pain control, few of them are carrying out systematic research into its effectiveness. Nevertheless, the studies that are reviewed below significantly add to our understanding of the application of hypnotic techniques to painful conditions. The chapter will conclude with a discussion of research and future developments.

Hypnoanaesthesia

Although Esdaile used mesmerism over 140 years ago as the sole anaesthetic agent in over 300 surgical operations, the development of inhalant anaesthetics spelled the death-knell for this form of 'painless surgery' in the 19th century as it was far less reliable and applicable than ether or chloroform. Nevertheless, hypnosis continued to be practised and over the last 25 years has enjoyed a new lease of life as a means of pain control now that psychological variables have been highlighted as crucial determinants of pain experiences.

The 1970s witnessed a mushrooming of interest in the application of hypnotherapy to both psychological and physical disorders. Although it became a legitimate therapeutic tool in the armamentarium against pain, the field continued to abound in anecdotal case studies appealing mainly to clinicians. Nevertheless, as has been pointed out (Hart 1984) hypnosis is still underused, even in pain clinics, probably owing to:

1 The belief that it is too time-consuming.
2 The disbelief in its effectiveness.
3 Misconceptions about the nature of hypnosis.
4 Early clinical failures.
5 Fear of ridicule.
6 The development of chemical anaesthetics.
7 Paucity of hypnotic training in medical and dental schools in spite of the BMA's approval of it in 1955.

The field of therapeutic hypnosis remains exciting and promising, however, as 'no other psychological technique is as efficacious in creating comfort out of discomfort, with none of the adverse side effects associated with medical treatment of comparable efficacy' (J. Barber 1986: 151).

Psychological approaches to acute and chronic pain

According to Pearce and Richardson (1987), until relatively recently psychological approaches to the treatment of pain were not used to treat disease with organic pathology. However, as modern theories of pain consider psychological factors to be important in pain perception, and with the realization that medical approaches often have little to offer chronic pain patients, clinicians have acknowledged the crucial role of psychology in the assessment and treatment of pain. While acute pain, defined as being predictable, of short duration and having signal value, usually responds well to traditional medical approaches, evidence is gathering that education and preparation of the patient and rehearsal of coping strategies, including hypnotic methods, can greatly enhance a patient's ability to cope effectively with acute noxious stimuli (Zeltzer and LeBaron 1986). Among acute pain suffering, the discomfort of surgery, childbirth, post-operative pain, dysmenorrhoea, headache and burns can be greatly relieved using hypnotic methods (Hilgard and Hilgard 1975, 1983).

Chronic pain, defined as being unpredictable, of at least six months' duration, unresponsive to traditional medical procedures and having no signal value, is far more complicated as it has an overall impact on the functioning of the individual. Nevertheless, as an adjunct within a rehabilitation programme including physiotherapy and cognitive–behaviour modification, hypnosis can greatly assist a clinician in the effective management of discomfort due, for example, to spinal injury, cancer, arthritis, rheumatism, the neuralgias and abdominal pain of unknown origin.

Baker (1987) claims that much of the growth of interest in hypnotherapy over recent years is due to the fact that careful experimental work has established hypnosis as a measurable phenomenon. In this respect, Hilgard and Hilgard (1975, 1983) have repeatedly shown a clear relationship between degree of hypnotizability and response to hypnotic suggestion for analgesia and anaesthesia. From 5 to 20 per cent of the population are considered hypnotizable enough to benefit from hypnotic treatment for pain. Much of the research, however, uses experimentally induced pain and thus appears far removed from the clinical setting, in which highly motivated patients are complaining of pain conditions that are compromising their day-to-day functioning.

A growing number of clinicians influenced by the late Milton H. Erickson claim that hypnotizability is clinically irrelevant to a person's ability to utilize hypnosis in the control of pain as long as indirect, permissive and naturalistic suggestions are used (J. Barber 1980). While Baker (1987) agrees that the current trend is away from regressive, uncovering and abreactive aspects of hypnosis towards a more permissive and humanistic approach in helping clients to use their own inner resources for problem solving, he also fears that the cultism associated with Erickson threatens to re-mystify hypnosis.

Orne (1983) suggests that hypnotizability is probably more relevant to pain relief when the alteration of physiological responses associated with acute pain in particular is the focus of treatment. For chronic pain, hypnotic susceptibility is probably not as important since changes in motivation, expectation, attitude and attribution are of more interest. Convincing evidence exists that hypno-anaesthetic effects are not simply due to relaxation or placebo (Hilgard 1980, Orne 1980). While cognitive approaches can be used within a hypnotic context, hypnosis is not cognitive therapy, but rather involves a dramatic shift in consciousness that produces perceptual and sensory alteration (J. Barber 1986). Orne (1983) claims that hypnosis is probably not useful in the treatment of functional pain but many clinicians now question the usefulness or indeed, veracity of the organic–psychogenic distinction in the aetiology of pain. That is, while clearly much acute pain is due to sensory input, its perception is also greatly affected by past experience with pain, and by fear, anxiety and expectation. Chronic pain is also very much determined by psychological factors such as the social consequences of expressing pain behaviours, mood and compensation and litigation issues. Thus, there are psychological aspects to all experiences involving pain.

Cognitive–behavioural methods

According to Wardle (1988), Melzack and Wall's (1965) cognitive evaluation of pain as a higher central process acting on the subjective experience parallels the cognitive conceptualization of pain from which cognitive-based treatment programmes are derived (Meichenbaum and Turk 1976). This model proposes that pain is accompanied by thoughts and images that are subject to both positive and negative distortions which can influence pain experience and pain behaviour. The various psychological treatment approaches can be subdivided around their points of intervention (Pearce 1984). Table 6.1 shows that foci for treatment have been sensory input (i.e. physiology), cognitions (i.e. subjective experiences) and consequence (i.e. behavioural), targeted respectively by relaxation training, biofeedback and hypnotherapy; cognitive–behaviour therapy and hypnotherapy; and contingency management. Although Pearce (1984) did not originally include hypnosis as a treatment for sensory input, abundant evidence exists to demonstrate the possibility of somatosensory change via hypnotic suggestion, especially with acute pain (Hilgard and Hilgard 1983).

The plausible relationship between tension and pain has not been convincingly demonstrated, but there are reports on the usefulness of relaxation and biofeed-

Table 6.1 Psychological approaches to pain management

Components of pain	Psychological treatment
Physiological (e.g. tissue damage; EMG/blood flow changes)	Relaxation training Biofeedback Hypnotherapy
Subjective experiences (e.g. sensations & feelings of distress & discomfort)	'Pain-directed' cognitive methods Hypnotherapy
Behavioural (e.g. wincing & taking pills)	Contingency management (operant conditioning)

(Pearce 1984)

back for pain reduction. While EMG biofeedback (feedback of changes in muscle activity) has not been found to be superior to relaxation training in headache reduction, Chesney and Shelton (1976) found both to be effective in decreasing headache frequency, severity and reliance on drugs. There is no doubt that general relaxation training is effective for tension headache and superior to medication alone (Blanchard *et al.* 1979).

Turk and Genest (1979) have summarized the cognitive strategies that have been used in experimental studies to alter the subjective aspects of pain. These are presented in Table 6.2.

Table 6.2 Cognitive strategies used in pain management

Strategy	Task	Example
Imaginative inattention	Imagine scenes incompatible with pain	Lying on a beach
Imaginative transformation	Relabel sensations as less distressing	Tingling, numbness, warmth, cold
Transformation of context	Imagine sensations occurring in different, more appropriate, context	Building a snowman, spy shot in the arm
Attention diversion		
(a) Internal	Attend to alternative thoughts	Mental arithmetic, recite poem
(b) External	Attend to alternative external event	Count ceiling tiles, focus on external object
Somatization	Focus on sensations in a detached way	Write a biology report about the sensations

(Turk and Genest 1979, as summarized by Pearce 1984)

Interestingly, it was the application of hypnosis in the 19th century that generated many of these cognitive strategies, as suggestions were administered for patients to ignore or transform the sensory input from the painful site. While hypnotized subjects were found to be better able to tolerate painful stimuli (T.X. Barber 1963), it was the similar finding with 'waking analgesia', where subjects were asked to respond as if hypnotized, that encouraged Scott and Barber (1977) to investigate the efficacy of cognitive strategies for pain reduction. They found that dissociation, coping imagery, distortion, and imaginative transformation all decreased pain responses. According to Pearce (1984), however, no conclusive findings have yet emerged with regard to which type of cognitive strategy is most effective. One reason for the variability in the results may be the lack of face validity in asking subjects to use strategies that make little sense (e.g. using imaginative inattention to deny the existence of pain). Chaves and Barber (1974) found that some subjects had developed more effective strategies for themselves than the ones under investigation. Control subjects might therefore be able to call upon more meaningful and useful strategies than experimental subjects.

While the unique contribution of cognitive strategies is still under investigation, in clinical settings they are normally used as part of a multi-modal package of treatment, often within the context of stress inoculation training (Meichenbaum and Turk 1976). This approach is based on the hypothesis that stress or anxiety may produce psychological changes that contribute to pain and therefore, teaching clients how to reduce stress will have a concomitant pain-reducing effect. Treatment starts with an educational phase in which models of pain (e.g. the Gate Control Theory) are introduced, inculcating the suggestion of pain's controllability by giving information on psychological factors. Next, a description of cognitive strategies is given, as in Table 6.1, followed by a training phase, in which the various cognitive approaches are taught and rehearsed. Clients are encouraged to reinforce themselves for applying the strategy or strategies which they find most effective. Finally, the new skills are applied in response to either imagined or induced pains.

The advantage of stress inoculation lies in the individuality of the strategies adopted by clients. While stress inoculation has yet to be adequately evaluated, there is evidence that it reduces pain from tension headache and migraine (Holroyd *et al.* 1977). The lack of studies applying cognitive stress management to other chronic pain conditions such as low back pain may be due to the lack of face validity for such patients, who believe their pain to be due to physical causes. On the other hand, it is generally accepted that headache is related to stress, and cognitive strategies may therefore have more face validity with this type of problem.

Behaviour modification

The behavioural aspects of chronic pain have been the focus of treatment by Fordyce (1976) who conceptualizes pain behaviours (e.g. grimacing, moaning, limping, seeking medication, and inactivity) as being maintained by their reinforcing consequences and thus modifiable by operant conditioning principles. Patients are brought into hospital for 2 to 8 weeks, during which time long-standing habitual pain behaviours are ignored by staff, while 'active' or 'well' behaviours (e.g. activity, smiling and exercise) are praised. Analgesic medication is gradually reduced via the 'pain cocktail', a strong-tasting but pleasant drink masking the flavour of the drug. It is administered on a time-contingent, as opposed to a pain-contingent, basis. The active ingredient is reduced over time with the patient unaware of exactly when this takes place. The aim of such a programme is not to reduce pain, but to increase the likelihood of patients' re-engaging in normal activities. Fordyce *et al.* (1973) offer supporting evidence for the effectiveness of their approach, but generally the research has lacked methodological rigour (e.g. absence of control groups and use of retrospective pain ratings). Also, Melzack and Wall (1982) complain that Fordyce's dismissal of the issue of felt pain as a philosophical problem is unacceptable.

Cairns and Pacino (1977) found that activity levels in chronic back pain patients returned to baseline levels on withdrawal of treatment in a study of the effect of contingent social reinforcement. This suggests that this method is unlikely to generalize beyond the treatment environment. Therefore, family members are included whenever possible in chronic pain clinics to teach them how to use the principles involved. Unfortunately, there have not been any controlled studies comparing contingency management with other methods. A number of multi-method outcome studies have incorporated operant conditioning along with a host of other treatment approaches (e.g. relaxation training, biofeedback and physiotherapy), thus preventing any reliable estimate of the efficacy of each ingredient. In view of the lack of sound research in this area, Melzack and Wall (1982) called for controlled studies demonstrating that:

1 The active procedure is more effective than placebo;
2 The therapeutic changes have clinical significance;
3 The effects are generalizable outside the clinic; and
4 Treatment has a long-lasting effect as shown by respectable follow-up studies.

Lastly, the immense cost of such in-patient programmes as advocated by Fordyce, and the lack of evidence of their effectiveness make their development in Britain unlikely, although Gwyther (1989) has described an in-patient Pain Management Unit at St. Thomas's Hospital, London.

Hypnotherapeutic approaches: general principles

Hypnosis can be a quick, effective and safe method to increase pain threshold and pain tolerance, especially in good hypnotic subjects, and when traditional methods have either failed or are contraindicated. It can also help avoid surgery and the reliance on and abuse of medication. Other factors in its favour are its relatively low cost and its ability to help increase a patient's sense of mastery, independence and self-control over discomfort. Hypnosis can also deal effectively with the emotional aspects of pain and can uncover the 'meaning' of chronic pain via hypnoanalytic methods.

Pain threshold is determined by physiological factors while pain tolerance is largely due to cultural and psychological variables. Hypnosis can increase pain threshold by way of a number of specific techniques including hypnoanaesthesia, hypnoanalgesia, hypnotic substitution, hypnotic displacement, dissociation, direct or indirect suggestion for abolition of pain, time distortion, reinterpretation of painful experience, suggested diminution of pain, distraction, paradoxical intervention, self-hypnosis and regression (Rossi 1980). Pain tolerance, on the other hand, can be increased hypnotically using fear and anxiety reduction suggestions, ego-strengthening, decreasing the anticipation of pain, and amnesia for painful memories. This has implications for intervening in the pain–tension–pain cycle.

The application of hypnotic methods to acute, as opposed to chronic pain appears to have changed over time. That is, while Esdaile used hypnosis in the mid 19th century during surgical procedures, Freud's influence in the early 20th century suggested that hypnoanalytic methods could be useful in uncovering the psychodynamics involved in both psychological disturbance and chronic pain disorders. The Gate Control Theory heightened awareness of the contribution of psychological factors to all pain, however, and from the 1970s, hypnosis has been used increasingly for the alleviation of acute pain of known physical origin. The basic strategy for acute pain is to decrease accompanying fear and utilize specific hypnotic techniques (see below) to increase the pain threshold. In addition, self-hypnosis is taught as a means of coping with pain in the future. Chronic pain is far more complicated than acute pain. Nevertheless, hypnosis can assist the clinician in the effective management of chronic discomfort by:

1 Discovering the 'meaning' of pain for the patient;
2 Offering the experience of hypnoanalgesia to show that this is possible;
3 Teaching self-hypnosis with safeguards; and
4 Remobilizing the patient using a cognitive–behavioural programme.

This final point refers to the concept of multiple convergent therapy (Melzack and Wall 1982) whereby treatments for chronic pain have been found to be more effective if used in combination with other therapies. As hypnotic techniques focus on the alleviation of pain, as opposed to remobilizing the client, their addition to contingency management programmes could be very useful in view of Melzack and Wall's (1982) objection that behaviour modification packages marginalize suffering. As there is nowadays a greater emphasis on self-determination in psychotherapy, the inclusion of self-hypnosis instructions to empower clients with a sense of independence and control is now commonplace for both acute and chronic pain. The one exception to this ethos of permissiveness is when hypnosis is used in an emergency situation, when an authoritarian approach is more likely to facilitate acceptance of suggestion.

Wallace (1987) claims that the following information is needed to establish a collaborative relationship with adults prior to teaching self-hypnosis at the Birmingham Accident Hospital Burns Unit:

1 The coping strategies that have already been found useful by the patient and the patient's faith in the possible effectiveness of psychological methods.
2 The patient's description of the intensity, duration and frequency of the pain; this enables his or her own language and metaphors to be used by the therapist in treatment.
3 The patient's perception of time and its relation to the experience of pain, in order to capitalize on the phenomenon of time distortion.
4 The patient's capacity for creative imagination and for suspending disbelief, as these are highly related to hypnotizability.
5 That the patient has a realistic understanding of hypnosis and any misconceptions have been corrected.

Wallace's fourth point (above) is very topical as clinicians such as J. Barber (see Barber 1977, 1980) have challenged the established research findings of Hilgard and Hilgard (1975) that pain relief via hypnosis is highly related to an individual's hypnotizability. While Barber (1977) originally argued that hypnotizability was irrelevant to clinical outcome for pain if naturalistic and indirect suggestion were used, his latest research (Price and Barber 1987) suggests that highly hypnotizable subjects can more easily alter the sensory aspects of pain, while the affective and motivational aspects of pain are unrelated to hypnotic capacity. This is a useful distinction in pain perception and may explain Barber's (1977) unreplicated finding that 99 out of 100 patients in a dental setting successfully used hypnosis as their sole anaesthetic agent during a variety of dental procedures. Although he did not measure hypnotizability, one can hypothesize that subjects with low hypnotizability responded to the relaxation and distraction components of the hypnotic procedure, thereby reducing fear and anxiety. Evidently, however, they often requested that the dental procedure be stopped while Barber reinforced the therapeutic suggestions. Presumably, more highly hypnotizable subjects responded with sensory alteration, producing a more complete analgesia. Barber's (1986) criteria for using hypnosis in pain reduction are:

1 That the patient will not abuse hypnosis in a way which causes harm to himself or herself, such as by masking new pain of signal value;
2 That pain reduction will not disrupt the patient's life by compromising the family system, self-esteem or secondary gains; and
3 That the patient is willing to take the initiative in his or her own treatment, as much effort is required.

Hypnotic techniques for pain control

Hypnosis should only be used for pain reduction after a medical screening has determined that there is no physical disorder being masked (Gibson 1989). With acute pain, the reason for the discomfort is often obvious, such as a painful medical procedure, but chronic pain should always be initially investigated by a physician. If a patient needs to be alert during a medical procedure, or if chemical anaesthetics are contraindicated, or if traditional medical treatments have failed, hypnosis is positively indicated, especially for patients who are highly hypnotizable.

Patients with low hypnotizability may also gain significant benefit from pain-reducing hypnotic suggestions for reasons mentioned above. Hypnosis is not a panacea, however, and realistic expectations in both therapist and patient are of utmost importance. Hypnosis provides a context within which the practitioner applies his or her therapeutic approaches. Thus, clinicians should not use hypnosis for conditions outside their area of expertise.

The following is a list of the more commonly used hypnotic techniques, from Hilgard (1980) and J. Barber (1986):

Direct diminution
The suggestion is made that the pain will lessen and gradually go away, although probably not completely. Metaphors can be used that utilize the patient's conceptualization of pain intensity or quality by suggesting the 'volume' be turned down, heat cooled, and so on.

Anaesthesia
Suggestions are given to render part of the body insensitive to pain and to transfer this anaesthesia to the painful area. Glove anaesthesia is often used in this

respect, whereby a hand is made numb via suggestion of coolness and memory of anaesthesia, followed by the patient's being asked to place this anaesthetized hand over the painful area and to allow the anaesthesia to transfer. It is easier to produce numbness in an unaffected part of the body first, rather than in the painful area. While there is no physiological reason to account for the successful transfer of anaesthesia in this manner, in the author's experience patients do not question this; rather, they are only too pleased with the usually successful result. This can be accomplished by using either direct suggestion (e.g. 'as I stroke your right hand, it is becoming numb, with no sensation at all') or indirect suggestion (e.g. 'I wonder if you can remember the sensation of having a hand in snow? It will be interesting to see if it will be your right or left hand that becomes numb first, or second').

Displacement

In suggesting that pain can move from one part of the body to another, the goal is to make the unpleasant sensation more tolerable and to imply that alteration in other dimensions (e.g. intensity) is possible. It is well known, for example, that pain in the extremities is less frightening than pain in the abdomen (Karle and Boys 1987). Humour can also be introduced by displacing pain into a finger or ear lobe. A permissive suggestion for displacement is:

> You may have already noticed that the pain moves, ever so slightly, and you can begin to notice that the movement seems to be in an outwardly spiralling circular direction. As you continue to attend to that movement, you may not notice until later that the pain has somehow moved out of your abdomen and seems to be staying in your left hand.
>
> (Barber 1986: 157)

Dissociation

Suggestions are given for a complete separation from pain, which is especially useful if the patient is immobilized or suffering from multiple painful sites. The patient imagines going somewhere else, leaving his or her body and the suffering behind while engaging in something interesting or enjoyable. A suggestion for dissociation might be as follows:

> While part of you is sitting in that chair, the rest of you can step out of your body, walk over to the window and describe for me what you see outside . . . Later on today, when you want to feel more comfortable, you can simply close your eyes and take yourself off in your mind's eye to somewhere you would rather be, such as your favourite museum you told me about.

Substitution

Substituting another sensation (e.g. itching, pressure, or warmth) for pain can assist in a reinterpretation of unpleasant sensation. Success is more likely if the substituted sensation is not totally pleasant as this would be somewhat implausible to the patient. Like displacement, once a successful substitution is achieved, this demonstrates that change is possible in other aspects of the pain as well.

Barber (1986) points out that cancer patients in particular may need some sensation for reassurance that they and the medical team will be aware of any change in their physical condition in order to treat it appropriately. Sensory substitution was achieved unwittingly by the present author from a finger anaesthetic suggestion in a 36-year-old woman suffering from severe organic pain in her neck and shoulder, with the following suggestion:

> As you place the two anaesthetized fingers onto the back of your neck, notice how the feeling of numbness replaces the discomfort that was there. When the numbness from your fingers has gone into your neck and replaced the pain, you will notice your fingers returning to normal but leaving your neck feeling comfortable and insensitive.

In the following session, the patient reported an odd sensation of feeling both fingers on the back of her neck, but was pleased to report a lack of pain. It was explained that her unconscious mind had obviously used the suggestions in a beneficial manner, even though no suggestion had been made for the sensation of finger pressure to replace the pain.

Neurophysiological metaphor

By having something specific to do along with a simple rationale for its effectiveness, patients can gain pain relief using physiological metaphors. In the 'wires and switches' technique, the suggestion is made for the patient to imagine a control centre in the brain or in the painful area, with switches controlling the nerves sending messages about the pain. By imagining turning off the switches, the suggestion is that pain relief will take place as no sensory messages will be sent. Hilgard (1980) claims this technique is successful with both adults and children.

Time distortion

Suggestions for time distortion capitalize on naturally occurring experiences of time passing quickly (e.g. when bumping into an old friend, or being engrossed in a good book or film) or slowly (e.g. waiting for a taxi in the rain). Once the patient is hypnotized, the suggestion is that when pain occurs, time will pass quickly; during pain-free intervals, however, time will go very slowly, in order to produce a subjective sense of being comfortable for longer periods.

Self-hypnosis

It is far easier to teach people how to hypnotize themselves if it is first suggested within a hetero-hypnotic context that this is possible. Soskis (1986) offers a protocol for teaching self-hypnosis which can easily be applied to pain control. Eye closure is followed by hand-levitation suggestions, followed by the suggestion that the lightness in the hand is spreading to the rest of the body as the hand returns to its normal feelings and position, with three deep breaths. A count from 1 to 10 is then accompanied by suggestions for muscular relaxation and imaginative transformation of going somewhere pleasant. Suggestions are then administered that the patients can repeat this procedure to achieve a hypnotic state of relaxation on their own and to enable them to achieve their own goals; they are to end the session by a count from 5 to 1.

As self-hypnosis is an integral part of most hypnotic pain control, it behoves the clinical practitioner to become familiar with such procedures. The author finds it useful to have patients practise self-hypnosis before leaving the clinic and to put on audiotape the suggestions for home use.

Specific applications

Cancer

Hypnosis has been used to combat both the disease process and the side-effects of chemotherapy associated with cancer (Gravitz 1982, Walker *et al.* 1988). Simonton *et al.* (1986) describe techniques for learning positive attitudes, relaxation, visualization, goal-setting, managing pain, exercise, and building an emotional support system for cancer patients. These approaches, including hypnosis, are based on the finding that emotional responses to stress can play a role in compromising the immune system, thus contributing to some cancers. As these physiological processes can be altered with visualization techniques used in a hypnotic context, psychological and physical well-being can thus be enhanced by patient participation and treatment.

In this way, Newton (1982) has found that some patients can significantly alter the course of their disease. Kraft (1990, in preparation) describes how hypnosis can be very helpful in alleviating both physical and emotional suffering in terminally ill patients suffering from cancer. Self-hypnosis is advocated as a method to give back control to these patients, who usually feel helpless. Kraft finds dissociation to be an effective anaesthetic but emphasizes the need for a general psychotherapeutic approach to deal with the strong feelings that dying patients need to express, quite often concerned with unfinished business associated with both their childhood and their parents. These studies and this general application of hypnosis are discussed further in the chapter on medical applications (Chapter 8).

Headache

Hypnotic suggestion for relaxation and somatosensory change has been used to treat tension headache and migraine, respectively. For example, Alladin (1988) found that hand-warmth suggestions were an effective treatment for chronic migraine headaches, but not significantly better than relaxation training. These methods are discussed by Gibson and Heap (1990) in their chapter on applications of hypnosis to psychosomatic medicine, and in Chapter 8 of this book.

In her hypnotic treatment of 'difficult' tension headache and migraine patients at Salford Royal Infirmary, Parker (personal communication) describes eight steps in treatment. Pain ratings are made by the patient on both a 0 to 10 scale and a visual analogue scale before and after treatment. The protocol is as follows:

Session 1
Discussion with patient about hypnosis, myths surrounding its use and why and how hypnosis will be used. The reasons for using a hypnotizability scale are reviewed.

Session 2
Clear up any points and worries raised in session 1. Administer Stanford Hypnotic Clinical Scale: Adult, in order to assess hypnotizability.

Session 3–6 (or longer if needed)
Hypnosis for pain control commences; self-hypnosis starts in session 4. The basic format is:

  (i) Induction – via counting 1 to 10.
 (ii) Relaxation – suggestions for both physical and mental comfort.
(iii) Deepening – various techniques (e.g. counting and breathing; descending stairs or lift).
(iv) Pain control techniques – various methods including dissociation, sensory reduction and analgesia.
 (v) Ego-strengthening – as in Hartland (1971).
(vi) Self-hypnosis instructions.
(vii) Post-hypnotic suggestions.
(viii) Dehypnotizing.

Lastly, Rooney (1988) describes a hypnotic method for alleviating headaches in prisoners who react violently to the stress of being in prison. Following the induction and deepening procedure, he suggests that the sensation of pain transfer into the patient's hand as it rests on his head. The individual is then told to tense the muscles of the hand by forming a fist, and this is followed by the suggestion that when the fist is relaxed the pain will disappear.

Burns

In her review of 16 American burns units, Wallace (1982) was surprised to find diverse practices adhered to dogmatically and the virtual absence of non-pharmacological methods of pain relief such as hypnosis. In her application of hypnosis in selected cases at the Birmingham Accident Hospital Burns Unit, she claims that 'pain control, or the lack of it, is the most overwhelming and overriding concern to burns patients once the initial shock of the accident and admission to a Burns Unit are surmounted' (p. 50). Discomfort comes from both damage to skin and nerve endings, and from painful nursing and medical procedures. Wallace ascertains information on the patient's coping strategies, description of pain, perception of time, creative imagination, and understanding of hypnosis prior to administering hypnotic suggestion. The induction serves to focus attention away from the pain, and the hypnotherapeutic task is seen as building on existing strategies and experiences in order to facilitate reduction in unpleasant sensation. Self-hypnotic techniques are an integral part of the programme and these must adjust for various interruptions on the

Unit, including noise from machinery, changes in temperature, and medical procedures.

Wallace (1982) describes the treatment of a woman hospitalized after a chip-pan fire produced burns to forty per cent of her body. The focus of hypnotic treatment was the constant pain in one hand, due to a deep full-thickness burn. Preliminary questioning gave the therapist insight into the hypnotic techniques that would probably be most effective. Induction was by eye fixation and a count from 1 to 5 with deep breaths to facilitate eye closure. Imagery of descending 13 steps at home was used to deepen the hypnosis, followed by arm levitation and then arm lowering into an imaginary bucket of ice-water to produce glove anaesthesia. A combination of direct suggestion for anaesthesia and its transfer, dissociation, self-hypnosis, and post-hypnotic suggestion for anaesthesia were successfully used to control pain levels. The unpredictability of pain during dressing changes was a major problem with this patient, however. That is, whether medical staff were available or not determined when the dressings were changed and under what conditions (e.g. with or without a chemical anaesthetic). Wallace felt that this undermined her patient's ability to prepare herself by using the most appropriate hypnotic technique. She concludes that hypnosis can provide pain relief at least as great as and without the side-effects of pharmacological methods in a willing and enthusiastic hypnotizable patient in a conducive environment.

Spinal injury

Alden (in preparation) uses hypnosis for both acute and chronic pain control in her work as a clinical psychologist at the Royal National Orthopaedic Hospital, Middlesex. She describes her approach as 'client-centred' with an emphasis on the utilization of the patient's description of their problem and their personality, beliefs and behaviour to facilitate therapy. Both direct and indirect techniques are used. Hypnosis is used in the management of acute pain due to certain medical procedures and for post-operative or trauma pain. An example of Alden's approach for acute pain is as follows.

A 50-year-old man with C6/7 spinal cord injury was having difficulty in physiotherapy. As a result of his injury, his biceps muscles functioned well but he had little triceps function. This resulted in his arms remaining in a permanently flexed position. Despite all efforts on the physiotherapist's part he had developed contractures of the elbows and found attempts to straighten out his arms too painful to tolerate. He also refused to tolerate the wearing of splints at night to help straighten his arms. Psychological assessment indicated that he was well motivated to resolve the problem and had a strong belief in the effectiveness of hypnosis. He had been hypnotized at a stage show and told the therapist that he had enjoyed the experience for which he had some amnesia. The therapist suggested that the patient could enter trance by bringing to mind this previous experience. As he was interested in electronics, a simple explanation of the Gate Control Theory was given using the analogy of wiring. He was able to enter a deep trance and imagined pain in terms of circuits and electric currents. He felt it would be appropriate to switch the current off and did so by imagining some switches on his chest and switching them off. As a result he was able to cope with his physiotherapy in comfort. He also practised self-hypnosis to help him tolerate the splints and to feel more relaxed generally. The result was straighter arms.

Alden claims that fear, anxiety, or other psychological factors will often influence the experience of post-operative or trauma pain. Direct inductions are often found to be effective because of the high level of motivation and willingness to accept hypnosis. An explanation of the Gate Control Theory is normally offered, which Alden finds facilitates the application of suggestion for anaesthesia, distraction, dissociation, and the 'switch box' technique.

Alden feels that for chronic pain, hypnosis is at its most effective when incorporated and integrated into a total pain management programme. The psychologist is a member of the rehabilitation unit, consisting of medical, physiotherapy, occupational therapy, nursing and social work staff. Alden assesses core beliefs as well as anxiety, depression, and the patient's learning history as it is relevant to pain. The McGill Pain Questionnaire (Melzack 1975) is used to shed light on the patients' descriptive language and affective components of their discomfort. Because most chronic pain patients have a strong belief in their inability to deal with pain, Alden believes that indirect approaches are often necessary for successful hypnotic inductions. The discovery by patients of their ability to decrease pain in trance, and especially learning that they can continue to do so afterwards often breaks through the core belief of a lack of control. Even when analgesic suggestions are unsuccessful, decreasing anxiety levels often produce a decrease in pain.

Painful medical procedures and surgery

Hypnosis may be used to alleviate the pain of certain medical and surgical procedures. In Britain there has been particular interest by some psychologists in researching into the use of hypnosis with children undergoing difficult medical interventions and this work is reported later.

At the beginning of this chapter mention was made of the surgical operations of the Scottish surgeon and mesmerist James Esdaile who practised in India in the 1840s. Another British advocate of the use of mesmerism in surgery during that period was Dr John Elliotson who practised at University College London. Although the accounts of this form of 'painless surgery' are impressive and convincing, they have been called into question by a number of modern writers such as Gauld (1988) and Gibson (1988).

Waxman (1989) lists both advantages and disadvantages of the use of hypnosis in the surgical setting. On the positive side, he claims that hypnosis can decrease pre-operative fear and anxiety, has no toxic effects, eliminates danger from inhaled anaesthetics, diminishes shock, does not interfere with the cough reflex, and controls post-operative pain, discomfort and nausea. However, the disadvantages are that hypnosis is a time-consuming and often difficult method of inducing anaesthesia; it is uncommon to achieve the deepest level of hypnosis essential for major surgery; and extra training is required to learn the approach. Nevertheless, Waxman advocates the use of hypnosis in helping to overcome fear and anxiety associated with surgery, capitalizing on its relaxing effects. Examples include minor surgical procedures, such as incisions, suturing, burn dressings, lumbar and abdominal punctures, cystoscopy, and dental extractions.

Scott (1976) advocates the use of hypnosis as an analgesic in reconstructive surgery and pedicle grafting, allowing patients to maintain unusual postures for long periods of time. He found that training patients in self-hypnosis often obviated the need for analgesic medication. Glove anaesthetic suggestions are given, using the imagery within hypnosis of the patient dipping his or her hand into a bucket of ice and transferring the numbness to the area to be operated on. Direct suggestions are given to facilitate the adoption of unusual postures while grafting takes place.

Obstetrics

All non-pharmacological methods assisting in pregnancy and childbirth aim to decrease fear, pain and discomfort. Recent accounts by British authors of this application of hypnosis include Waxman (1989) and Gibson and Heap (1990). Waxman (1989) devotes 27 pages to the use of hypnosis in obstetrics, listing the advantages as:

1 Increasing mental and physical relaxation.
2 Producing no depression of respiration or circulation in the mother or child.
3 Shortening the first stage of labour.
4 Increasing resistance to obstetric shock.
5 Not interfering with the normal mechanics of labour.
6 In light and medium stages, decreasing pain by relieving fear and tension.
7 In deep stages, producing partial or complete analgesia and anaesthesia by direct suggestion.
8 Increasing control over the rate of expulsion of the baby's head and shoulders.
9 The possibility of a painless episiotomy.
10 Promoting a usually smooth and uneventful post-operative recovery.
11 Stimulation of lactation and facilitation of breast feeding by direct suggestion.

Research developments

While much of the research into the relevance of hypnotizability and the difference between direct and indirect suggestion for pain control is American (see above), this section will briefly review two British studies teasing apart the effectiveness of various hypnotic procedures for managing acute and chronic pain in children. Clinicians in this country have also used hypnosis in the alleviation of pain associated with such disorders as irritable bowel syndrome and migraine, and these are covered by Wilkinson in Chapter 8.

Painful medical procedures

Ioannou (in preparation) has studied the psychological assessment and treatment of acute pain in chronically ill children. A pilot study was carried out at Guy's

Hospital on the discomfort and anxiety associated with blood tests for six kidney transplant children aged 6–16 years. A hypnotic procedure using the pain switch-box method (Hilgard and LeBaron 1984), favourite activity imagery, rehearsal of blood test and post-hypnotic suggestion was compared with a cognitive-behavioural package consisting of reinforcement, relaxation and breathing exercises, distraction, education, rehearsal of cognitive coping statements, and behavioural rehearsal with dolls. Results indicated a trend for global ratings of pain and anxiety to decrease in both groups, with the cognitive–behavioural subjects being slightly more successful.

The main study, at Addenbrooke's Hospital, Cambridge, extended the pilot research to 50 diabetic children aged 6–16 years. Every three to six months, these children received blood tests, during which they typically felt little control over the procedure as compared to finger pricks and insulin injections. Following assessment, experimental subjects received either a hypnotic procedure or a cognitive–behavioural intervention immediately prior to the next blood test. The cognitive–behavioural procedure is as described above for pilot subjects. Control subjects had one additional baseline assessment prior to either hypnosis or cognitive–behavioural intervention. Assessment of pain and anxiety via global ratings was made after each blood test by trained observers, parents and the child. In addition, a behaviour check-list was completed by a trained observer, and heart-rate measurements were taken by the researcher. Preliminary results suggest that while global ratings for control subjects do not change over time, half of the subjects in both the hypnosis and cognitive–behavioural groups increased their ability to control the pain and anxiety associated with venepunctures.

Sokel *et al.* (1990) also describe the use of hypnosis in a 6-year-old boy with multiple medical problems who had become phobic of venepunctures. This child was one of 50 children who had been referred to the Pain and Symptom Management Team, formed in September 1988 at the Hospital for Sick Children, Great Ormond Street, London (see Chapter 10 on applications to children). The authors state that pain in children has been a relatively neglected area but in the last two years clinical and research interest has mushroomed. Hypnotherapy has been used as an adjunctive treatment for children suffering from asthma, eczema, migraine, pain of both known and unknown origin, nausea associated with painful medical procedures, and anxiety. The key to successful hypnotic treatment is felt by the team to be the engagement of the child in developmentally appropriate imagery. Following medical evaluation, a psychological assessment is carried out on each child, which may indicate that alternative methods, such as family therapy, marital therapy, or individual therapy, should be carried out to resolve underlying conflicts, excessive dependencies, or manipulations.

The hypnotic approach incorporates progressive relaxation with selective focusing of attention on guided images. Suggestions are also given of pain or symptom relief and feelings of well-being and control. Between September 1988 and March 1989, 14 (39%) of the 36 children treated with hypnosis were considered 'much improved' and 15 (41%) were rated as 'improved'. In 7 (20%) no appreciable change had occurred; but no child was considered to be worse following hypnotherapy.

This same hospital team (Sokel 1989) described a case series of six children aged between 7 and 14 years with severe recalcitrant handicapping abdominal pain. Following psychological and medical interviews, the children were taught self-hypnosis along the same lines as described above. Within a mean period of 18 days, all children were able to use the self-hypnotic techniques to decrease or remove the pain in order to enable a resumption of normal activities. Individual and family therapy was then offered to work on underlying causes.

Future directions

While Melzack and Wall (1982) concluded that 'the evidence . . . shows convincingly that psychological approaches can have powerful effects on pain' (p. 355), they felt that using two or more techniques (including medication) tends to have a cumulative effect. Thus, they claimed that 'multiple convergent therapy' was increasingly becoming the standard psychological approach to pain management. The British research reviewed in this book clearly demonstrates the effectiveness of various psychological therapies for painful conditions, and hypnotic methods in particular. Future research will very likely extend the use of hypnosis to physical illness and medical procedures that have not heretofore been treated in this way (e.g. burns, immunologic disorders and chronic illness). However, while there probably remains little doubt amongst psychologists and psychiatrists that hypnosis can have a therapeutic effect on emotional problems, the medical profession has been more resistant to challenges to the dualistic mind–body ethos. Nevertheless, since the 1970s hypnosis has increasingly been used either solely or as an adjunctive treatment to decrease anxiety and pain during medical investigations and to combat disease processes. While research developments using sound methodology will no doubt extend the application of hypnosis to various medical disorders, perhaps even more important is that physicians make use of existing research findings in their clinics. For example, it was commented earlier that although hypnosis has been shown to be useful in the alleviation of pain due to burns, Wallace (1987) found very few American burns units incorporating any psychological methods in treatment regimens.

Developments over the last 10 years also suggest that hypnosis will be used increasingly with both children and the geriatric population, and in group and family therapy settings (Baker 1987). The trend towards a more humanistic and permissive approach in hypnosis has been demonstrated by an increased emphasis on self-hypnosis. This enhances the patient's sense of mastery and aids generalization and maintenance of therapeutic gains, thus satisfying the current demand for greater effectiveness of psychotherapeutic intervention in general.

Research still needs to demonstrate the unique contribution of hypnosis, however, and to elucidate which types of suggestion (e.g. direct versus indirect) are most effective for various conditions. The selective application of hypnosis is more likely to be guided in the future by the literature on the predictive value of hypnotizability for disorders such as acute pain, warts, and asthma (Wadden and Anderton 1982). A rational approach to applying hypnosis will increase the likelihood of successful outcome and prevent history repeating itself whereby hypnosis could be dismissed owing to its being oversold as a remedy for all ills.

References

Alden, P. (in preparation). The use of hypnosis in the management of pain on a Spinal Injuries Unit, *Proceedings of the Seventh Annual Conference of the British Society of Experimental and Clinical Hypnosis.*

Alladin, A. (1988) Hypnosis in the treatment of severe chronic migraine, in M. Heap (ed.) *Hypnosis: Current Clinical, Experimental and Forensic Practices*, London: Croom Helm.

Baker, E.L. (1987) The state of the art of clinical hypnosis, *International Journal of Clinical and Experimental Hypnosis* 35: 203–14.

Barber, J. (1977) Rapid induction analgesia: a clinical report, *American Journal of Clinical Hypnosis* 19: 138–47.

—— (1980) Hypnosis and the unhypnotizable, *American Journal of Clinical Hypnosis* 23: 4–9.

—— (1986) Hypnotic analgesia, in A. Holzman and D.C. Turk (eds) *A Handbook of Psychological Treatment Approaches*, New York: Academic Press.

Barber, T.X. (1963) The effects of hypnosis on pain. A critical review of experimental and clinical findings *Psychosomatic Medicine* 25: 303–33.

Blanchard, E., Theobald, D., Williamson, D., Silver, B. and Brown, D. (1979) Temperature biofeedback in the treatment of migraine headaches, *Archives of General Psychiatry* 35: 581–8.

Cairns, D. and Pacino, J.A. (1977) Comparison of verbal reinforcement and feedback in the operant treatment of disability due to chronic low back pain, *Behavior Therapy* 8: 621–30.

Chaves, J.F. and Barber, T.X. (1974) Cognitive strategies, experimenter modeling and expectation in the attenuation of pain, *Journal of Abnormal Psychology* 83: 356–63.

Chesney, M.A. and Shelton, J.L. (1976) A comparison of muscle relaxation and electromyogram biofeedback treatment for muscle contraction headache, *Journal of Behavioural and Experimental Psychiatry* 7: 221–5.

Fordyce, W.E. (1976) *Behavioral Methods for Chronic Pain and Illness*, St. Louis: C.V. Mosby.

Fordyce, W.E., Fowler, R.S., Lehmann, J.F., Delateur, B.J., Sand, P.L. and Treischmann, R.B. (1973) Operant conditioning in the treatment of chronic pain, *Archives of Physical Medicine and Rehabilitation* 54: 399–408

Galvin, R.M. and Thompson, D. (1984) Unlocking pain's secrets, *Time Magazine*, 11 June.

Gauld, A. (1988) Reflections on mesmeric analgesia, *British Journal of Experimental and Clinical Hypnosis* 5: 17–24.

Gibson, H.B. (1988) Gauld's (1988) reflections on mesmeric analgesia, *British Journal of Experimental and Clinical Hypnosis* 5: 25–7.

—— (1989) Hypnosis in musculoskeletal medicine, Paper presented to *The Ninth International Congress of Federation Internationale and the British Association of Manipulative Medicine*, September, London.

Gibson, H.B. and Heap, M. (1990) *Hypnosis in Therapy*, London: Lawrence Erlbaum.

Gravitz, M.A. (1982) Hypnosis and cancer (special issue), *American Journal of Clinical Hypnosis* 25: 87–187.

Gwyther, M. (1989) *The Place Where It Hurts*, Observer Magazine, October. London: Chelsea Bridge House.

Hart, B. (1984) Hypnosis for Pain Control, in A. Broome (ed.) *Proceedings of the First International Conference of the Pain Interest Group*, Liverpool.

Hartland, J. (1971) *Medical and Dental Hypnosis*, 2nd edn, London: Baillière Tindall.

Hilgard, E.R. (1980) Hypnosis in the treatment of pain, in G. Burrows and R. Denner-
    stein (eds) *Handbook of Hypnosis and Psychosomatic Medicine*, Amsterdam: North-Holland
    Biomedical Press.
Hilgard, E.R. and Hilgard, J.R. (1975) *Hypnosis in the Relief of Pain*, Los Altos, Calif.:
    William Kaufmann.
—— (1983) *Hypnosis in the Relief of Pain*, 2nd edn, Los Altos, Calif.: William Kaufmann.
Hilgard, J.R. and LeBaron, S. (1984) *Hypnotherapy of Pain in Children with Cancer*, Los Altos,
    Calif.: William Kaufmann.
Holroyd, K.A., Andrasik, F. and Westbrook, T. (1977) Cognitive control of tension
    headache, *Cognitive Therapy in Research* 1: 121–33.
Ioannou, C. (in preparation) *Psychological assessment and intervention of acute pain in chronically
    ill children*, Ph.D. thesis, University of Leicester.
Karle, H.W.A. and Boys, J.H. (1987) *Hypnotherapy: A Practical Handbook*, London: Free
    Association Books.
Kraft, T. (1990) Use of hypnotherapy in anxiety management in the terminally ill: a
    preliminary study, *British Journal of Experimental and Clinical Hypnosis* 7: 27–33.
—— (in preparation) Hypnotherapy for the terminally ill: review of the first thirty cases,
    *Proceedings of the Seventh Annual Conference of the British Society of Experimental and Clinical
    Hypnosis*.
Meichenbaum, D. and Turk, D. (1976) The cognitive–behavioral management of anxiety,
    anger and pain, in P.O. Davidson (ed.) *Behavioral Management of Anxiety, Depression and
    Pain*, New York: Brunner/Mazel.
Melzack, R. (1975) The McGill Pain Questionnaire: major properties and scoring
    methods, *Pain* 1: 275–9.
Melzack, R. and Wall, P.D. (1965) Pain mechanisms: a new theory, *Science* 150: 971–9.
—— (1982) *The Challenge of Pain*, London: Penguin.
Newton, B.W. (1982) The use of hypnosis in the treatment of cancer patients, *American
    Journal of Clinical Hypnosis* 25: 104–13.
Orne, M.T. (1980) Hypnotic control of pain: toward a clarification of the different
    psychological processes involved, in J.J. Bonica (ed.) *Pain*, New York: Raven Press.
—— (1983) Hypnotic methods for managing pain, in J.J. Bonica, U. Lindbloom and
    A. Iggo (eds) *Advances in Pain Research and Therapy*, New York: Raven Press.
Pearce, S. (1984) A review of cognitive behavioural methods for the treatment of chronic
    pain, in A.K. Broome (ed.) *Proceedings of the First International Conference of the Pain Interest
    Group*, Liverpool.
Pearce, S. and Richardson, P.H. (1987) Chronic pain: treatment, in S.J.E. Lindsay
    and G.E. Powell (eds) *Handbook of Clinical Adult Psychology*, Aldershot: Gower Press.
Price, D.D. and Barber, J. (1987) An analysis of factors that contribute to the efficacy
    of hypnotic analgesia, *Journal of Abnormal Psychology* 96: 1–6.
Rooney, G. (1988) The use of hypnosis with violent prisoners, in M. Heap (ed.) *Hypnosis:
    Current Clinical Experimental and Forensic Practices*, London: Croom Helm.
Rossi, E.L. (1980) *The Collective Papers of Milton H. Erickson on Hypnosis*, Vol. 4, New York:
    Irvington.
Scott, D.L. (1976) Hypnosis in pedicle graft surgery, *British Journal of Plastic Surgery*
    29: 8–13.
Scott, D.S. and Barber, T.X. (1977) Cognitive control of pain: effects of multiple cognitive
    strategies, *Psychological Record* 27: 373–83.
Simonton, O.C., Simonton, S.M. and Creighton, J.L. (1986) *Getting Well Again*, London:
    Bantam Books.
Sokel, B. (1989) Self-hypnosis in the treatment of severe abdominal pain of no discernible
    medical cause, Paper presented at *The First European Conference on Pain in Children*,
    Maastricht.

Sokel, B., Lansdown, R. and Kent, A. (1990) The development of a hypnotherapy service for children, *Child Care, Health and Development* 16: 227–33.

Soskis, D.A. (1986) *Teaching Self-hypnosis: An Introductory Guide for Clinicians*, London: W.W. Norton.

Turk, D.C. and Genest, M. (1979) Regulation of pain: the application of cognitive and behavioral techniques for prevention and remediation, in P.C. Kendall and S.D. Hollon (eds) *Cognitive–behavioral Interventions: Theory, Research and Procedures*, New York: Academic Press.

Wadden, T.A. and Anderton, C.H. (1982) The clinical use of hypnosis, *Psychological Bulletin* 91: 215–43.

Walker, L.G., Dawson, A.A., Pollet, S.M., Ratcliffe, M.A. and Hamilton, L. (1988) Hypnotherapy for chemotherapy side effects, *British Journal of Experimental and Clinical Hypnosis* 5: 79–82.

Wallace, L.M. (1982) Psychological management of pain in American burn units, *Psychology and Pain* 1: 6–17.

—— (1987) Hypnosis and pain control on an English burns unit, *Intensive Care Nursing* 3: 50–55.

Wardle, J. (1988) Pain, in F.N. Watts (ed.) *New Developments in Clinical Psychology*, Leicester: British Psychological Society and Wiley.

Waxman, D. (1989) *Hartland's Medical and Dental Hypnosis*, 3rd edn, London: Baillière Tindall.

Zeltzer, L. and LeBaron, S. (1986) The hypnotic treatment of children in pain, in D. Raith and M. Wolraich (eds) *Advances in Developmental and Behavioural Paediatrics* 7: 197–234.

7

Hypnotherapy and sexual problems

MARCIA D. DEGUN AND GIAN S. DEGUN

Introduction

A sexual problem may be defined as an inability to derive pleasure and satisfaction from sexual activity individually or in a relationship. This may be due to some impairment or inadequacy of the sexual response as judged by a client or by the partner. Such problems may reflect ignorance and lack of proper knowledge of sexual functioning, or what may be termed unrealistic expectations which can usually be rectified by re-education and counselling. On the other hand some physiological components of the sexual response may be involved and further psychological intervention and therapy may be required. In the latter case the problem is usually termed a 'sexual dysfunction'. Sexual dysfunctions have been classified as primary or secondary, primary being present throughout the whole sexual life and secondary becoming manifest any time after a problem-free period, and occurring either in certain situations only or in all. This chapter will be devoted to this latter group of dysfunctions. Sexual behaviours which arise from different sexual orientations will not be considered here.

A variety of global terms have been used to describe sexual dysfunctions such as 'frigidity' and 'impotence'. A more acceptable classification is presented in Table 7.1 which is based upon the model of Masters and Johnson (1970), Kaplan (1979) and Dennerstein (1980). The causes of these dysfunctions may be physical or psychological. In the assessment of the problem it is important to include physical causation before looking for psychological factors to treat. The authors will not be concerned with the organically caused dysfunctions and the medical treatment of these conditions, though it is recognized there may be interactions between organic and psychological causes.

First it seems appropriate to discuss briefly the general psychological factors in the causation of sexual problems. These have been classified into five main groups as follows: previous learning, contemporary or current conditions, psychological reaction to organic factors, deficient or false information, and deficient or inappropriate stimulation (Jehu 1979). The last two can perhaps be

Table 7.1 Classification of sexual dysfunctions

Phase	Male	Female
1 Desire	Low sex desire or Impaired sex desire	Low sex desire or Impaired sex desire
2 Arousal or Excitement	Failure to achieve erection (erectile dysfunction)	Impaired sex arousal Lack of vaginal lubrication
Penetration	Failure to maintain erection	Pain Vaginismus Dyspareunia
3 Orgasm	Premature ejaculation Ejaculatory incompetence (retarded ejaculation)	Anorgasmia
4 Resolution	Dysphoria	Dysphoria

more readily tackled by re-education and counselling. Previous learning includes traumatic experiences, restrictive upbringing, and adverse family relations, all of which cause anxieties about sexual urges and behaviour. Contemporary conditions may consist of psychological stress, such as fear of harm or failure, or of contravening moral and religious codes. Situations which involve stress, anxiety, depression, guilt, or anger can also contribute to avoidance behaviour in sexual encounters, thus leading to discord and dysfunction. The factors which lead to discord include deficient reinforcement, rejection and dominance–submission conflicts. Having a sexually dysfunctional partner and the consequent stress reactions of rejection, anxiety, anger and aggression can also lead to sexual problems. Psychological reactions to organic factors, such as illness, ageing and surgery, may be similar in kind: that is, anticipation of harm or failure, depression, impairment of self-concept, rejection, anxiety and partner discord.

Over the past 20 years or so several advances have been made in the therapeutic approaches to sexual problems. In the 1950s and early 1960s most sex therapy was based on psychoanalytic theory which viewed sexual problems as a manifestation of unconscious intrapsychic conflicts and therefore therapy was individually based. With the advent of behaviour therapy based on learning theories and classical conditioning (Wolpe 1958), sexual difficulties were seen as learned maladaptive responses which could be unlearned. Wolpe (1958) used desensitization to reduce anxiety conditioned to sexual behaviour. Alternative methods of sex therapy were introduced in the USA from 1970 onwards by Masters and Johnson, whose approach was based on scientific observations of human sexual functioning and was largely behavioural but also educational in nature. They attempted to dispel some of the myths about sexual functioning which they considered to have four phases: excitement, plateau, orgasm and resolution. The dysfunctions could be classified according to these phases (see Table 7.1). Their main focus was upon the couple or the marital relationship as they did not consider that there could be an uninvolved partner where there was some form of sexual inadequacy (Masters and Johnson 1970). Therefore both partners participated in therapy. In addition the effectiveness of therapy was considered to be dependent upon a male and female co-therapy team, as they believed only a woman could understand a woman's sexuality and sexual problems and a man could understand the man's sexuality and sexual problems. They emphasized two important factors in the sexual dysfunctions, namely performance anxiety and lack of clear communication between couples. The aim of the therapy was to rectify the above problems and the therapy was carried out away from the couple's home in a relaxed environment.

The work of Masters and Johnson has never been exactly replicated in Great Britain, but it has been widely used in modified form. The British have not always used conjoint therapy, and the intensive therapy in isolation has also not been repeated here, largely because of its impracticality financially and otherwise. The therapy sessions here are usually at weekly or fortnightly intervals. However, the other general principles and tenets of the therapy have been accepted and applied by British therapists.

Kaplan (1974) developed this approach further by considering what she called 'remote' as opposed to 'immediate' causes, that is, psychological events in the individual's history which seemed responsible for the sexual dysfunction. In this way she broadened the behavioural and educational approach to include psychotherapy (Kaplan 1974). She also introduced a more flexible approach by seeing clients singly or as couples and also as a single therapist. Another major contribution was her recognition of the importance of the desire phase of sexual functioning as distinct from the arousal or excitement phase. Consequently she reclassified sexual functioning into three phases: desire, arousal and orgasm.

Masters and Johnson and Kaplan revolutionized sex therapy in the USA and have greatly influenced therapists in this country. The so-called new sex therapies have been introduced into marital sexual dysfunction clinics of Relate – formerly the National Marriage Guidance Council. A training programme, spearheaded by clinical psychologists and sex counsellors, has led to the availability of sex and marital therapy for a wide range of clients and according to some accounts (Cole 1985) most sex therapists seem to follow a modified version of the approaches of Masters and Johnson and Kaplan. The majority of therapists (Cooper 1986) work singly with couples and there is little evidence to suggest that co-therapists are more effective than single therapists (Crowe *et al.* 1981, Mathews *et al.* 1983).

Behavioural methods have survived the expansion and development of the new sex therapies (Jehu 1979, Hawton 1982), although in one survey (Cooper 1986) therapists dealing with sex problems preferred a more eclectic approach similar to that advocated by Kaplan (1974). The behaviour therapist attempts to understand the events surrounding the onset of the sexual dysfunction, the current events sustaining the problem, and the consequences of the behaviour. Therapy focuses on the anxieties which may have been produced by sexual traumas, irrational beliefs or unrealistic expectations of performance. These anxieties are treated by systematic desensitization in imagination and *in vivo* (Jehu 1979, Lazarus 1980).

Cognitive therapists have more recently contributed to the development of sex therapies (Araoz 1980, Kowalski 1985). They focus on the faulty assumptions about sex which can adversely affect sexual functioning: for example, myths that are perpetuated in the media, sex magazines and peer groups can contribute to performance anxiety. Giving information and correcting irrational beliefs which determine sexual dysfunctions are the major tasks of cognitive therapists. Araoz (1980, 1983) who broadly follows an Ericksonian experiential approach considers that the cognitive aspect represents a fourth phase of sexual dysfunction after the three phases of Kaplan's model; that is, the thoughts a person has after failing to achieve an orgasm may well influence future sexual responses – for example, 'I have failed again and will never get over this'. Araoz calls this 'negative self-hypnosis' (see later and Chapter 5). Such cognitions eventually affect all three phases of sexual functioning and Araoz advocates a form of cognitive restructuring before embarking upon more traditional sex therapy utilizing elicited positive self-statements to counteract negative cognitions. His innovations are being adopted in this country though no published account is yet available.

Since Kaplan emphasized the importance of considering unconscious processes and defence mechanisms in sexual dysfunctions, the psychodynamic approach is now being intregrated into sex therapies, whereas in the past it tended to be applied alone. The emphasis now is upon understanding conflicts which interfere with personal and intimate relationships, thereby influencing attitudes and changing belief systems.

Cooper (1986) carried out a survey of British sex therapists with the aim of finding out their therapeutic methods. Out of a total number of 145 respondents, 33 used a psychodynamic method alone. Of the 111 therapists who used an eclectic approach 22% reported using a psychodynamic approach combined with the procedure of Masters and Johnson and Kaplan and a further 33% used it in an eclectic way with other methods.

It can be seen from this brief account of the therapeutic approaches to sexual dysfunction that sex therapists are increasingly intervening at different levels of personal and sexual functioning, and as Cooper (1986) rightly observes most therapists are not 'purist' but work in a broad-based way. Bancroft (1985) believes that the field of sex therapy shows a healthy eclecticism and has broken down the barriers between the behavioural and psychodynamic approaches, thus providing a comprehensive therapeutic package for all clients. This development must be welcome because it protects the client from being forced into a model that he or she does not fit.

Hypnotherapeutic approaches: general principles

The major hypnotic procedures used in the treatment of sexual problems can be classified under four headings:

1 Hypnoanalysis.
2 Direct symptom removal.
3 Hypnosis as an adjunct in behaviour therapy.
4 Cognitive and experiential approaches.
5 Eclectic approaches.

1 Hypnoanalysis

Psychodynamic therapists who view psychosexual problems as the consequence of intrapsychic conflicts use hypnosis for the purpose of exploration and uncovering the unconscious material. They believe that deep-seated unresolved past events or traumas are the main causes of psychosexual problems. Although Freud himself originally used hypnosis for the development of his theories, he later abandoned it in favour of free association, but his contemporaries continued to use it as a means of uncovering the presumed historical causes which have been repressed in the unconscious. In order to gain access to the repressed material a method commonly used is hypnotic age-regression which enables the therapist to target the critical period in the client's life. During the hypnotic sessions the client is encouraged to elaborate, identify and relate the emotional content of the experience (Alexander 1974, Smith 1975, Wijesinghe 1977, Ward 1980, Miller 1986) and this is presumed to release the fears and anxieties associated with the experience. The therapist then reinterprets the significance of these events to the client who with this new knowledge and insight is encouraged to restructure his or her reality and thus to achieve a more satisfactory life adjustment.

Therapists using a psychodynamic framework employed different hypnotic techniques. Wijesinghe (1977) used free association, Mirowitz (1966) questioned the client and used ideomotor techniques to retrieve information (see Chapter 2), and Alexander (1974) induced age-regression by asking the client in hypnosis to relive a painful day. Depending on the nature of the problems uncovered these therapists employed appropriate suggestions to help resolve them. Dream analysis is also used in hypnosis to uncover an underlying cause or conflict, and suggestions are made to resolve it (Ward 1980, Degun and Degun 1988).

The psychodynamic approach is not always concerned with past conflicts but can be used with present events as well. Levit (1971) and Crasilneck (1979) considered that some sexual dysfunctions arise from anger towards the spouse and subsequent guilt; these negative emotions then act as a 'turn-off' for sexual feelings. Levit (1971) used hypnosis to facilitate ventilation of repressed negative feelings. For example, a client was asked to build up his anger in hypnosis and at a given signal was required to clench his fist and strike the arm of the chair, thus facilitating the expression of hitherto repressed anger. Afterwards the client was given suggestions to express his feelings more appropriately. Ventilation of feelings may be one of several aims of hypnoanalysis. For example, Deabler (1976) listed five important aims: (a) to uncover unconscious conflict; (b) to release fears which inhibit sexual arousal; (c) to restructure associations and orientation to sex objects; (d) to dispel inhibiting identifications, for example, with the mother in the case of oedipal conflicts; and (e) to provide ego-building and ego-strengthening suggestions.

2 Direct symptom removal

Some psychodynamic therapists have relinquished hypnoanalysis in favour of direct symptom removal in some cases of sexual dysfunction. This also involves the use of hypnotic suggestions but these are directed towards the symptoms rather than historical causes. One method involves visualization of sexual encounters with the partner with suggestions of improved sexual performance (Schneck 1970). Post-hypnotic suggestions are also incorporated. Hypnotic recall and detailed visualization of previous positive sexual experiences coupled with hypnotic time distortion to prolong the pleasure have been used by other therapists (Mirowitz 1966, Cheek 1976). They used self-hypnosis to reinforce these experiences and found that this was an important component of therapy where direct symptom removal was attempted.

Another variation on this theme is the introduction of positive imagery of having successful sexual intercourse combined with positive self-statements. The hypnotic experience is made more vivid by the therapist's description of feelings and sensations appropriate to the situation (Richardson 1968).

3 Hypnosis as an adjunct in behaviour therapy

Behaviour therapists have used hypnosis as an adjunct in a variety of ways, in particular with systematic desensitization (Wolpe 1958, Dengrove 1980, Fuchs 1980, Degun and Degun 1982). The presumed value of hypnosis in this procedure is to facilitate relaxation and vivid imagery. Compared to Jacobson's relaxation technique, hypnotic induction has been found to be less time-consuming and more effective (Dengrove 1980, Clarke and Jackson 1983).

Systematic desensitization follows the classical model (Wolpe 1958) in which the graded hierarchy of sexual scenes and situations where appropriate are constructed and presented in the hypnotic state. The items of such a hierarchy might contain elements of sexual foreplay and involvement or scenes of progressive social and physical involvement (Beigel 1971, Fabbri 1976, Fuchs 1980, Degun and Degun 1982). Post-hypnotic suggestions are used to facilitate *in vivo* (real-life) performance of the imagined situation.

Other therapists have used graded dilators under hypnosis instead of finger insertion in cases of vaginismus (Fuchs 1980). In anorgasmia, Dengrove (1980) employed manual and self-stimulation with vibrators and hypnotic rehearsal prior to *in vivo* practice. He also found that hypnosis facilitated relaxation, time distortion, dream induction and vivid imagery of pleasurable sexual experiences and led to an increase in intensity of sexual feeling and enjoyment of sexual dreams through post-hypnotic suggestions. Misra (1985) included four stages in his method of using systematic desensitization with hypnosis:

1 Hypnosis with ego-strengthening.
2 Video-hypno-sensitization: that is, the client, whilst hypnotized with eyes open, watches a graded series of videotaped scenes depicting most aspects of normal sexual relationships.
3 Hypno-conditioning with slides: that is, the client, whilst hypnotized with eyes open, watches a graded series of slides of sexual situations which he or she has to practise at home.
4 Hypnotic recall: that is, the client is asked, whilst hypnotized, to imagine vivid past successful and happy heterosexual experiences.

Both Fabbri (1976) and Misra (1985) consider hypnosis contributes in a major way to the process of systematic desensitization. Fabbri stated that systematic desensitization is the main therapeutic framework for resolving sexual anxieties, whether phobic or secondary to guilt, anger, or hostility, and that hypnosis reinforces the conditioning process by post-hypnotic suggestion. Misra (1985) maintains that hypnosis produces deep relaxation, heightens visual imagery and allows for revivification and recall of past experiences. Most therapists have employed self-hypnosis to reinforce the post-hypnotic suggestions and other assignments given during the hetero-hypnotic session.

4 Cognitive and experiential approaches

Cognitive–behavioural therapists have emphasized the importance of mental processes such as images and thoughts. Araoz (1980) has introduced the concept of 'hypnosex therapy'; although he claims to be experiential (see below), in our view his approach is mainly cognitive–behavioural since he uses cognitive restructuring in his therapy, and indeed other approaches such as the psychodynamic (see later). He believes that sexual difficulties can arise from a person's cognitions which may be self-hypnotic in a negative way. Negative self-statements and negative sexual imagery may create and perpetuate symptoms and this happens in particular after sexual failure has been experienced, when the person believes he or she is inadequate and may have an inner image of sexual failure. This becomes a form of covert self-reinforcement which acts as a 'turn-off' in all future sexual encounters. Araoz calls this 'negative self-hypnosis' and, as mentioned earlier, considers that it represents a fourth phase in addition to Kaplan's three phases of desire, arousal and orgasm, though he also recognizes that inner conversations and imagery may be present in all other phases, thus affecting sexual feelings and behaviour at all the sexual stages. Kowalski (1985) has also found that negative mental processes play a major role in sexual problems such as low sex desire. However, Araoz considers that the negative self-hypnosis has to be treated before embarking on any other sex therapy, either individual or conjoint. In his approach to therapy he uses hypnosis initially for the rehearsal of negative self-statements in order to create the corresponding negative mood and feelings, thus dramatizing for the client the adverse effects of this process. The hypnotic state is then employed to elicit counter-active positive statements and imagery: for example, the therapist may say to the client 'Now we have seen the negative side let the more positive side of your personality come out. Let that side say something about the problem.' In hypnosis the client can focus on these alternative statements and become involved in positive imagery, and self-hypnosis is taught to reinforce this cognitive restructuring. Araoz makes clear that 'hypnosex therapy' is no substitute for Masters and Johnson's therapy, but may be used first in order to produce some early improvements.

In the experiential psychotherapeutic framework the therapist deals in a concrete way with the client's sense of immediate experience which is not emotions, words, or muscle movements but a 'feel' of the complexity of situations and difficulties. Erickson and his followers have used the experiential approach in conjunction with traditional sex therapy techniques (Erickson *et al.* 1976). They use indirect hypnotic inductions in which the client's own language is utilized and metaphors or parables are introduced tailored to the individual's needs and problem. These are termed multiple-embedded metaphors. They are cleverly created stories intended to confuse the client's conscious mind but to engage the unconscious because resolutions are presented in the story content which could be of importance and significance to the client. In this way the therapist hopes to draw upon the client's unconscious resources. Gilmore (1987) described and illustrated the procedures in cases of sexual dysfunction. In the initial hypnotic trance a metaphor was used which matched the client's present life situation. It had a protagonist and some sort of conflict and was designed to turn the client away from his current fears and towards the story. A second metaphor was then presented with a different protagonist and different conflict. This was also abandoned by the therapist for a third metaphor (the 'Vortex'). By now the client was confused and it was therefore assumed that the therapist could give direct suggestions which were likely to be taken up. Conclusions containing solutions to the first and second metaphors were then presented. This procedure was presumed to help resolve the sexual problems through the client's inner resources.

5 Eclectic approaches

Surveying the literature of sex therapies we have found that there are a number of therapists who combine the behavioural and psychodynamic approaches. By doing so their therapies seem to have become more eclectic and broader based. The reports are mostly anecdotal and often contain large numbers of clients (Fabbri 1976, Crasilneck and Hall 1985). However, there are few controlled studies, except for that of Obler (1982) who reported a study comparing an integrated approach (i.e. individual therapy by systematic desensitization with hypnosis and the parallel use of hypnoanalysis with psychodynamic interpretations) with the co-therapist and couples approach of Masters and Johnson. Both the immediate and long-term results (at a four-year follow-up) indicated the superiority of the integrated approach. In fact, those receiving the Masters and Johnson therapy were no better than untreated controls after four years. The important therapeutic factors were considered to be dynamic exploration, reduction of anxiety, and historical analysis of the problem. The author favoured behavioural techniques with hypnoanalysis.

6 Indications and contraindications for using hypnosis

Unfortunately sex therapists who have used hypnosis have not specified the criteria for selection of clients: that is, there is no mention of the use of hypnotizability scales. Hypnotizability of the client is an obvious positive indication for introducing hypnosis into therapy, although much depends on the nature of the intervention and the appropriate use of hypnosis to facilitate the process. Bridges *et al.* (1985) have reported an interesting finding that women who scored high on hypnotizability scales reported less ability to control thoughts and movements near the end of coitus. There might be an inverse relationship between hypnotizability and general inhibitory control. Whether this has prognostic significance in sex therapy with hypnosis would be interesting to know.

Before deciding the contraindications of using hypnosis the therapist must assess the motivational factors. Where the client has an internal locus of control, hypnosis might be a very useful adjunct. On the other hand, where the client is unprepared to face up to the reality of the problem and simply seeks hypnosis as a magic wand it might be contraindicated. There is some consensus of opinion that hypnosis should not be used to treat any problem where there is evidence in the client of latent psychosis, severe depression and suicidal ideation (Crasilneck and Hall 1985); see also Chapter 4 on applications to depression.

Specific applications of hypnosis in the treatment of sexual dysfunctions

In this section we will be mainly concerned with the phases of sexual functions already mentioned in our Introduction (see Table 7.1), the aetiological factors in the disorders arising within these phases and the therapies which have been applied to them with the use of hypnosis.

Sexual dysfunctions of the desire phase

Kaplan (1979) defined sexual dysfunction of the desire phase as the evocation of anxiety very early in the sequence of desire–excitement–orgasm. The focus on negative thoughts acts as a 'turn-off' to all sexual desire. Causes of sexual dysfunctions are considered to be mild, moderate, or deep (Kaplan 1979). Mostly, the causation of inhibited sex desire seems to be deep-rooted fears involving pleasure and love, intimacy, rejection, or intense performance anxiety. The relationship problems arising from anger, mistrust, hostility, power struggles and early childhood injury can also be important variables. Not surprisingly, treatment of the deep-rooted dysfunctions of the desire phase have been largely reported by psychodynamic therapists (Wijesinghe 1977, Oystragh 1980, Miller 1986). Hypnotic age-regression was used by all three authors in case studies which were all female. Oystragh treated a woman of 28 years who displayed absence of sexual desire and failure to obtain orgasm. By hypnotic age-regression the client abreacted two incidences of rape in her childhood and during the hypnotic sessions her emotions and feelings related to these incidents were relieved by the method of suggested automatic writing. It was also suggested to the client that she would vividly imagine sexual intercourse and remember the enjoyable aspects of sex. This case had a positive outcome with six-month follow-up. A similar case involving incest was reported by Wijesinghe (1977) where other methods such as Masters and Johnson's and systematic desensitization did not produce any change. Hypnotic recall of the incestuous events in childhood alleviated her negative feelings, her sexual desire returned and she also reported experiencing orgasm with her husband. Finally, a very complex case of a woman with loss of sexual desire arising from incestuous experiences in childhood was reported by Miller (1986), using age-regression, abreaction, dream suggestion, and dissociation of aspects of herself (the client) into part-selves with subsequent reintegration. These all contributed to the client's gaining insight and facilitated mature, satisfying sexual relations.

As discussed earlier, Araoz (1980) considers low sex desire to be due to faulty cognitions or negative self-hypnosis (NSH). In Araoz's view most clients present with complaints of the second and third phases of sexual function (i.e. excitement or orgasm) because in this culture everyone is supposed to want sex. None the less, a certain number of these clients may be experiencing lack of sexual desire which goes unrecognized. Araoz reported the case of a male with premature ejaculation and then erectile dysfunction who basically had no desire for sexual intercourse. Hypnosis was used for three main purposes: (a) revivification, that is, suggesting reliving a period when he was sexually aroused (to facilitate cognitive and feeling changes); in this case nothing was elicited; (b) to uncover at what point in his history and for what developmental reasons there was no sex desire; again this produced no information; (c) to imagine a life with greater sexual interest (mental rehearsal). These attempts to facilitate cognitive changes proferred little as the client had devoted most of his time and energies to intellectual pursuits. Araoz finally employed a 'pleasure hierarchy' or list of items of the relatively more pleasurable aspects of sexual encounters with his wife. These were imagined in hypnosis and post-hypnotic suggestions were given to the effect that these feelings would return before going to bed with his wife and the chain of reactions would be elicited by his wife's embrace. In three to four sessions, together with a self-hypnosis tape, sexual desire increased. In this account one can see two processes taking place during hypnosis: first, switching of focus from the intellectual to the emotional life and secondly, modification of early childhood negative experiences into something positive and pleasurable. This is akin to approaches used in cognitive therapy. Although Araoz has adopted a cognitive approach to sexual dysfunctions he has recognized the importance of uncovering past traumatic events and their significance to the client. The focus in his approach to therapy has been the 'turn-off' self-statements which he considers affect in particular the desire phase. Apart from the uncovering technique used by Wijesinghe (1977) there is no other British publication of hypnotherapy of sexual dysfunctions of the desire phase.

Sexual dysfunctions of the excitement phase

The dysfunctions of the excitement phase arise when anxiety is evoked at varying points in the course of love-making when the person is already sexually aroused. Among males it manifests as impotence or erectile dysfunction and retarded ejaculation. Erectile dysfunction can arise from overconcern for the partner, transient fear of rejection, lack of assertiveness, guilt over masturbation, unrealistic sex expectations, and mild power struggles (Kaplan 1979). Retarded ejaculation can result from anger towards women and lack of trust in the relationship.

Impotence may be primary (that is, the male has never been able to maintain an erection) or secondary (when sexual intercourse has been successfully completed in the past but subsequently failure has ensued owing to inability to maintain an erection). Primary impotence is more rare (Kaplan 1974). Kaplan stressed the importance of emotional and cognitive conditioning which may follow a single episode of impotence: that is, the man remembers his failure and fears that he will not be able to function fully in future, and his performance anxiety inhibits his sexual function. Physical factors such as fatigue, excessive alcohol, and tranquillizers and other drugs may be responsible for a single episode or several episodes of failure. Other physical causes embrace some neurological and endocrine disorders, but Kaplan (1979) reported that 85% of cases of impotence in the USA were psychogenic. Masters and Johnson (1970) discovered other factors that also lead to dysfunctions of the excitement phase, namely, secondary impotence following premature ejaculation, religious teaching about the sin of sex, and orientation to homosexuality. Crasilneck and Hall (1985) included aetiological factors, guilt over an extramarital affair, fear of producing pregnancy, fear of venereal disease, and traumatic events in childhood, such as being scolded for sex play and fear of father's anger and castration in the case of unresolved oedipal conflict. Whilst sex therapy for this condition has been used in Britain (Cole and Dryden 1988) as well as in the USA, the scene here is sadly lacking in the therapeutic application of hypnosis.

Crasilneck and Hall (1985) are two authors who have studied hypnotherapy with a large number of clients with impotence. They attempted direct symptom removal by hypnotic suggestions that erections would become hard and rigid. Arm rigidity was suggested together with the words 'if you can produce this hardness in one part of your body you can produce it in your penis . . . You will begin to feel hard erections whenever you are sexually aroused.' During each hypnotic session the client was allowed to ventilate his feelings concerning the problem and was helped to gain intellectual and emotional insight thus resolving the problem. Explanations about the physiology of penile erection were also given during hypnosis. The relative efficacy of the two parts of the hypnotic session was not assessed, but of 400 clients, 80% improved at a four-month follow-up. Fuchs *et al.* (1985) used arm levitation as the hypnotic induction method in cases of male impotence, the authors considering this to be a symbolic expression of an elevated and erect organ. Various suggestions were given during hypnosis, concluding with 'You will immediately experience the feeling that your penis is elevating like your stiff arm'.

The combination of direct symptom removal in conjunction with uncovering techniques seems to have been popular in the treatment of psychogenic impotence. Schneck (1970) described a young man who had previously had fantasies of wrestling with other young men which had been accompanied by erection and then ejaculation. A later relationship with his girlfriend presented problems when he was unable to maintain an erection. The client was asked in hypnosis to visualize repeatedly sexual encounters with his partner and to describe each step unfolding from beginning to end. During this process the therapist emphasized the aspects of the scene which needed improvement and the client was encouraged not to delay penetration. When he was able to have intercourse, the wrestling fantasies were elicited in hypnosis and suggestions were made that he would see them converted into heterosexual activity. As his heterosexual performance improved the wrestling fantasies receded. The direct suggestions given in hypnosis and the probing questions about his sex life were reported by the client to be significant factors in his improvement.

Deabler (1976) reported a similar case of loss of erection at intromission. Using uncovering and ideomotor techniques, Deabler discovered that the client had guilt over adolescent fantasies of masturbating in front of his nude mother and found that the client was imagining having sex with his mother. The therapist then attempted to foster a guilt-free attitude towards his wife when having sex with her. This client recovered completely, although no direct symptom removal was employed. Deabler concluded that hypnosis is effective in uncovering the unconscious conflicts, releasing the fears and anxieties, associations and orientation towards sex objects. He found that dispelling inhibiting identifications and providing ego-strengthening suggestions helped the development of a masculine role.

Impotence has been treated by hypnotic uncovering techniques by Mirowitz (1966) who also used hypnosis to help the client relive satisfactory sexual experiences and reinforced this with self-hypnosis. A similar approach was used by Alexander (1974) in a case of male impotence. Ventilation of feelings of anger towards the spouse was found to be therapeutic in a case of impotence reported by Levit (1971). Beigel (1971) in his treatment of impotence combined hypnotic elicitation of repressed memories with a desensitization procedure using erotic pictures and guided imagery of sexual situations in the hypnotic state. There appears to be no account in the literature of the systematic use of hypnotherapy for impotence in Britain.

The category 'sexual dysfunctions in the excitement phase in women' has been omitted in Kaplan's classification (1979). However, vaginismus and dyspareunia can be classified under this heading; certainly they seem to the present authors to arise from a loss of desire or lack of excitement or arousal. Dennerstein (1980) put these problems into a special category of 'penetration' problems. Vaginismus is defined by Kaplan (1979) as a conditioned spasm of perivaginal musculature – a reaction to fear evoked by vaginal penetration; in dyspareunia there is a painful spasm of certain genital muscles. Causes include guilt over sexual pleasure, anger with the partner, fear of penetration, and others of a deeper nature such as sexual conflicts (Kaplan 1979).

Hypnotherapy for vaginismus, both in the United States and the UK, has been largely behavioural (Schneck 1965, Fuchs 1980, Degun and Degun 1982). Schneck (1965) reported two cases, one of which had not responded to hypno-analysis. Hypnotic relaxation with visualization of sexual encounters and post-hypnotic suggestion of relaxation were successful in alleviating symptoms of pain on partial penetration in one of his cases. His treatment regime consisted of gradual steps in imagination, of accepting loveplay, superficial genital contact, longer periods of genital pressure, graded partial penetration, and eventual complete penetration and full coitus. A similar process of systematic desensitization was used in 14 cases of vaginismus by Fuchs (1980), whose procedure of *in vitro* desensitization is described earlier in this chapter. In his *in vivo* method he used graduated dilators during hypnosis without imaginal scenes. Although Fuchs did not compare the two methods of desensitization objectively, he favoured the *in vivo* method as neither deep trance nor imaginal scenes were needed; also the partner became active in the desensitization procedure, and this helped the wife to build up her confidence (see earlier).

In Britain Degun and Degun (1982) reported the efficacy of a simple systematic desensitization procedure with hypnosis in conjunction with conjoint Masters and Johnson sex therapy. Hypnotic suggestions of relaxation of the pelvic musculature were given and the client then imagined inserting her finger in the vagina as far as she could. Post-hypnotic suggestions were given of having the same relaxed feeling when doing this *in vivo*, and after the hypnosis she was left alone to attempt insertion of her finger in the vagina. She was encouraged to repeat the procedure at home and to penetrate her finger deeper during future hypnotic sessions. This was followed by conjoint sex therapy, and during the genital sensate focusing the husband was encouraged to attempt finger insertion. Although both therapists were involved in Masters and Johnson sex therapy the female therapist alone carried out the systematic desensitization with hypnosis. In both cases of vaginismus, fewer sessions were needed to help the client overcome the problem than were used by other therapists such as Fuchs (1980). In later cases both therapies were combined in the same session, the first half being devoted to conjoint feedback and counselling and the second half to desensitization.

Misra (1985) also used systematic desensitization with hypnosis for the treatment of vaginismus and dyspareunia. His methods are described in the previous section, but it is worthy of note that his particular techniques had been applied to a whole range of psychosexual dysfunctions in both males and females and across all phases and did not necessitate a co-therapist.

Sexual dysfunctions of the orgasm phase

Sexual dysfunctions in this phase are caused by anxiety evoked at the highest peak of arousal. In the male it manifests as premature ejaculation due to a failure to perceive erotic sensations at the stage just prior to orgasm, thus causing inadequate control. The causes include performance anxiety, anger towards the partner and sometimes pressured conditions in earlier sex experiences. In women it manifests as inhibition of orgasm which may be due to 'orgasm watching', self-consciousness and spectatoring, ignorance of sexual physiology, and lack of assertiveness. Other identified causes include fear of rejection or loss of control, or frightening fantasies about orgasm. As Crasilneck and Hall (1985) have pointed out, orgasm in the female is not an all-or-nothing phenomenon and some women are able to enjoy sexual experiences without achieving orgasm. The quality of orgasmic experience varies considerably, even in those women who do achieve orgasm, as the enjoyment of the sexual act is dependent upon the entire sexual situation and setting. However, some women expect orgasmic experience to be an ecstatic one for them, whilst others expect that mutual orgasm should always be achieved. These kinds of unrealistic expectations can readily be eliminated by education and counselling.

As in the case of male premature ejaculation, pressured conditions, such as inadequate time, tiredness, distractions, and lack of privacy contribute to this problem, and fear of pregnancy can play a part too. Withholding of the sexual response in women can be an expression of hostility towards the partner as it can be in the case of premature ejaculation in men. Negative attitudes of parents towards sex combined with a punitive upbringing may adversely affect the sexual feelings of the child, who comes to view sex as bad, ugly, or dirty, thus leading to sexual dysfunction in adult life.

Targeting the symptom of anorgasmia by the use of hypnosis seems to be a favourite approach as it does in some cases of male impotence mentioned earlier, and there have been various ways of doing this. Crasilneck and Hall (1985) favoured the combined approach of exploration of 'deeply unconscious' factors by hypnosis as well as modifying the sexual inhibition itself. After hypnotic induction the woman was told she would be able to completely relax her vagina. Suggestions were made to increase the sensitivity of the vagina and clitoris and to heighten the experience of pleasure during sexual intercourse. The authors also involved the husband in the therapeutic sessions; thus the shared awareness and sensitivity helped towards a satisfactory outcome. Orgasmic dysfunction can produce a lot of anxiety and feelings of inferiority and insecurity in the male partner, thus undermining his sense of masculinity; as stated above, making him a partner in the therapy helps him to understand the general nature of the problem.

Richardson (1968) employed hypnotic imagery to enable anorgasmic women to achieve orgasm. This was accompanied by direct suggestions that when the woman began intercourse she would shut her eyes, exclude extraneous thoughts and become an active participant in sexual intercourse. In some cases a situation was structured verbally in hypnosis and then suggestions of imagining vividly sexual stimulation and coitus were introduced. Images of orgasm were accompanied by post-hypnotic suggestions of increasing the intensity of orgasm. Direct post-hypnotic suggestions could also be used to speed up or decrease the time of reaching an orgasm and to increase the desire and frequency. Although Richardson mentioned the use of hypnoanalysis and psychotherapy, he clearly believed in the important influence of direct suggestion on the capacity to experience orgasm.

When the sexual dysfunction is due to anger or hostility emanating from the partner's remarks made during the earlier sexual encounters, uncovering techniques may be used. For example, during hypnosis Miller (1979) suggested to his patient that she would relive a sexual encounter and ventilate her feelings. In addition to this he administered a placebo tablet (said to be a powerful sexual stimulant). This he believed would break the vicious circle and increase hope and positive anticipation. The relative efficacy of the two parts of the treatment was not assessed.

Alexander (1974) believed that preoccupation with successful performance of the male can produce impotence in men and anorgasmia in women. Because of the intense concern of a woman to please her partner, her voluntary intentions might interfere with the involuntary pleasurable aspects of sex; hence, the most accepted suggestion for anorgasmia is 'you must please yourself'. Alexander (1974) reported two cases of anorgasmic women who had spent a lot of their time trying to please others. Direct suggestions to please themselves in hypnosis were effective in both cases, with the outcome being maintained at three-year follow-up. This approach broke the inhibiting effect of watching and being in the role of spectator.

Kroger and Fezler (1976) have also favoured a direct symptomatic approach to problems of anorgasmia, impotence and premature ejaculation. They put great emphasis on what they termed 'sensory recall' in hypnosis. Past sexually arousing pleasant experiences were recalled during hypnosis and the therapist then heightened the sensitivity and receptivity of the client by inclusion of further sexual imagery. Recall of erotic imagery also inhibited anxiety-producing thoughts. Hypnotic time distortion was also successfully used in the treatment of premature ejaculation: the therapist trained the client to prolong imagined time of an erection and an image of a non-sexual nature was then introjected to be rehearsed during intercourse in order to delay ejaculation. Smith (1975) maintained that producing symptom relief in anorgasmia gives new hope and motivation though it is no substitute for insight therapy or behaviour modification. He produced quite a long discourse with the client during hypnosis, extolling the pleasures and virtues and purposes of sex. This seemed to have a beneficial effect on the general attitude of the client and set the scene for further joint counselling of the couple.

Dengrove (1980) emphasized the importance of focusing the female client on pleasures of sex rather than thinking about orgasm. Manual and self-stimulation were encouraged and facilitated by hypnotic suggestion and hypnotic rehearsal. Systematic desensitization to sexual foreplay was used both in imagination and *in vivo*. A vibrator was incorporated into the *in vivo* situations to condition vaginal orgasm and perineal musculature control was taught to anorgasmic women. Beigel (1980) described the 'squeeze' and 'delay' techniques for premature ejaculation. In the 'squeeze' technique the woman was required to hold the erect penis firmly between two fingers and a thumb. The thumb should be placed on the frenulum and the two fingers either side of the ridge where the glans meets the shaft of the penis opposite to the thumb. She had to squeeze the penis really hard for a few seconds and not to be afraid if some pain is caused. This squeezing stopped the urge to ejaculate in the male and he would lose part of his erection. After 15 to 30 seconds she had to stimulate the penis again and once more apply the squeeze technique. She had to repeat this procedure several times and enjoy 15 to 20 minutes of sex play without ejaculation. Other strategies were included, such as change of positions and settings, with hypnosis being mainly used to facilitate pleasurable erotic fantasies and self-stimulation.

Although some authors have reported recovery of orgasmic function by hypno-analysis alone (Levit 1971, Ward 1980) there is some evidence for success with an integrated approach – that is, hypnoanalysis with a behavioural and symptomatic approach (Obler 1982). In two cases of anorgasmia Ward (1980) was able to facilitate recovery by resolving problems of guilt arising in early childhood. Levit (1971) used hypnosis in marital crisis intervention; in clients who had been impotent or anorgasmic hypnosis helped in facilitating awareness and expression of anger thus resolving sexual conflict and leading to satisfactory sexual functioning.

Obler (1982) studied 26 anorgasmic women. His integrated approach consisted of systematic desensitization to sexual situations, with hypnosis, for half of one therapeutic session, whilst the second half was devoted to free association in which the client provided relevant material for later exploration, and this took two months. Then deeper hypnosis was used during which the client was allowed to abreact to significant items and to the relevant material uncovered by free association. These were then discussed and reinterpreted to the client in the non-hypnotic state which took another 20 weeks. This therapeutic approach seemed to be quite lengthy but according to the author it was superior to Masters and Johnson's therapy, as it enabled seven of the eight women treated by hypnosis to experience satisfactory orgasm even after a four-year follow-up. Only two out of eight women benefited from Masters and Johnson's therapy and these relapsed after two years. Dynamic exploration and reduction of anxiety were considered by Obler to be the most important therapeutic variable in the treatment of anorgasmia. Further details of this study are reported in the next section.

Sex therapy in Britain has advanced considerably since the early 1970s and the British have adopted sex therapies developed in the United States, such as Masters and Johnson (1970) and Kaplan (1974, 1979) and modified them to suit the different social, cultural and individual needs (Cole and Dryden 1988). It is surprising, then, to find a paucity of literature on the use of hypnosis with these therapies in Britain. The present authors attribute this to the absence of training for psychologists in hypnosis and hypnotic techniques in this country until 1978, when, with the formation of the British Society of Experimental and Clinical Hypnosis, facilities for training in the use of hypnosis were made available to clinicians and counsellors. No doubt very many clinical psychologists are using hypnosis in their therapeutic work, but there are few published accounts (Wijesinghe 1977, Degun and Degun 1982). As can be seen from the American literature there is no dearth of different ways in which hypnosis can be a most useful adjunct. It appears to facilitate systematic desensitization with relaxation and imagery, is an excellent medium for the recall and mental rehearsal of positive sexual experiences, and has obvious value for uncovering and exploring relevant historical material and effecting experiential and cognitive changes, thus shortening the length of therapeutic interventions.

Research developments

Hypnosis has been used widely in the treatment of sexual problems but there is a lack of controlled trials to establish specifically the efficacy of hypnosis as an adjunct in sex therapy (Mathews *et al.* 1976, Lazarus 1980). Since hypnosis has not been used in Britain by sex therapists, at least until the beginning of the 1980s owing to the lack of training facilities mentioned in the previous section, it is not surprising that in Britain there is an absence of research into hypnosis with sex therapy. No controlled trials have been published in Britain – only the anecdotal case studies already mentioned (Wijesinghe 1977, Degun and Degun 1982, Misra 1985).

There is only one study, that of Obler (1982), where hypnosis was an important component of a research project and this was carried out in the United States.

The main aim of Obler's work was to establish whether integrating behavioural and psychodynamic approaches with hypnosis would be more effective than the co-therapist couples approach of Masters and Johnson. The integrated approach with hypnosis was to analyse the root of the sex problem, whereas Masters and Johnson's therapy was to create a relaxed sexual environment through exercises and stimulation. Out of 42 anorgasmic women, Obler selected 26 for the study. All the women and their partners completed pre- and post-treatment assessment measures which consisted of a 20-item questionnaire focusing on responses in sex foreplay, sexual intercourse, and anxiety in social and sexual situations. He divided the 26 clients into three groups: experimental group 1, who received 42 weeks of the integrated approach (E1); experimental group 2, who received 16 weeks of Masters and Johnson's therapy (E2); and a control group, who received no treatment but were promised therapy at the end of the trial. All agreed to the offer. A detailed description of the procedures used in the integrated approach with hypnosis is given in an earlier section of this chapter. The results indicated no change in the control group, but improvement in both the experimental groups: 7 out of 8 clients in group E1 reported success in orgasm at the end of the trial, and 2 out of 8 did so in group E2. However, E1 received more therapy concerned with deeper analysis of the problem and the female clients were seen alone. At a four-year follow-up, 6 out of the 7 in group E1 maintained their reported improvement, whereas the 2 who had initially improved in group E2 regressed to pre-treatment level and had, in fact, reported the relapse after only two years. Analysis of the results at four-year follow-up showed that there was no difference between group E2 and the controls, and that group E1 was superior to group E2 in producing orgasmic success. Obler's conclusion was that the integrated approach was better for long-term success.

In this study the clients were assessed quite thoroughly in the beginning with a questionnaire and psychological testing, but as this was a controlled comparison there was no attempt to consider the individual needs of clients and to allocate treatment on the basis of any psychological criteria. The Obler study is flawed by the fact that group E1 received 42 weeks of therapy, whereas group E2 received only 16 weeks. If Obler had controlled the number of sessions for both groups the results might have been of greater significance. It is difficult to assess the efficacy of hypnosis in this study as there is little information about the application of hypnosis in a standardized form. Even the author does not make any direct claim about the use of hypnosis in facilitating therapy.

Future developments

Now that training of sex counsellors has been made widely available throughout Britain and hypnosis and hypnotic techniques are being taught to non-medical therapists, one would expect to see major research developments in the future. The problems in the 1960s and 1970s when only doctors and dentists could receive recognized training in hypnosis now no longer exist. There is a need for therapists who deal with sex problems to conduct controlled trials to assess the efficacy of the various treatments with and without hypnosis. As hypnosis has been found to be a very important therapeutic adjunct in behavioural psychotherapy and a major factor in the Ericksonian techniques, it is time that British therapists embark on research projects to establish the usefulness or otherwise of hypnosis in their work.

As there are so many components of hypnosis and a variety of ways in which it can be used, and furthermore, as sex therapy has embraced so many different approaches and orientations, it is not surprising that we find numerous areas for exploration, some of which may include the following:

1 The effectiveness of post-hypnotic suggestion.
2 The usefulness of hypnosis and self-hypnosis compared to the more common relaxation methods (e.g. Jacobson Relaxation Technique, Autogenic Training and the Alexander Technique).
3 The relative value of imaginal versus *in vivo* procedures particularly in behavioural psychotherapy.
4 The efficacy of individual versus conjoint therapy.
5 The importance of the exploration and uncovering of historical causes as opposed to behavioural methods.
6 The relationship of hypnotizability to outcome in sex therapy.
7 The relationship of hypnotizability to the outcome of sex therapy for particular sexual dysfunctions.

This is by no means an exhaustive list, but in our view these are some of the fruitful areas for research.

References

Alexander, L. (1974) Treatment of impotency and anorgasmia by psychotherapy aided by hypnosis, *American Journal of Clinical Hypnosis* 17: 33–43.
Araoz, D.L. (1980) Clinical hypnosis in treating sexual abulia, *American Journal of Family Therapy* 8: 48–57.
—— (1983) Hypnosex therapy, *American Journal of Clinical Hypnosis* 26: 37–41.
Bancroft, J. (1985) Marital sex therapy, in W. Dryden (ed.) *Marital Therapy in Britain Vol 2. Special Areas*, London: Harper & Row.
Beigel, H.G. (1971) The hypnotherapeutic approach to male impotence, *Journal of Sex Research* 7: 168–76.
—— (1980) Premature ejaculation, in H.G. Beigel and W.R. Johnson (eds)'*Application of Hypnosis in Sex Therapy*, Springfield, Ill.: Charles C. Thomas.
Bridges, C.F., Critelli, J.W. and Loos, V.E. (1985) Hypnotic susceptibility, inhibitory control and orgasmic consistency, *Archives of Sexual Behaviuor* 14: 373–6.
Cheek, D.B. (1976) Hypnotherapy for secondary frigidity after radical surgery for gynaecological cancer: 2 case reports, *American Journal of Clinical Hypnosis* 19: 13–19.
Clarke, J.C. and Jackson, J.A. (1983) *Hypnosis and Behavior Therapy: The Treatment of Anxiety and Phobias*, New York: Springer.
Cole, M. (1985) Sex therapy – a critical appraisal, *British Journal of Psychiatry* 147: 337–51.
Cole, M. and Dryden, W. (eds) (1988) *Sex Therapy in Britain*, Milton Keynes: Open University Press.
Cooper, G.F. (1986) *Survey of Sex Therapists in Britain*, Birmingham: Training and Consultancy Services.

Crasilneck, H.B. (1979) The use of hypnosis in the treatment of psychogenic impotency, *Australian Journal of Clinical and Experimental Hypnosis* 7: 147–53.

Crasilneck, H.B. and Hall, J.A. (1985) *Clinical Hypnosis: Principles and Applications*, 2nd edn, New York: Grune & Stratton.

Crowe, M.J., Gillan, P. and Golombok, S. (1981) Form and content in the conjoint treatment of sexual dysfunction: a controlled study, *Behaviour Research and Therapy* 19: 47–54.

Deabler, H.L. (1976) Hypnotherapy of impotence, *American Journal of Clinical Hypnosis* 19: 9–12.

Degun, M.D. and Degun, G. (1982) The use of hypnosis in the treatment of psychosexual disorders: with case illustrations of vaginismus, *Bulletin of the British Society of Experimental and Clinical Hypnosis* 5: 31–6.

—— (1988) The use of hypnotic dream suggestion in psychotherapy, in M. Heap (ed.) *Hypnosis: Current Clinical, Experimental and Forensic Practices*, London: Croom Helm.

Dengrove, E. (1980) Hypnotherapy of sexual disorders in women, in H.G. Beigel and W.R. Johnson (eds) *Application of Hypnosis in Sex Therapy*, Springfield, Ill.: Charles C. Thomas.

Dennerstein, L. (1980) Hypnosis and psychosexual dysfunction, in G. Burrows and L. Dennerstein (eds) *Handbook of Hypnosis and Psychosomatic Medicine*, Amsterdam; Elsevier/North-Holland Biomedical Press.

Erickson, M.H., Rossi, E. and Rossi, S. (1976) *Hypnotic Realities*, New York: Irvington.

Fabbri, R. Jr. (1976) Hypnosis and behavior therapy: a co-ordinated approach to the treatment of sexual disorders, *American Journal of Clinical Hypnosis* 19: 6.

Fuchs, K. (1980) Vaginismus: therapy by hypno-desensitization, in H.G. Beigel and W.R. Johnson (eds) *Application of Hypnosis in Sex Therapy*, Springfield, Ill.: Charles C. Thomas.

Fuchs, K., Zaidise, I., Peretz, B.A. and Paldi, E. (1985) Hypnotherapy in male impotence, in D. Waxman, P.C. Misra, M. Gibson and M.A. Basker (eds) *Modern Trends in Hypnosis: Proceedings of the 9th International Congress of Hypnosis and Psychosomatic Medicine*, New York: Plenum Press.

Gilmore, L.G. (1987) Hypnotic metaphor and sexual dysfunction, *Journal of Sex and Marital Therapy* 13: 45–57.

Hawton, K. (1982) The behavioural treatment of sexual dysfunction, in Symposium on Sexual Dysfunction, *British Journal of Psychiatry* 140: 94–101.

Jehu, D. (1979) *Sexual Dysfunctions – A Behavioural Approach*, Chichester: Wiley.

Kaplan, H.S. (1974) *The New Sex Therapy*, New York: Brunner/ Mazel.

—— (1979) *Disorders of Sexual Desire*, London: Baillière Tindall.

Kowalski, R. (1985) Cognitive therapy for sexual problems, *British Journal of Sexual Medicine* 12: 64–6, 90–3, 131–5.

Kroger, W.S. and Fezler, W.D. (1976) *Hypnosis and Behavior Modification: Imagery Conditioning*, Philadelphia: J.B. Lippincott.

Lazarus, A.A. (1980) Psychological treatment of dyspareunia, in S.R. Leiblum and L.A. Pervin (eds) *Principles and Practice of Sex Therapy*, London: Tavistock.

Levit, H.I. (1971) Marital crisis intervention: hypnosis in impotence/frigidity cases, *American Journal of Clinical Hypnosis* 14: 56–60.

Masters, W.H. and Johnson, V.E. (1970) *Human Sexual Inadequacy*, London: J.A. Churchill.

Mathews, A., Bancroft, J., Whitehead, A., Hackmann, A., Julier, D., Bancroft, J., Gath, D. and Shaw, P. (1983) The behavioural treatment of sexual inadequacy: a comparative study, *Behaviour Research and Therapy* 14: 427–36.

Miller, A. (1986) Hypnotherapy in a case of dissociated incest, *International Journal of Clinical and Experimental Hypnosis* 24: 13–28.

Miller, M.M. (1979) *Therapeutic Hypnosis*, New York: Human Sciences Press.

Mirowitz, J.M. (1966) The utilisation of hypnosis in psychic impotence, *British Journal of Medical Hypnotism* 17: 25–32.

Misra, P.C. (1985) Hypnosis and sexual disorders, in D. Waxman, P.C. Misra, M. Gibson and M.A. Basker (eds) *Modern Trends in Hypnosis: Proceedings of the 9th International Congress of Hypnosis and Psychosomatic Medicine*, New York: Plenum Press.

Obler, M. (1982) A comparison of a hypno-analytic/behaviour modification technique and a co-therapist type treatment with primary orgasmic dysfunctional females: some preliminary results, *Journal of Sex Research* 18: 331–45.

Oystragh, P. (1980) Hypnosis and frigidity: utilization of automatic writing, in H.G. Beigel and W.R. Johnson (eds) *Application of Hypnosis in Sex Therapy*, Springfield, Ill.: Charles C. Thomas.

Richardson, T.A. (1968) Hypnotherapy in frigidity and para-frigidity problems, *Journal of the American Society of Psychosomatic Dentistry and Medicine* 15: 88–96.

Schneck, J.M. (1965) Hypnotherapy for vaginismus, *International Journal of Clinical and Experimental Hypnosis* 13: 92–5.

—— (1970) Psychogenic impotence with a hypnotherapy case illustration, *Psychosomatics* 11: 352–4.

Smith, H.D. (1975) The use of hypnosis in treating inorgasmic sexual response in women – the report of five cases, *Journal of the American Institute of Hypnosis* 16: 119–25.

Ward, W.O. (1980) Successful treatment of frigidity through hypnosis, in H.G. Beigel and W.R. Johnson (eds) *Application of Hypnosis in Sex Therapy*, Springfield, Ill.: Charles C. Thomas.

Wijesinghe, B. (1977) A case of frigidity treated by short-term hypnotherapy, *International Journal of Clinical and Experimental Hypnosis* 25: 63–7.

Wolpe, J. (1958) *Psychotherapy by Reciprocal Inhibition*, Stanford, Calif.: Stanford University Press.

8

Hypnosis in medicine

J.B. WILKINSON

Introduction

Altered states of consciousness as aids to healing date back to ancient times and were part of early Egyptian and Greek cultures. Through the centuries in various Eastern ethnic groups complex exercises in meditation and relaxation evolved, akin to what we would call hypnosis. In the West interest in such mental states really began in the third quarter of the 18th century with Anton Mesmer, a physician who worked first in Vienna, but moved to Paris when the University of Vienna repudiated his theory of animal magnetism which stipulated that good health depended on maintaining a correct relationship with heavenly bodies and that the magnet was capable of restoring this if it was disturbed. The cure was supposed to be due to a mysterious fluid which entered the patient's body via the magnet, or magnetized object, thus healing the condition. This theory was later condemned as fraudulent by a Royal Commission set up by Louis XVI in Paris. But in spite of this lack of scientific basis for his treatment there is no doubt that Mesmer obtained good results in many cases, almost certainly because the patients were hypnotized with a consequent increase in suggestibility.

In Britain 'mesmerism' was adopted by a well-known physician at University College Hospital, London, namely John Elliotson, but in spite of some success this treatment led to friction with the hospital authorities and he was forced to resign. However, he continued in private practice, concentrating mainly on psychoneurosis and functional disorders, and believing that mesmerism worked through a physical agent, animal magnetism. It was James Braid, a Manchester surgeon, who produced a more rational theory for its success. After careful studies he perceived the subjective nature of mesmeric phenomena and that these were not dependent on magical powers possessed by the therapist. He considered mesmerism to be a form of 'nervous sleep' and therefore named it 'hypnotism' (from the Greek 'hypnos', meaning sleep). This name has persisted although we now know that hypnosis is not the same as sleep.

Interest in hypnosis continued in the last quarter of the 19th century mainly in France, through the work of Liébault in Nancy and Bernheim in Strasbourg. They came to believe that hypnosis produced its effects by suggestion acting on and through the patient's mind, and that it was a normal state between sleep and full consciousness. Later, Freud used hypnosis but then abandoned it in favour of his own technique of psychoanalysis; this was a setback to the therapeutic use of hypnosis, although it was employed to a limited extent in both World Wars, and in Korea, for treating shell-shocked or battle-weary personnel. Since then there has been growing interest in the use of hypnosis in medical conditions in Britain and Europe, as well as North America and Australia, and the work of Maher-Loughnan *et al.* (1962) in the treatment of asthma with self-hypnosis stimulated many clinicians to use hypnosis for all kinds of psychosomatic illness.

It is, however, not as widely used as it should be, probably because it is more time-consuming than using drugs. There is also a lingering prejudice against hypnosis because of the activities of stage hypnotists, and of others who use it with an inadequate grounding in psychology or medicine. But used in the form of self-hypnosis it has a great deal to offer in increasing patients' confidence and morale, and in establishing rapport between patient and therapist.

Hypnotherapeutic approaches: general principles

The altered state of consciousness which we call hypnosis enables the patient to achieve a deeper level of mental and physical relaxation than is possible in full consciousness; it is not, therefore, sleep and there is no loss of consciousness. There is increased suggestibility in hypnosis but this is limited – people will only accept suggestions which appear sensible and reasonable; anything else is likely to be ineffective and potentially damaging to the therapist–patient relationship, though in practice there is usually no problem provided there has been full discussion with the patient about the aims and expectations of treatment. The heightened attention of the patient in hypnosis is progressively narrowed down to what is being said by the therapist, which gives added force to any suggestions which are being made. People are referred for hypnotherapy because they want to change in some way – for example, reduce general anxiety, lose an unpleasant symptom, or alter behaviour which they feel is unsuited to their pattern of life. Therefore they will usually accept suggestions directed to this aim; motivation is of course immensely important, but on the whole most sick people want to get better.

It has now become accepted by most clinicians who use hypnotherapy that self-hypnosis is desirable in the great majority of cases. Its advantages are obvious: there are more frequent treatments, as the patients in effect learn to treat themselves; it is less time-consuming for the therapist; it lessens patient–therapist dependency but greatly increases rapport; and lastly (and perhaps most importantly) it is a form of self-help which raises morale and increases the confidence of the patient, which must surely be the aim of all treatment in this field. Self-hypnosis is easily taught to those who are well motivated towards recovery.

It is important that in medical conditions with mainly physical symptoms organic illness should first be excluded by careful history-taking, physical examination and further investigations as required. If hypnosis is thought to be a suitable approach to treatment, a full discussion and explanation of this with the patient (or parents of a child) is essential; more treatment failures are due to lack of this factor than to any other, as misconceptions about hypnosis are common and must be removed at the start. It is not usual to induce hypnosis at the first session; it is better to allow patients to go home with an information sheet couched in simple terms so that they can decide at leisure whether or not to take on the discipline of this form of treatment. They should also be asked to keep a diary of the frequency and severity of their symptoms.

If patient and therapist are agreed that hypnotherapy is desirable then induction of hypnosis can take place at the second session, using a non-authoritarian, passive technique, it being made clear to patients beforehand that they will be *helped* into hypnosis and not *made* to do anything, that they are in fact in control all the time, with their minds alert even if they feel very relaxed. Properly prepared in this way, induction should not take more than three or four minutes with deepening procedures, if required, taking a few more minutes. With the patient in hypnosis, suggestions of general relaxation and lessening of tension are made, and that deeper relaxation will occur at later sessions. After coming out of hypnosis the patient's experience is discussed, and if all is satisfactory hypnosis is reinduced and self-hypnosis taught as a post-hypnotic suggestion (PHS): that is, a suggestion made during hypnosis that something specific will happen at a future time. It is suggested that when the PHS or signal is used self-hypnosis will occur, will last approximately 15 minutes, and will then end automatically and spontaneously. Signals might include eye-fixation and a reverse count from ten to zero, or the repetition of words such as 'calm' or 'rest'. The patient is then asked to use the signal in the consulting room and go into self-hypnosis, after which reinforcing suggestions of mental and physical relaxation are given on the lines of Hartland's ego-strengthening routine (Hartland 1971). This procedure, described in chapter 2 of the present book, includes suggestions of reduced tension and anxiety, greater ability to think calmly and clearly, increasing self-confidence and ability to cope with life's problems, and improved sleep pattern, all tailored to suit the patient's needs.

Reinforcement sessions are repeated at weekly intervals for two or three weeks, with the patient practising self-hypnosis at home at least once a day. Diaries are discussed at each treatment session, the patient's attention being drawn to any improvements. In clinical work it is most important to concentrate on a lessening of *general* tension first, without mention of specific symptoms. To suggest early removal of the latter is likely to strain the patient's credulity and in fact seldom works; they should be dealt with later, and usually as the level of tension and anxiety is reduced the specific symptoms improve spontaneously. The patient should be told that improvement is likely to take time and that it seldom goes up in a straight line – it is more usual for it to be in a series of steps, and there may at times be backward ones (temporary setbacks) which must be accepted and coped with. The intervals between the reinforcing sessions are gradually increased, the patient taking on more and more of the treatment as time goes on. Daily self-hypnosis should continue for at least three months after the first signs of improvement, and then the number of self-treatments can slowly be reduced in line with progress. For most complaints of a mainly somatic nature, patients need about six sessions in the first two months and about twelve sessions in the first year, but there is obviously considerable variation according to need. Maher-Loughnan (1980) found that 75% of 103 patients with a wide variety of psychosomatic conditions had begun to improve within twelve weeks of starting self-hypnosis, and 72% had achieved complete remission or 80% improvement within one year. Patients under 20 responded more quickly, and there was no difference between sexes. It has been suggested that patients may report symptoms as improving when they are not, in order to please the therapist: in fact, in the author's opinion, they do not want the therapist to overrate progress and phase out treatment too soon. Follow-up should continue until the patient no longer feels the need for support, after which the way is left open for treatment to be resumed if symptoms recur.

Choice of cases

The symptoms must be severe enough to warrant the discipline of daily self-hypnosis. Patients need not be deep-trance subjects, as with mainly somatic symptoms satisfactory results can be obtained with only a light depth of hypnosis, but in cases where psychological problems are clearly important, at least a medium depth is required. Children aged 9 and over, provided they are reasonably intelligent, and have sufficiently troublesome symptoms to motivate them to use self-hypnosis regularly, make good subjects (see Chapter 10 concerning applications to children). Cases of psychosis are best avoided, and those with a significant element of depression should be started on suitable antidepressive treatment before self-hypnosis is introduced: if anxiety is treated first the depression may be accentuated.

It will thus be clear that medical conditions with a marked psychological element – that is, psychosomatic illness – respond best to hypnotherapy as outlined above, and the more important of these conditions will now be discussed.

Specific applications: procedures and research findings

The respiratory system

Asthma

This is a condition characterized by variations over short periods of time in resistance to air-flow in the bronchi. These episodes occur in people who are over-responsive to environmental stimuli, and are usually accompanied by expiratory wheezing, but a cough may be the only symptom, especially in children. More than 10% of the population in Britain will give a history of wheezing at some time in their lives, usually with a virus infection causing temporary narrowing due to increased reactivity of the bronchi. A diagnosis of asthma requires that the symptoms should be sustained or recurrent, and the prevalence in the population is then approximately 5%. These vulnerable individuals have developed or inherited a liability to respond in a certain way not only to external irritants but also to the stresses and strains of everyday life.

Asthmatic attacks may be precipitated by exercise, allergy (hypersensitivity), infection and emotion; as the attack develops, constriction of the bronchi occurs due to contraction of muscle in their walls. There is also swelling of the mucous membrane lining the bronchi, with secretion of mucus into the lumen with inflammatory cells, all of which causes further obstruction to air-flow. The common allergens are pollens especially those of grass, also moulds, house dust mites, and animal fur and dander, but mechanical irritants such as dust and fumes may also cause wheezing. Infections causing attacks are usually due to viruses, but bacteria may also be involved. Emotion as a factor is difficult to assess, but no one can be wholly objective about their own wheezing, so anxiety is a common and powerful aggravating factor in the development of the asthmatic attack. Whatever the immediate trigger, early breathing discomfort causes a vicious circle of anxiety, more wheezing, more anxiety; and the hyperventilation (overbreathing) which accompanies the anxiety complicates and aggravates the situation. Rees (1956) studied 441 cases of asthma with 321 controls, and found that in the former group there was a significantly higher incidence of marked anxiety, timidity, sensitiveness and obsessional traits. In children, faulty parental attitudes tended to precipitate asthma in the child, the commonest being over-protection; rejection and perfectionism were less common. In a high proportion of cases these personality traits and attitudes antedated the onset of asthma. The common factors precipitating attacks were anxiety with tension, pleasurable excitement, frustration, anger, resentment, humiliation, depression, laughter, guilt feelings, joy and elation. In the asthma group as a whole, psychological factors were aetiologically important in 70%, infective factors in 68%, and allergic factors in 36%.

It seems therefore that asthma is due to a combination of excessive irritability of nerves supplying the bronchi, and the release of various broncho-constrictor substances (e.g. histamine) from mast cells, macrophages and other inflammatory cells (Barnes 1987). Anxiety, suggestion and conditioning have all been shown to play a part, singly or together, in the aetiology of asthma (Cohen 1971). The bronchial tree in asthma is certainly hyperactive, and Groen (1976) quotes the studies of Dekker and himself which showed that wheezing could be induced by exposing such patients to situations which had a special emotional meaning for them. These attacks produced in the laboratory were indistinguishable from those precipitated by inhalation of allergens, or from the patients' 'spontaneous' attacks.

More than one factor may cause asthma at any one time: for example, attacks may start as a result of allergy or infection, and persist through anxiety and fear generated by the unpleasantness of the illness; or psychological factors may be of equal importance right from the start. Therefore a comprehensive history must be taken in each case, covering the following:

1 Family – relationships with and between parents, and with sibs; also school records and so on.

2 Marriage state – if applicable; relationships with spouse, children, or step-children; housing problems, if any.
3 Bereavements – especially if recent.
4 Job satisfaction; relationship with colleagues; possible financial problems.
5 Previous illnesses – especially chest infections; possible allergy; possible depression.

If the above questions are asked, a reasonably accurate picture of the patient's life-style and problems can be obtained.

Management of asthma During the past 25 years the treatment of asthma has become increasingly pharmacological, with less attention being paid to its psychological aspects. In acute asthma, drug treatment is essential and life-saving, and as regards long-term maintenance it has improved the quality of life for many. But side-effects do occur in those on long-term steroids, and the mortality from asthma rose annually in the UK by an average of 4.7% in the 5–34 age-group between 1974 and 1984, the increase being greater among male patients (Burney 1986). Failure by patient or doctor to recognize the severity of an attack is the chief reason given for the change, but this can hardly be the whole answer as general clinical management has not changed for many years. The missing factor in treatment could well be insufficient attention to the emotional side of the patient's illness. Failure to provide retraining could also be important, where asthmatic breathing is a conditioned response. For all the reasons given earlier, self-hypnosis as used by Maher-Loughnan *et al.* (1962) is uniquely placed to help the asthmatic patient; it also facilitates the exploration of sensitive material in the reinforcement sessions if this is necessary, and provides a method of retraining. It is essentially *preventive* treatment: it is not for use during the acute attack when all available measures including steroids must be used. The time to consider the introduction of self-hypnosis is ideally when a firm diagnosis of asthma has been made and it seems likely that long-time steroid maintenance treatment may be required. It does seem that many patients become 'hooked' on steroids, and then the results with hypnotherapy are less satisfactory, although it may help to reduce steroid dosage. As emphasized earlier, general reduction in tension and anxiety with ego-strengthening, and feedback of improvement as it occurs, to restore the patients' self-confidence and coping abilities must be the aim at the start. Direct symptom removal should at all times be avoided, as to suggest to an asthmatic patient that he is not wheezing or 'tight', when in fact he is, will almost certainly reduce respiratory drive; the author has seen marked deterioration occur from this practice.

Outcome studies In the first controlled study of the use of *self*-hypnosis in asthma, Maher-Loughnan *et al.* (1962) showed its superiority in reducing the frequency and severity of attacks in 27 cases of asthma, as compared with 28 controls given the latest isoprenaline inhaler (Medihaler), the trial lasting six months. In the British Tuberculosis Association (1968) multi-centre trial on 252 moderate or severe asthmatic patients, independent clinical assessors considered that 59% of the self-hypnosis group improved, as compared with 43% of those taught relaxation breathing exercises by the same physicians; this trial lasted one year and there was continuing improvement in both groups in the second six months, more especially in the female hypnosis group. Physicians experienced in hypnosis obtained better results than those who were not. Air-flow measurements in these trials could only be done once a month; this is not adequate, but subjective assessment by diary-keeping, of frequency and severity of attacks and use of bronchodilators, does give a sufficiently accurate record of progress in the great majority of cases. Maher-Loughnan (1970) described the treatment of 173 successive cases of asthma with self-hypnosis over a six-year period: 82% were much improved or remitted entirely. The present author in an unpublished series of 70 cases of perennial asthma in 1972 found that 27% were relieved of their symptoms or very much improved, and a further 36% significantly improved, using self-hypnosis. In 30 cases emotional factors were thought to be especially important and 67% of these did well; patients under 50, and those who were medium-level or deep hypnotic subjects, did best. This series showed the less satisfactory results in patients already committed to steroids, and this was confirmed by Collison (1975). In his series 121 cases were treated with self-hypnosis; 21% became free of attacks, a further 33% had a good response with worthwhile decrease in frequency and severity of asthma, or a decrease in drug requirements; and half of the 46% who had a poor response had a marked subjective improvement in well-being. Forty-four out of 56 who had a nil or poor response were on continuous steroids. More recently Morrison (1988), in a careful study of 16 asthmatic patients, 12 of whom had suffered for over ten years, found that after one year of hypnotherapy with self-hypnosis, there was a fall in admissions to hospital from 44 in the year before starting therapy to 13 in the year after; duration of stay was reduced for 13 patients by 249 days; and prednisolone was withdrawn in 6 and reduced in 8 (increased in none).

Discussion   The British Tuberculosis Association (1968) concluded that it was hard to separate psychological triggers from the others, since in the Pavlovian sense most, including allergic triggers, have some element of conditioning attached to them. 'The view that a daily self-hypnotic regimen replaces old habits by new conditioning would explain the uniformity of responses to treatment of asthma, whatever the trigger.' There has, however, been a growing feeling for some years, particularly amongst those who are interested in the treatment of both asthma and hyperventilation (see below), that the latter may play a much more important part in the developing asthmatic attack than had been previously realized; it can cause broncho-constriction in those with hyperactive air-ways, due to cooling and probably also to an increased intake of allergens or other airborne irritants (Clarke and Gibson 1980). It also makes respiration less efficient by shifting the pattern of breathing from the diaphragm to the upper thorax.

Asthma has been dealt with at length in this chapter not only because it is the best documented of the psychosomatic illnesses treatable by hypnotherapy but because it is a potentially dangerous condition and exemplifies the many problems created by multi-factorial illnesses. Furthermore, the principles of treatment outlined above are applicable to other similar illnesses.

Chronic hyperventilation

The term 'hyperventilation' means breathing in excess of bodily needs, and it is the natural reaction to fear and anxiety, stemming as it does originally from primitive man's 'fight or flight' mechanism. We still have this reaction to unpleasant, frightening, or worrying situations, but as the increased breathing is often, in modern life, not followed by physical activity, it is inappropriate, and leads to the breathing out of too much carbon dioxide (CO_2) from the body so that the partial pressure of CO_2 in the blood (PCO_2) falls. This causes a change in the acid–alkali balance (pH) in the blood towards the alkaline (respiratory alkalosis) which can have profound effects, especially on the nervous system directly, but also by causing some constriction of the muscle in the walls of the cerebral arteries which produces a slight decrease in oxygen supply to the brain (Lum 1976, 1981, 1987). A wide variety of symptoms are produced by these changes in the pH of the blood, as any part of the nervous system may be affected, and it is this range of apparently unrelated symptoms which gives the clue to the diagnosis; this can be confirmed by capnography which is the continuous monitoring of PCO_2 levels while watching the responses on the tracing to stimuli such as forced voluntary overbreathing and thinking of stressful situations (Nixon and Freeman 1988). These stimuli cause a significant lowering of PCO_2, and the subsequent recovery to resting levels is slower than in normal subjects. Hyperventilation produces a breathing pattern which is rapid, shallow, unstable and irregular; it is also inefficient as it is largely confined to the upper chest, neglecting the use of the diaphragm, and it is commonly interrupted by sighs or yawns. However, it may be quite unobtrusive and difficult to spot, so the diagnosis is often missed, very much to the detriment of the patient who may become involved in uncomfortable investigations and unnecessary treatments to no avail. A combination of self-hypnosis with relaxed diaphragmatic breathing is the best way of tackling this problem, coupled with a full explanation to the patient of the mechanisms involved (Wilkinson 1988). This is most important because the symptoms, which are real and caused by physiological changes, have often previously been dismissed as 'nerves', or even as malingering, and this merely increases the patient's apprehension and frustration leading to more hyperventilation, a typical 'vicious circle'. Hyperventilation is also discussed in Chapter 3 in relation to hypnosis and anxiety.

It is of interest, and perhaps significant, that the symptoms of hyperventilation are identical to those of the post-viral fatigue syndrome (myalgic encephalomyopathy or ME), although muscle fatigue is more prominent in the latter. The symptoms include headache, dizziness, blurring of vision, 'pins and needles' of extremities or face, palpitation (often with rapid pulse), chest pain, inability to get enough air (commonly at rest), sighing and yawning, constriction in the throat, belching, heartburn, abdominal distension, bowel disturbance (usually looseness), muscle cramps or twitching, tension in neck, shoulders and back, poor concentration, anxiety, feelings of unreality, agoraphobia and panic attacks. It is possible that many such patients developed the habit of hyperventilation after their initial viral infection – a common occurrence and one which would explain the persistence of symptoms. A combination of rest with graded exercise, self-hypnosis, and breathing control exercises shows encouraging results in a high percentage of these patients, and this is important because no conventional treatment is available and they are liable to involvement in useless and often expensive therapies.

The cardiovascular system

The problems to be considered in this section include chest pain, palpitation not attributable to serious heart disease, the re-education of the patient who has recovered from an attack of coronary thrombosis, and raised blood pressure (hypertension).

Angina
Anxiety, usually through the mechanism of hyperventilation, can produce chest pain very similar to that of true angina of effort (Evans and Lum 1977), and in some cases can aggravate the latter (Freeman and Nixon 1985).

Palpitation
Palpitation is the consciousness of one's heart beating, and is commonly caused by disturbed and sometimes irregular heart rhythm, but also the too rapid pulse rate of tachycardia. Again, anxiety may cause or aggravate the situation, acting through an imbalance in the autonomic nervous system, and associated with an increase in adrenalin production.

Post-coronary thrombosis rehabilitation
Patients who have had a coronary thrombosis and who combine anxiety about their health with an inability to alter their life-style to meet their changed circumstances, are a perennial problem in cardiology. The position was well summarized by Nixon (1976) with the Human Function Curve (Fig. 8.1), which applies also to all whose circumstances drive them into a state of exhaustion.

Hypertension
Similar problems face patients with raised blood pressure who must learn to relax mentally and physically, and adjust their way of life to the point where their pressure remains in or near the normal range. Deabler *et al.* (1973) found a significant lowering of pressures in six previously untreated patients and nine patients stabilized on antihypertensive medication, when treated in sessions including muscular relaxation followed by hypnosis; a control group given no treatment of any kind, but asked to attend hospital as out-patients, showed no improvement. Blood pressure levels were reduced by relaxation but brought within the normal range by hypnosis; self-hypnosis was taught after four of the eight sessions to maintain the improvement, which included a decrease in symptoms such as anxiety, headache and insomnia.

All the above cardiac conditions benefit from self-hypnosis and breathing control, as this will help to lower arousal levels, so that the patient can exert more control and recover from what has previously been a fruitless and exhausting struggle to change deeply rooted habits (King 1988).

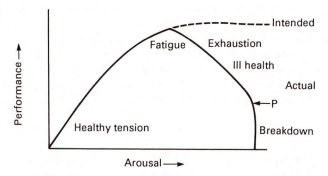

P – The point at which even minimal arousal may precipitate
a breakdown

Figure 8.1 'Human function curve' showing the effects on human functioning of increasing levels of arousal (Based on Nixon, 1976)

The nervous system

Migraine

Migraine affects approximately 15–25% of the population and is characterized by intermittent, often severe headache, commonly starting on one side of the head and spreading to involve the whole. It is usually associated with nausea, and sometimes vomiting, and in about 10% of cases is preceded by visual disturbances. Various causes have been attributed to it, including allergy, hormonal changes and emotional factors. It is therefore a multi-factorial illness and in one group of patients hyperventilation is a factor; this is not altogether surprising as constriction of the cerebral arteries is thought to be the first stage in the development of a migraine headache, followed rapidly by dilatation of the arteries. Treatment usually consists of pain-killing tablets of various kinds, together with an ergot derivative, ergotamine, which has a powerful constricting effect on blood vessels. Such treatment is variable in its effects and often unsatisfactory. Anderson *et al.* (1975) used self-hypnosis with ego-strengthening and suggestions of gradual improvement in 47 randomly allocated patients with migraine, the controls being given prochlorperazine (Stemetil), a drug mainly used for vertigo, nausea and vomiting; there were monthly assessments and an independent evaluation after one year of continuous care. The number of attacks, and the number of patients who suffered blinding attacks, were significantly lower in the hypnosis group as compared with previous treatment: prochlorperazine seemed as effective as the previous treatment.

Alladin (1988) has reviewed the subject of hypnotherapy and migraine, comparing the hypnotic techniques of induced warmth, glove anaesthesia (numbness), and direct suggestion of improvement, with a group trained in relaxation only. Fifty sufferers (ten per group) were investigated over ten weekly sessions, augmented in the treatment groups by 'home practice' using audio tapes; the fifth group were waiting-list control patients. There was a thirteen-month follow-up appointment. Warmth was generally more effective than suggestion or numbness, but was superior to relaxation only in frequency and intensity of migraine during treatment, and there were no differences between the groups at follow-up. There was a tendency for the suggestion and numbness groups to relapse in the period before follow-up. All four groups did better than the controls. It is suggested that any procedure that reduces sympathetic arousal will have a direct effect on the neuro-vascular mechanism of migraine. Warmth is a para-sympathetic response, and hypnotic relaxation is well known to reduce levels of arousal. This suggests that this treatment is superior to drugs and that it has no side-effects.

Tinnitus

This is an often distressing condition in which there is intermittent or continuous noise in one or both ears. Its pitch may vary but is commonly described as being 'hissing' or 'whistling'. It is common, especially in the elderly, and very resistant to treatment. Apart from its known association with drugs like quinine and salicylates (aspirin) in big doses, its cause is unknown. The persistence of the noise and its interference with hearing can lead to considerable tension and frustration. There have been earlier reports of success with hypnotherapy but a controlled trial of 14 patients at Guy's Hospital (Marks *et al.* 1985) produced a good result in only one patient, although 36% were able to tolerate the symptoms better. The patients were randomly assigned to three forms of hypnosis:

1 Hetero- and self-hypnosis with ego-strengthening and imagery related to the subjective nature of the patients' tinnitus, aimed at a decrease in perception of the volume of sound (e.g. turning down the valve of a gas cylinder);
2 Hetero- and self-hypnosis with ego-strengthening only;
3 Hetero- and self-hypnosis with ego-strengthening and imagery of banks of switches on a telephone switchboard and operating these to produce a decrease in the tinnitus.

In spite of the disappointing results of this trial it is probably worth trying some type of visual imagery with hypnosis, but if no improvement is evident after two or three sessions, success is unlikely.

Skin conditions

Warts

These are viral in origin and respond to suggestions under hypnosis that they will disappear. Sinclair-Gieben and Chalmers (1959) treated 14 patients, concentrating treatment to one side of the body, the other side acting as control. Nine of the 10 in whom medium or deep levels of hypnosis could be achieved lost their warts on the treated side, those on the control side remaining unchanged. In this series the warts appeared to shrivel up and disappear without scarring, and it seems probable that the effect was related to alterations in blood-flow via the autonomic nervous system. Condylomata acuminata (venereal warts) which occur on the external genitalia are caused by a virus similar to the one which causes skin warts. Hypnosis was used by Ewin (1974) in four cases with complete success, the emotional aspects of the condition being dealt with before suggestions of cure were given. Straatmeyer and Rhodes (1983) describe the successful treatment of a 48-year-old woman with a background of stress, in four sessions, suggesting anaesthesia coming into each wart like a painless injection with itching and burning diminishing; then suggestions that the warts were shrivelling and shrinking, drying up and beginning to disappear, and that before long they would be gone completely; and lastly that her confidence was growing, that the warts were indeed leaving and that soon she would be free of them for ever. The problem in assessing treatment for warts is that they can and do disappear spontaneously but it may be that hypnosis helps by reducing blood-flow in the tiny skin vessels, thus cutting off nourishment to them. Gibson in Chapter 3 of this book provides further discussion of hypnosis and warts.

Eczema

This is a skin condition, occurring mainly in allergic subjects, in which inflammation of the skin occurs, often with very severe itching. The subsequent scratching leads to soreness and often 'weeping' of the skin, with considerable discomfort and frequent loss of sleep. Various medicaments have been tried with varying success, the most successful being steroid creams or ointments, but it is undesirable to use these long-term if it can be avoided. Hypnotherapy can be used in four ways: (1) as support, using ego-strengthening; (2) direct suggestion of reduction in itching, burning, anxiety and insomnia; (3) the suggestion that as soon as the patients' fingers touch their skin they will be aware of this, even at night, and therefore will be able to prevent scratching; and (4) that there will be improved blood-flow through the skin, with better nourishment causing healing and a decrease in the sensitivity of the nerves. If there are emotional conflicts these must be explored and resolved if possible as they are potent causes of keeping the condition going. Hartland (1971) has given an excellent review of this problem and concludes that the results of treatment range from excellent to poor, an opinion with which the present author would agree.

Gastrointestinal conditions

Peptic ulcer (gastric and duodenal)

Ulcers of this kind represent a break in the mucous membrane lining the stomach and duodenum, giving symptoms of upper abdominal pain commonly relieved by food or antacids, and by drugs such as cimetidine (Tagamet) or ranitidine (Zantac) which reduce the production of acid gastric juice; these drugs therefore have a powerful healing effect. Smoking tends to interfere with healing. After the ulcer has healed it is liable to recur, especially the duodenal type, unless cimetidine or ranitidine are continued as maintenance treatment. Colgan *et al.* (1988) studied 30 patients with rapidly relapsing duodenal ulceration whose ulcers had healed with ranitidine; the drug was then continued for a further ten weeks during which time half of the patients received hypnotherapy by random selection, the two groups being matched for age, sex, smoking habits and alcohol consumption. Follow-up of both groups was continued for twelve months after the ranitidine was stopped. After one year, 8 (53%) of the hypnotherapy patients, and 15 (100%) of the non-hypnotherapy patients had relapsed. The hypnosis group was given seven sessions plus an audiotape for self-hypnosis; the other group were seen as often but received no hypnotherapy: after the ten weeks and the stopping of ranitidine, all were reviewed over three months, with the active group receiving hypnotherapy at each visit. All subjects had an endoscopy at the end of the study, or sooner if symptoms recurred. This study shows that hypnotherapy is helpful in maintaining remission in patients with duodenal ulcers who are particularly prone to relapse. The authors suggest that it may operate by increasing 'coping' abilities, thus reducing stress, or that hypnotically induced relaxation may reduce gastric acid secretion, probably by correcting an imbalance in the autonomic nervous system.

Irritable bowel syndrome
This is a condition in which there is abdominal pain or discomfort associated with a disturbed bowel habit, but with no apparent organic disease. Feelings of abdominal distension are common and there may be either constipation or bowel looseness. It affects up to 15% of the population, and 75% respond to medication designed to reduce muscle spasm in the bowel, together with substances to increase the bulk of the faeces. There is frequently obvious anxiety, and sympathetic handling with explanation of bowel function is helpful for many but 25% remain inconvenienced and uncomfortable. Whorwell *et al.* (1984) have done the first controlled trial of hypnotherapy for this condition, studying 30 patients with long-standing refractory illness. The subjects were randomly assigned to treatment with either hypnotherapy or psychotherapy and a placebo. Hypnotherapy consisted of seven half-hour sessions of decreasing frequency over a three-month period, with an audiotape for daily self-hypnosis after the third session. Suggestions were directed solely at general relaxation and control of bowel movement, with no attempt at analysis. (Before hypnosis the patient was given a simple account of intestinal smooth-muscle physiology.) In hypnosis, feelings of induced warmth in a hand resting on the abdomen was related to asserting control over bowel function. Reinforcement by visualization was used if the patient had this ability, and the sessions ended with ego-strengthening suggestions. Patients in the control group received a placebo (not specified) and seven half-hour sessions of supportive psychotherapy from the same physician; these included discussion of symptoms and an exploration of any emotional problems and stressful life-events. All patients were asked to keep diary cards recording daily the frequency and severity of abdominal pain and distension, and any disturbance of bowel habit. At the end of treatment, symptoms were either mild or absent in all hypnotherapy patients, the difference between the groups becoming significant by the fourth week of treatment for bowel habit, abdominal distension and well-being, and by the fifth week for pain. The control group showed a small but significant improvement in all symptoms except bowel habit. Harvey *et al.* (1989) studied 33 patients with refractory irritable bowel syndrome, using four 40-minute sessions of hypnotherapy over seven weeks; the patients were also taught self-hypnosis for twice-daily use at home. Seventeen were given group and 16 individual therapy. Twenty of the 33 improved, 11 becoming almost symptom-free, and improvement was maintained up to three months without further formal treatment. Hypnotherapy in groups of up to eight patients was as effective as individual therapy. These studies show the value of hypnotherapy

in this troublesome condition, and the problem has been usefully reviewed by Walker (1988).

Terminal illness

Hypnotherapy has been used in the USA for many years to help to alleviate the anxiety and pain associated with illness due to cancer, and with the procedures involved in the treatment of children with leukaemia; it also seems to help with the nauseating effects of chemotherapy. We in the UK have lagged behind in this respect although some general practitioners use it for such patients dying at home. However, Walker *et al*. (1988) studied 14 patients who were suffering severe side-effects from chemotherapy for malignant disease, especially nausea and vomiting which typically worsened after each monthly treatment. After a full history had been taken and rapport established, hypnotherapy was started consisting of two to six sessions of 10–15 minutes each, another 15–20 minutes being devoted to reviewing progress. The patients were trained in 'cue controlled' relaxation and were given an audiotape for use at home. During hypnosis suggestions were made of increasing ability to relax, to be more calm and confident about chemotherapy, and that the patient would achieve a greater degree of control on a moment-to-moment basis, giving a greater ability to cope with the treatment, as the side-effects would become less troublesome and less frequent. When possible the first two or three sessions of hypnotherapy were carried out before the next chemotherapy treatment, the last one as near to it as possible. Most patients received nausea management training while in hypnosis. (Walker 1984); they were helped to experience nausea by means of suitable imagery and suggestion, and then the nausea was alleviated by direct suggestion and gentle abdominal self-massage; this gives the patient practice in eliminating nausea. The conditioned nausea and vomiting improved in 11 and 9 patients respectively, and the pharmacologically induced nausea in 8 and 5 cases respectively; all 14 patients improved as regards insomnia, irritability and anxiety.

Also in the UK, Kraft (1990) has reported the treatment of 12 terminally ill patients in a nursing home, all cases of cancer of various kinds, with an age range of 30–77. All were severely ill and 9 died within nine weeks of starting treatment, which was focused on reduction in anxiety. Kraft made a careful assessment of the personalities of the patients and their stage of adjustment to the prospect of an almost certainly limited future. There were three patients with obsessional personalities who benefited little from hypnotherapy and preferred psychotherapy, but the rest found hypnotherapy very helpful, not only as regards alleviation of anxiety, but also in reducing breathlessness and pain. This was a preliminary study with encouraging results and a larger one is planned (see Kraft, in preparation).

Future developments

The above type of work with terminally ill patients will, one hopes, become more widely used. We are, after all, an ageing population with increasing opportunity to develop cancer and other malignant conditions; also AIDS looms over us. It would be good if such treatment could be started at an earlier stage in the illness. Since the work of Hans Selye in the 1950s (Selye 1956), it has become increasingly clear that psychological factors can affect the immune system; and the Simontons (Simonton *et al.* 1978) taught their patients to replace depression and despair with hope and anticipation, using 'relaxation and mental imagery'. This involved very positive images of white blood cells attacking and destroying cancer cells weakened by radiotherapy or chemotherapy, then flushing them out of the body – that is, this technique was used in conjunction with conventional treatments. They also discussed mind–body relationships with their patients and strategies for coping with stress, thus increasing confidence and self-esteem. They do not describe this method as 'hypnosis', but in the present author's opinion there seems little doubt that most of their patients achieved an altered state of consciousness akin to hypnosis. At any rate it improved the quality of life for most of the patients, and the median survival times for breast, bowel and lung cancers doubled as compared with the US national average. Even better results were obtained by Newton (1982) at the Newton Center for Clinical Hypnosis in Los Angeles, where hypnosis and self-hypnosis were used in a working association with oncologists. This work emphasizes the importance of using hypnosis as an adjunct to conventional treatment; not only is the combination likely to be more effective but hypnosis will become more acceptable to clinicians as a result. Newton (1982) has written the Introduction to the 25th Anniversary Commemorative Volume of the American Journal of Clinical Hypnosis (1982–3), and a description of his work occurs in the body of that volume which includes papers on other aspects of the problem and is required reading for anyone working in this field.

For medical conditions in general, the use of hypnosis is likely to increase, mainly in those illnesses with a significant psychosomatic element. The public is becoming increasingly unhappy about the long-term use of tranquillizing drugs, and it is interesting that in the author's consulting hypnotherapy practice 20–25% of patients are self-referred, even though they come with doctors' letters. In other words, the idea has come from the patient (or the parent of a child) in the first place, very often because a relative or a friend has previously been treated successfully with hypnosis. There is also an increasingly positive attitude to good health, which welcomes methods of self-help such as self-hypnosis.

References

Alladin, A.(1988) Hypnosis in the treatment of severe chronic migraine, in M. Heap (ed.) *Hypnosis: Current Clinical, Experimental and Forensic Practices*, London: Croom Helm.
American Journal of Clinical Hypnosis (1982–3) Special Issue: Hypnosis and Cancer 25, 2 and 3.
Anderson, J.A.D., Basker, M.A. and Dalton, R. (1975) Migraine and hypnotherapy, *International Journal of Clinical and Experimental Hypnosis* 23: 48–58.
Barnes, P.J. (1987) Mechanisms of asthma, *Medicine International* 37: 1522–5.
British Tuberculosis Association (1968) Hypnosis for asthma – a controlled trial, *British Medical Journal* 4: 71–6.

Burney, P.G.J. (1986) Asthma mortality in England and Wales: evidence for a further increase, 1974–1984, *Lancet*, 9 August, 323–6.

Clarke, P.S. and Gibson, J.R. (1980) Asthma, hyperventilation and emotion, *Australian Family Physician* 9: 715–19.

Cohen, S.I. (1971) Psychological factors in asthma: a review of their aetiological and therapeutic significance, *Post-graduate Medical Journal* 47: 533–9.

Colgan, S.M., Faragher, E.B. and Whorwell, P.J. (1988) Controlled trial of hypnotherapy in relapse prevention of duodenal ulceration, *Lancet*, 11 June, 1 (8598): 1299–1300.

Collison, D.R. (1975) Which asthmatic patients should be treated with hypnotherapy? *Medical Journal of Australia* 1: 776–81.

Deabler, H.L., Fidel, E., Dillenkoffer, R.L. and Elder, S.T. (1973) The use of relaxation and hypnosis in lowering high blood pressure, *American Journal of Clinical Hypnosis* 16: 75–83.

Evans, D.W.E. and Lum, L.C. (1977) Hyperventilation: an important cause of pseudo-angina, *Lancet*, 22 January, 155–7.

Ewin, D.M. (1974) Condyloma acuminatum: successful treatment of four cases by hypnosis, *American Journal of Clinical Hypnosis* 17: 73–83.

Freeman, L.J. and Nixon, P.G.F. (1985) Chest pain and the hyperventilation syndrome – some aetiological considerations, *Postgraduate Medical Journal* 61: 957–61.

Groen, J.J. (1976) Present state of the psychosomatic approach to bronchial asthma, in O. Hill (ed.) *Modern Trends in Psychosomatic Medicine, Vol. 3*, London: Butterworth.

Hartland, J. (1971) *Medical and Dental Hypnosis and its Clinical Applications*, London: Baillière Tindall.

Harvey, R.F., Hinton, R.A., Gunary R.M. and Barry, R.E. (1989) Individual and group hypnotherapy in treatment of refractory irritable bowel syndrome, *Lancet* 1: 424–5.

King, J.C. (1988) Hyperventilation – a therapist's point of view: discussion paper, *Journal of the Royal Society of Medicine* 81: 532–6.

Kraft, T. (1990) Use of hypnotherapy in anxiety management in the terminally ill: a preliminary study, *British Journal of Experimental and Clinical Hypnosis* 7: 27–33.

—— (in preparation) Hypnotherapy for the terminally ill: review of the first thirty cases, *Proceedings of the Seventh Annual Conference of the British Society of Experimental and Clinical Hypnosis*.

Lum, L.C. (1976) The syndrome of chronic habitual hyperventilation, in O. Hill (ed.) *Modern Trends in Psychosomatic Medicine, Vol. 3*, London: Butterworth.

—— (1981) Hyperventilation and anxiety states, *Journal of the Royal Society of Medicine* 74: 1–4.

—— (1987) Hyperventilation syndromes in medicine and psychiatry: a review, *Journal of the Royal Society of Medicine* 80: 229–31.

Maher-Loughnan, G.P. (1970) Hypnosis and autohypnosis for the treatment of asthma, *International Journal of Clinical and Experimental Hypnosis* 18: 1–14.

—— (1980) Hypnosis: Clinical application of hypnosis in medicine, *British Journal of Hospital Medicine* 23: 447–55.

Maher-Loughnan, G.P., Macdonald, N., Mason, A.A. and Fry, L. (1962) Controlled trial of hypnosis in the symptomatic treatment of asthma, *British Medical Journal* 2: 371–6.

Marks, N.J., Karle, H. and Onisiphorou, C. (1985) A controlled trial of hypnotherapy in tinnitus, *Clinical Otolaryngology* 10: 43–6.

Morrison, J.B. (1988) Chronic asthma and improvement with relaxation induced by hypnotherapy, *Journal of the Royal Society of Medicine* 81: 701–4.

Newton, B.W. (1982) The use of hypnosis in the treatment of cancer patients, *American Journal of Clinical Hypnosis* 25: 104–13.

Nixon, P.G.F. (1976) The human function curve: with special reference to cardiovascular disorders, Part I and Part II, *Practitioner* 217, 765–70 and 935–44.

Nixon, P.G.F. and Freeman, L.J. (1988) The think test: a further technique to elicit hyperventilation, *Journal of the Royal Society of Medicine* 81: 277–9.

Rees, L. (1956) Physical and emotional factors in bronchial asthma, *Journal of Psychosomatic Research* 1: 98–114.

Selye, H. (1956) *The Stress of Life*, New York: McGraw-Hill.

Simonton, O.C., Simonton, S.M. and Creighton, J.L. (1978) *Getting Well Again*, New York: Bantam Books (UK edition 1986).

Sinclair-Gieben, A.H.C. and Chalmers, D. (1959) Treatment of warts by hypnosis, *Lancet* 2: 480–82.

Straatmeyer, A.J. and Rhodes, N.R. (1983) Condylomata acuminata: results of treatment using hypnosis, *Journal of American Academy of Dermatology* 9: 434–6.

Walker, L.G. (1984) Hypnotherapy for aversion to chemotherapy in patients with lymphoid tumours, in M. Heap (ed.) *Proceedings of the First Annual Conference of the British Society of Experimental and Clinical Hypnosis*.

—— (1988) Hypnosis in the treatment of the irritable-bowel syndrome, in M. Heap (ed.) *Hypnosis: Current Clinical, Experimental and Forensic Practices*, London: Croom Helm.

Walker, L.G., Dawson, A.A., Pollet, S.M., Ratcliffe, M.A. and Hamilton, L. (1988) Hypnotherapy for chemotherapy side-effects, *British Journal of Experimental and Clinical Hypnosis* 5: 79–82.

Whorwell, P.J., Prior, A. and Faragher, E.B. (1984) Controlled trial of hypnotherapy in the treatment of severe refractory irritable-bowel syndrome, *Lancet*, 1 December, 1232–4.

Wilkinson, J.B. (1988) Hyperventilation control techniques in combination with self-hypnosis for anxiety management, in M. Heap (ed.) *Hypnosis: Current Clinical, Experimental and Forensic Practices*, London: Croom Helm.

9

Hypnosis in dentistry

PAULINE E. NICOLAOU

Introduction

Although an appointment with the dentist does not always start with a needle or drill, for many, even the very thought of a check-up and possible filling can be traumatic. It follows that reduction in the level of fear and tension is desirable, increasing the acceptability of dentistry to the patient and resulting in greater job satisfaction for the dental team.

In addition to routine scaling and polishing, X-rays, injections, fillings, crowns, bridges and dentures, the dentist may be called upon to advise patients on a wide range of disorders and conditions. These can include temporomandibular joint pains, bruxism (teeth grinding problems), soft tissue afflictions such as aphthous ulcers, oral herpes, intraoral lichen planus (a disorder of the lining of the mouth) and various lumps and bumps including torus palatinus (natural overgrowth of bone in the centre of the palate in the embryonic stage of development), dental abscesses and malignant lesions. By their very nature certain conditions require treatment that may be uncomfortable, thereby increasing adverse reaction in the patient who may already be in a fairly nervous state, and this may make treatment that much more difficult to carry out.

Difficulties encountered by the dentist in his or her work range from the failed appointment of a worried patient to someone with a fear of bleeding to death. Some people are allergic to local anaesthetic and other materials used in the dental surgery and this increases their fear of pain.

Manifestations of dental fear

Nervous dental patients may show that they are frightened in many different ways:

1 Facial expression: no eye contact, looking unhappy, and so on.

2 Posture in the chair: sinking chin into chest, head twisting away from dentist, or unwillingness to lie back.
3 Feeling faint and sick: history of fainting with injections, and so on.
4 Talkativeness and other delaying tactics.
5 Gagging and coughing or repeated swallowing.
6 Rapid breathing and increased heart rate, which can easily be detected by observing the carotid artery.
7 Clutching at the dentist's arm, not opening the mouth, crying, and even biting the dentist.
8 Attending appointments too late for treatment.

Fear of dentistry is widespread and can be a major problem. A recent survey of patients attending general practices and dental clinics reported that 46% of those asked considered themselves to be anxious in the dental surgery (Green and Green 1985). It is fair to assume that of the patients who do not attend for dental treatment at all, and for those who attend only as an emergency, the anxiety level must be so high as to become a barrier to any form of routine dental care. Education of these patients in maintenance of dental health becomes impossible. Apart from the obvious, there are many strange and various manifestations of dental anxiety. For example, Clarke and Clarke (1987) report a case of hysterical blindness which developed following the administration of a local anaesthetic to a 10-year-old girl; they conclude that anxiety about dental procedures can result in a conversion reaction mimicking neurological disease, as well as the more usual phobic reaction.

Some causes of dental fear

There are many causes of fear of the dentist, the main ones of which are as follows:

1 *Hearsay*: stories of other people's bad experiences which may or may not be exaggerated in the telling; cartoons, television programmes and films depicting a negative expectation.
2 *Fulfilment of meaningless threats*: expecting the dentist to wreak retribution for past childhood wrong-doings ('If you are naughty the dentist will pull all your teeth out!').
3 *Shame and fear of failure*: for example, the patient may be ashamed of the state of the teeth, whether this is justified or not, or will feel foolish in front of the dentist and staff.
4 *Instruments*: imagining procedures that could take place with all the sharp instruments on view (and how many bigger ones are hidden away in cupboards?); the noise of some instruments, such as the drill and suction.
5 *Dominance*: mixed emotions towards power figures in the past, and feelings of helplessness.
6 *'Catastrophic' fears*: for example, having a heart attack in the dental chair, losing teeth, bleeding to death, and numbness and the numbed area not returning to normal.
7 *Pain*: this is the greatest fear. In a survey conducted by Woolgrove *et al.* (1980) on 243 patients, of the 54% who indicated some fear of the dentist, 30%

expressed fear of pain. Wardle (1982) reports that the most common reason given for fear was expectation of pain, whether it had been experienced in previous dental episodes or not.

8 *Maternal anxiety*: this can make the child patient anxious without knowing the reason for it. Anxious mothers may make anxious children. Children's anxieties are discussed in further detail below.

Problems and considerations in pharmacological management

When a patient is introduced to the idea of sedation it is advisable that the dentist consider the ideal basic requirements, namely safety, simplicity, optimal action, analgesia, amnesia (e.g. for difficult operations), acceptability, compatibility and cost (Ryder and Wright 1988). In addition to the usual range of topical (i.e. surface) and local anaesthetic agents other methods to enhance patient tolerance of dentistry can be considered.

From a pharmacological standpoint oral medication prior to the dental appointment can be prescribed, the most common being the benzodiazepines which are also chosen for intravenous sedation in the surgery. There are always disadvantages (Chaplin 1988), the main problem being the possibility of dependence in some patients.

Relative analgesia is the administration of a mixture of nitrous oxide, oxygen and air through a small nasal mask; this promotes a feeling of calm and relaxation. Many dentists have this method available for both children and adults; in some practices it is almost routine. This is a pleasant way of promoting relaxation and reduction of anxiety with no dangers or side-effects. The dentist, unless the patient prefers silence, continues to give reassurance and suggestions of relaxation, comfort and distraction, and in fact the gases may sometimes be dispensed with and the procedure then assumes the form of that carried out with the label of 'hypnosis'.

Gagging

Gagging can be a difficult problem in clinical dentistry, for example in intraoral examinations, taking radiographs, carrying out conservation procedures, and in the wearing of dentures and appliances (with the necessary impression taking). Most dentists deal with this in a reassuring manner, making concessions to the patient's comfort by allowing the patient to sit upright during the impression-taking procedure, giving advice on breathing and swallowing, and being generally sympathetic and encouraging. Where the problem is more severe other methods, such as anaesthetizing the palate or hypnotic procedures, need to be employed.

Children's anxieties and the aetiology of dental anxiety

Improved dental health makes children's dentistry far less of a problem than was the case two or three decades ago. Moderate dental anxiety is a common phenomenon (Feinman 1987) which accompanies normal childhood development experiences such as teething and loss of primary dentition. These events involve a wide range of psychodynamic processes which apparently cause a great proportion of the population to suffer a certain amount of dental anxiety, even before their first exposure to dental treatment. Some personality types are predisposed to a much higher than normal dental anxiety level as a result of these experiences. Dental phobia is an extreme instance of dental anxiety which creates a pattern of total avoidance behaviour even without a previous traumatic experience. Some children may be afraid of being alone with a 'stranger' – the dentist – or they simply may not know how they are expected to behave and feel embarrassed by this.

Kent (1984), researching into fear of dentistry, observed that some psychologists have put forward the hypothesis that prevalent fears reflect a biological predisposition to become anxious about situations and objects that threatened the human species during its evolutionary history. Although fears and phobias of animals are more common than intense fears about dentistry (Kent 1984), it makes sense to postulate that lying on one's back having someone place sharp instruments in the mouth posed a threat in our evolutionary past. Kent goes on to suggest that if fear of the dental setting is associated with a fear of being seriously hurt by another person, then having trust in the dentist to do the utmost not to cause harm is crucial. This view is consistent with the intense loyalty which anxious patients in particular feel for their dentist. On being questioned, about half reported that their anxiety was due to a painful experience in childhood, but the same proportion traced their fears back to the sort of dentist they had as a child, using adjectives such as 'cold', 'disinterested' and 'uncaring'.

The importance of recognizing psychogenic factors

Feinman (1987), a psychiatrist at the Eastman Dental Institute in London, has stressed the importance of the dentist's recognizing when symptoms such as persistent oral or dental pain have a psychogenic origin or are exacerbated by emotional factors such as chronic anxiety or depression. Research (Feinman 1987) suggests that patients with these types of symptoms make about twice as many visits to the dentist.

The problem of non-attendance

This problem may well be on the increase because of changes in the National Health Service such as the imposition of, or the increase in, charges to the patient. Dentists cannot promote the idea of dental health and continuing care to those who are not there to listen! In an excellent detailed survey by Lindsay *et al.* (1987) the conclusion is reached that behavioural management would be especially appropriate for at least fifty per cent of patients to help them accept dentistry without sedation or general anaesthesia, and it goes on to assert that behavioural pain management would be appropriate for almost everybody.

Confidence is everything. In this light, the dentist should give equal attention to both the patient's feelings towards the dental experience and the clinical considerations themselves. Patients usually respond positively to a kind and friendly attitude, when they are informed about what to expect in terms of treatment (necessary or desirable), cost, and the anticipated number of appointments.

General principles

As people with an apprehension of dentistry become more aware of the various means of coping with stress, hypnosis in dentistry is now becoming a realistic alternative to the invasive methods of sedation that are normally available. When placed in context with such aids to pain relief as topical anaesthetic, local anaesthetic, intravenous sedation and general anaesthesia, hypnosis drops into a ready-made niche.

Historical perspective on dental hypnosis

Throughout history the complaint 'toothache' has led people to try to rid themselves of their dental disorders by whatever methods or beliefs happened to be considered right at the time. In medieval days magic charms, witch-craft and pagan religions were commonly associated with the relief of pain and suffering.

Concerning the use of formal hypnotic procedures for such purposes it is customary to take as a historical starting point the activities of Franz Anton Mesmer (1734–1815) and his followers (see Chapter 6 on applications to pain and Chapter 8 on applications to medicine). In 1837 Dr Oudet, in France, is recorded as having made the first tooth extraction using mesmerism. In the USA the first known 'dental' operation using hypnoanalgesia was performed in 1864 by Dr Albert Wheeler to remove a nasal polyp. In March 1890 the *British Dental Journal* reported that under suggestion a total of forty teeth from various patients were removed under hypnotism by a Leeds dentist by the name of Arthur Turner (Bramwell and Turner 1890). In the years to follow, hypnodontic methods were used periodically, ether and chloroform providing alternative anaesthetic methods.

It was not until some way into the 20th century, however, that an interest in dental hypnosis in Britain was revived. In the *British Dental Journal* of 1938 Eric Wookey, a dentist practising in London, published his article 'Uses and Limitations of Dental Treatment'. Together with Harry Radin, an Essex dental surgeon, he lectured extensively throughout Great Britain. They founded the British Society of Dental Hypnosis in 1955 which, in time, attracted people from the medical profession. The group then assumed the name by which it is known today – The British Society of Medical and Dental Hypnosis. The BSMDH now has branches throughout the British Isles with a membership of over one thousand doctors and dentists. There is also a section of the Royal Society of Medicine devoted to the study and dissemination of ideas on hypnosis and psychosomatic conditions in medicine and dentistry.

Aims and rationale of dental hypnosis

The aims of hypnosis in dentistry are to teach the patient to cope with the dental situation to the best of his or her ability. The starting-point is the reduction of fear and tension thereby minimizing the effect of anything that is potentially painful or perceived as such. Reduction of tension cuts down the amount of fear and pain perceived or anticipated; so by producing relaxation and breaking the fear–tension–pain–fear cycle, hypnosis can break the vicious circle at any of the three points. The various ways in which a nervous patient can indicate fearfulness have already been described. Once the cause of the patient's fears has been established, much can be done to satisfy his or her needs, from continuous assurance and information, to the full hypnotic treatment. The treatment options may fall into one of three categories.

1 The routine patient is treated with kindness, consideration and compassion as soon as possible and commensurate with good clinical dentistry. No overt hypnosis is necessary or planned unless difficult or time-consuming procedures are to be undertaken.
2 If the patient manifests any outstanding symptoms of nervousness or provides a history of unduly sensitive teeth, even with anaesthetic, then help is offered in the following words: 'Would you like me to teach you a very quick and easy way to relax so deeply that while you are here nothing will bother or disturb you half as much as it used to? I use it to relax myself, would you like to see me do it first?' The answer is generally 'Oh yes please, when can we start?' The approach with children differs in that the wording goes 'Would you like to play a game while you are here today? I play this game with lots of children just about your age.'
3 The third group consists of patients referred by doctors and other dentists and for whom dentistry has been impossible for a number of years. Treatment may involve several sessions which may include behaviour modification, imagery conditioning, or the rehearsal techniques described by Smith (1977).

Before launching into a relaxation technique the dentist must consider the patient's feelings about the word 'hypnosis' if it is mentioned. It is only sometimes necessary to mention to a patient that hypnosis is employed. The dentist is providing several suggestions which the patient is at liberty to accept or reject as the need is felt. To allay any fears it may be wise to use the term 'medical hypnosis' to make quite clear the fact that this is a professionally accepted and endorsed method.

A few dentists like to have a special room set aside for hypnosis prior to entering the clinical setting, introducing the patient to the surgery when the treatment is ready to take place. Depending on the severity of the patient's anxiety it may be necessary to have training sessions in the dental chair before being ready for dental treatment. One criticism that is sometimes made of hypnosis is that it is too time-consuming, but in fact this need not be the case. Rapid induction methods combined with suitable post-hypnotic suggestions result in an overall reduction in time spent on treating anxious patients. Hypnosis with the proper safeguards built in does not encourage dependence. As Smith (1977) says, all hypnosis is self-hypnosis.

Hypnosis as a form of sedation is perfect for the dental situation; it costs nothing apart from the time spent and is simple, quick and acceptable. It is introduced to the patient as a natural inherent skill of his or her own which can be drawn upon at the right time in the right place for the right reason. From the operative point of view, induction and recovery can be rapid, and importantly, all the protective reflexes are maintained throughout. The patient feels better on leaving the dentist, and has increased confidence in his or her inherent ability to cope with difficult situations, rather than the after-effect and exhaustion of just having been through a traumatic experience. The anticipation of the next dental appointment is with pleasurable feelings.

Furthermore once the patients have learned a way of accepting dental treatment and absorbed the new-found skill, they can continue to employ it for their own benefit, not only during subsequent dental treatment when no formal induction is needed, but also in many other areas of life.

Induction and deepening techniques

Most dentists use eye fixation followed by progressive relaxation; with relaxation comes calm and ease. Counting and breathing can be combined with suggestions of calmness and descriptions of relaxing imagery throughout the duration of the operation, unless the patient indicates that he or she prefers the dentist to remain silent. Ego-enhancing suggestions are invaluable, as may also be demonstrations of hypnotic responsiveness such as arm levitation, automatic movements and limb catalepsy.

A neat way of showing the patient his or her suggestibility is the 'magic circle' technique which may be administered in the waking state. A circle is drawn on the back of the hand with a ball-pen, the patient is instructed to concentrate very hard to make this area as numb as it can possibly be, and the dentist then demonstrates with a sharp instrument or sterile needle the differing sensation on the skin inside and outside the circle. The patient is then informed that this circle is a personal possession and can be transferred to any part of the body for the right reason at the right time, usually for injection sites. The reaction produced is usually one of great delight, this method being particularly suitable for young teenagers, but applicable to all age-groups.

Visualization and fantasy are enjoyed especially by the very young. Suggestions such as bouncing balloons in a bucket of water or balloons floating to the ceiling before they 'pop and flop into a deep sleep' can be employed to encourage relaxation and co-operation. (See Chapter 10 by Ioannou on applications to children.)

The quicker methods of induction take only two to three minutes and for most dental procedures this is all that is necessary. Dental work can be carried out in the lightest 'trance', the patient being invited to reach whatever depth he or she requires. Patients who are already trained in their own self-hypnosis will give the signal when the dentist can start work, or post-hypnotic suggestions for relaxation may have been given in previous sessions of hypnosis. Most dentists, in fact, use a combination and a variety of induction techniques according to how the needs of the patient are assessed.

Although it has been stated that it is perfectly possible to continue dental work on a patient in the lightest possible stages of hypnosis, sometimes it is advisable to employ deepening techniques. These are useful when a more difficult or prolonged session is planned such as the removal of wisdom teeth, periodontal surgery or multiple crown preparations.

Hypnoanalgesia

Most dentists who use local anaesthetics consider that the time taken to achieve hypnoanalgesia is unreliable and unnecessary, their real objective in using hypnosis being to reduce fear and anxiety, thus promoting calm and comfort. Analgesia using hypnosis alone is variable and it does not automatically follow that a patient in a good depth of trance will not feel pain. However, there are many recorded cases of tooth extraction under hypnoanalgesia alone from Mesmer's time to the present day. With a combination of effective topical anaesthetic and hypnotic techniques, described later, the local anaesthetic can be extremely quick, convenient, effective and safe, and the patient may be sure of not feeling pain during the dental procedure. In general, dentists do not directly test for anaesthesia or any other hypnotic phenomenon, but use their clinical and subjective judgement in conjunction with the patient's appearance, behaviour and verbal reports or ideomotor signalling.

In the case of needle phobias and allergy to lignocaine derivatives (local anaesthetics) it is necessary to spend more time with the patient to achieve the depth of analgesia required. Smith (1977) advocates the use of self-suggested analgesia as this makes it possible for the patient to be totally independent of the hypnotist or dentist.

Hypnosis combined with other methods of sedation

Hypnosis is a valuable adjuvant to relative analgesia (RA) and intravenous sedation (IV), both in the reduction in pharmacological input required to reach the same depth of comfort and in improved healing after surgery with reduction in bleeding and concomitant swelling (Litchfield 1982). With RA, inhalations of even low levels of nitrous oxide result in a greater response, in anxious patients, to suggestions of relaxation, comfort and involvement in imagery, and this increased responsiveness is maintained once administration of gases has ceased.

Harris (1989), working in community dentistry in London with mentally handicapped patients, reported how she has success in gaining increased co-operation from these patients using not only RA but also hypnosis alone.

Other methods of relaxation

Morse (1984) finds that meditation combined with hypnosis is more effective in obtaining the results reported than by using hypnosis alone. His endodontic work involved 35 patients who were asked to relax, close their eyes and silently repeat a simple word of their own choice. As the patients were repeating their words a hypnotic induction was given which included suggestions of numbness. After deepening, 22 of the patients were able to direct the numb feelings to the specific area to be treated. With the other 13, glove anaesthesia was transferred to the relevant area of the mouth. Dental work was started 10 to 15 minutes from when the patient was seated. The effectiveness of the hypnoanalgesia was tested by deep investigation inside the live tooth. The criterion for successful analgesia was lack of movement of the patient. The overall result, with 6 cases requiring no anaesthetic at all, was judged to be successful in so far as of those who needed anaesthetic only half the usual amount was sufficient. The simplicity of the meditational approach may help allay any fears concerning hypnosis that may be present – for example, those relating to being 'out of control'.

Audiotapes may be purchased to play hypnotic inductions to the patient in preparation for treatment and during the treatment session itself. Patients may also be advised to bring into the surgery tape-recordings of their own choice of music to play through personal headphones; a relaxing atmosphere is thus encouraged and the distraction provided by the music helps relieve suffering. The advent of the Sony Walkman, in which tiny headphones plug into the ears, has been an absolute boon to the dentist. The patients drift off into a world of their own! For more anxious people a tailor-made tape is even more effective. Biofeedback machines, skin galvanometers and pulsimeters with auditory feedback are also helpful in the reduction of tension in a wide range of treatment modalities.

Contraindications and precautions

First it is imperative to take a good comprehensive history not only of the dental background of the patient but also medical details, how the patient has previously behaved in medical and dental settings, and what the patient considers to be a normal level of anxiety concerning dental procedures. A knowledge of family background can be useful, particularly in predicting how children will behave in the dental setting. People with depression and schizophrenia and those on drugs indicating mental instability are best avoided when considering hypnosis in case of adverse emotional reactions. Some religious sects object to hypnosis. It is not wise to consider hypnotizing anyone for curiosity alone, or in response to a challenge: 'I bet you can't hypnotize me – go on have a go!' Occasionally during a well-planned hypnotic induction there is resistance; hypnosis cannot be imposed on an unwilling subject.

Abreactions may occur in even the lightest trance, the commonest response being to burst into tears, and reassurance and guidance should be given. Suggestions are also given that this cathartic release will last as long as is necessary for the patient to obtain relief, bearing in mind that it is interrupting the real purpose of the session, namely dental treatment, and that the patient need only recall as much of the experience as is appropriate.

Recently in the dental press (Christian 1989) it has been noted that when the dentist is carrying out treatment, the presence of a chaperone is not so much desirable as essential. This advice was issued concerning the use of benzo-diazepines which when taken can result in sexual fantasies in one in every two hundred women sedated. The dentist, by the very nature of the job, necessarily has to touch the patient and enter the oral cavity of the patient who is lying down in the submissive position and may have the eyes closed as is usual in hypnosis. To protect both parties from misunderstanding, the presence of a chaperone could be considered to be mandatory, especially when, during the hypnotic procedure, visual imagery and fantasy are suggested. Even without fantasy a patient may become so grateful to the dentist there is danger of a strong positive transference or dependency. This is best pre-empted by building in the safeguard of self-dependence for the patient (e.g. teaching self-hypnosis and emphasizing that this is a procedure the patient does for himself or herself whenever he or she considers it useful).

Specific applications of hypnosis

In this section some of the most common problems encountered in dentistry will be examined or re-examined and the role of hypnotic procedures in alleviating these problems will be briefly described.

1 Dental anxiety

In the range from mild anxiety experienced by many people at the dentist (with the patient saying 'I am feeling a bit edgy today' or more familiarly 'I must be your worst patient') through to a near-phobic state, the first consideration is to secure a significant degree of relaxation. The pain threshold is invariably raised in relaxation, the patient experiencing the benefit straight away (see Chapter 6 on applications to pain).

The three categories of patient management were mentioned in the earlier discussion of general principles, but the first formality is to treat all patients as if they are entering a place where they are welcome. Perhaps this could be called the 'pre-hypnotic preparation'. It is fundamental to establish the normality of the situation and lay the foundation of a good two-way communication characterized by confidence, kindness and full attention to the patient. Semantics are crucial in the way of speaking to a patient in order to facilitate the positive motivation for success. For example, the dentist does not say 'This needle will not hurt' but rather 'You will feel a little pressure of my fingers on your gums but you can manage that quite easily now. There you are! Soon you will feel the comforting numbness in the right place for us to work on [not 'drill' or 'cut'] before you soon go back to school [or office, etc.] feeling good.' Many messages are contained in this short statement:

1 Alteration of conception of subjective sensations: hurt has been translated to pressure.
2 Encouragement to build on the success of having already coped with a difficult episode – very few people actually enjoy having injections.

3 Confirmation that what the patient is feeling is right, and it is a good feeling.
4 Time distortion, by anticipating the completion of dental work and suggesting that the good feelings will continue when the patient has left the surgery.

This way of communication could be called 'positive programming' or 'waking hypnosis' in that the patient is experiencing feelings that are suggested to him or her. The patient is experiencing subjective alterations in feelings simply owing to the fact that suggestions are made which he or she chooses to accept.

The second group mentioned under 'General Principles', namely the very anxious dental patients, may be illustrated by the description of a short case history. Mrs G came to my practice as she had heard that I specialize in nervous patients. She had been so petrified of 'the dentist' that she had allowed many of her back teeth to become decayed stumps, and she had gaps at the side which showed when she talked or laughed. She was a charming person in her early sixties who ran a small local business. At her first appointment she was trembling with nerves and she expressed her embarrassment at how awful her teeth must look to me, and said how many times she nearly picked up the telephone to cancel her appointment. I understood her problem and immediately said I could help her by increasing her confidence in herself and in her ability to cope with the dental situation with my guidance, and eventually to be happy with any dentist of her choice. Mrs G learned very quickly to go into hypnosis at our initial meeting, and agreed that if she felt as comfortable at the next session the roots could be extracted using a local anaesthetic administered by injection. I also explained to her what could be done for her mouth to improve her dental health and appearance thereby allowing her to make the most of herself and her own abilities. After six appointments the offending roots had all gone, she no longer needed hypnosis at her dental sessions and a small partial denture was nearing completion.

The third group of referred patients (see 'General Principles') are suffering from the more severe life-disturbing forms of anxiety, and need to be assessed very carefully to judge whether the anxiety is of such a nature that it requires specialized treatment.

Morcas (1984), a general dental practitioner in London, has described his treatment of severe dental anxiety by reciprocal inhibition. The patient was a 29-year-old woman who complained of choking, coughing, trembling and feeling cold at the thought of dental treatment. The sight and sound of the drill made her feel faint. Her treatment over the previous ten years had been only as an emergency patient when she required intravenous sedation. At her last treatment she had a badly swollen arm afterwards and was ill for 24 hours. A comprehensive hierarchy was drawn up. The patient made a list of experiences involving dental treatment: the top item was the most difficult to envisage (instruments in the mouth) and the lowest one was that which could be tolerated without physical symptoms (walking past the surgery door), there being about ten situations in between in descending order of difficulty. The patient underwent hypnotic induction and deepening and the least anxiety-evoking situation was then presented in imagination to the patient with suggestions of relaxation, until the image no longer produced anxiety. The process was repeated on each item in ascending order over seven visits until the patient felt that she could use self-hypnosis to receive local anaesthetic, after which she would alert herself in order to accept dental treatment in her waking state. Her comment at the end of treatment was 'I am so proud. I tell all my friends I am going to the dentist.'

This is obviously a very satisfying and rewarding experience for both the dentist and the patient, but in my opinion a less experienced hypnodontist would be advised to refer such a patient to the appropriate specialist.

2 Dental phobia

The ultimate progression of a particular anxiety is for it to become a phobia. A phobic reaction is one of avoidance and in dentistry this often amounts to total oral neglect, with the attendant clinical dental problems. Opinion is divided as to whether the dentist should be the one to treat a dental phobia. For example, rather surprisingly Rowley (1986) states that it is a mistake to think that a dental phobia is actually a dental problem; he regards it as a psychological problem in which the phobic object is the dentist, the drill and so on.

The phobia may indeed be directed towards a specific object, for example, it may be a needle phobia, but it may also concern the whole dental experience. Individuals with a dental phobia usually suffer from one or more other phobias. In general, except in cases of dental emergency, phobic patients are best referred for the appropriate psychiatric assessment and treatment prior to dental intervention. This issue is also discussed by Kleinhauz *et al.* (1986) who point out that the reports in the dental literature tend to group anxiety (fear and apprehension) and phobia together. They go on to say that the former is treatable in the dental surgery, and is usually very responsive to a sensitive and understanding approach, with or without hypnosis. The latter needs more investigation and treatment than can normally be provided in general practice. There have nevertheless been a number of individual case reports of the treatment of dental phobia by dentists themselves. For example, Fairfull Smith (1978) reports a family successfully treated with hypnotherapy for many problems including dental phobia in two members. Graham (1984) has used hypnosis combined with primal therapy and Baker and Boaz (1983) treated a dental phobic patient by replacing a traumatic memory with a pleasant one; after two sessions the dental phobia was considerably reduced. Other reports include Zwirn and Vartikovski (1978), who recommend indirect hypnotic techniques with uncooperative dental patients, Fairfull Smith (1978), and Hobbs (1982).

There have also been a number of surveys of treatment outcome. For example, Fairfull Smith (1982) described the treatment of 20 dental phobics referred to Glasgow Dental Hospital after all other methods had failed. He used self-hypnosis together with deep-relaxation suggestions, meditation and desensitization with reciprocal inhibition. The success was maintained at two-year follow-up. A Swedish survey (Hakeberg *et al.* 1990) of a ten-year follow-up of 14 patients showed successful treatment for dental phobia and avoidance, one group receiving systematic desensitization and the other premedication with Valium. A significant reduction in dental fear was found, with a better effect for the group which underwent systematic desensitization.

Needle phobics and those who fear injections may be grouped together with those who are allergic to local anaesthetic. Patients with these problems have a strong motive to succeed in using hypnosis and hypnoanalgesia as an alternative to injections.

3 Pain in dentistry

Hypnosis does not automatically produce anaesthesia, but by the very nature of the relaxation techniques used during induction and the distractions employed, painless dentistry is perfectly possible. In using hypnosis the patient learns not only to raise the pain threshold but also to eliminate the fear and promote relaxation (cf. the fear–tension–pain–fear cycle described under 'General Principles'). The sensation of painful, potentially painful, or uncomfortable stimuli can be altered by employing hypnotic techniques. This can be done by a number of means such as the use of direct suggestion (merely suggesting numbness and insensitivity of the relevant area), transference of glove anaesthesia, or images of the 'colour' of pain changing. In the case of transference of glove anaesthesia, the patient is instructed in the ways of producing a profound anaesthesia of the hand and is then asked to rub the tooth or teeth to be operated upon until that part becomes numb. In the procedure employing imagined colours it is suggested to patients that a colour of their own choice (perhaps red) is the colour of their pain, another colour (e.g. yellow) is 'comfort' and a third colour (e.g. blue) is so lacking in sensation, and pain-free, as to be 'completely numb'. The patient is taught to produce anaesthesia by imagining the appropriate area changing colour until numb and insensitive. Finally, the technique of imagining the 'switching off' of certain sensations in the body by turning off an imaginary switch in the 'main control' (the brain) is also useful in achieving anaesthesia. In these methods it is emphasized that the patients will only use them 'in the right place and at the right time'. For other methods of pain control the reader is referred to Chapter 6 by Hart on applications of hypnosis to pain.

4 Gagging and retching

When techniques for hypnoanalgesia are employed it is not only pain which may be controlled but also any unwanted sensations of the oral cavity, particularly when the palate is unduly sensitive; thus gagging and retching during dental procedures may be controlled. No single cause can satisfactorily explain all manifestation of these symptoms. In some cases they may be learned avoidance reactions and in others the manifestations of a defence mechanism. In the former case the dentist may use hypnosis to teach the patient a more adequate method of coping with the anxiety of dental intervention. Where a defence mechanism serves as an inadequate solution for some deep-seated psychodynamic conflict, referral for psychotherapy may be necessary to enable any form of dental treatment to be undertaken.

Conny and Tedesco (1983a, 1983b) emphasize that management of the problem depends on treating the cause and not merely the symptoms. Approaches include clinical techniques, prosthodontic management for denture-wearers, pharmacological and psychological intervention; multiple causes require multiple approaches.

Graham (1987) has a very individual approach to this problem which includes the use of hypnotic exploratory and uncovering techniques, distraction, Neuro-linguistic Programming, and other non-hypnotic procedures. Goldman (1989) described the use of hypnosis in the facilitation of dental treatment for a patient with an 'unusually low retching threshold'. Over several visits the 55-year-old man learned, with the use of hypnosis aimed at desensitization of the palatal mucosa, to accept dental treatment and to manage his own oral hygiene on an improved basis. Other advantages in different aspects of his life were also noted.

Muir and Calvert (1988) reported two case histories of children where not only gagging but also vomiting occurred during impression-taking. Both children had anxiety-related difficulties, but the parents had not sought advice and seemed unaware that anxiety could interfere with dental treatment. The children responded very well to treatment which consisted of simple relaxation exercises with the aid of tape-recorded instructions to be practised at home two or three times a day. GSR biofeedback (feedback of changes in sweating) was also used. (By this method the patient learns to relax by monitoring an auditory response to alterations in skin conductivity.) Parents and children in both cases were pleased that the children continued with wearing their orthodontic appliances. In common with hypnotic treatment methods the accompanying rewards of increased personal self-confidence in each instance meant that the child's quality of life improved in many unexpected areas.

5 Aphthous ulcers and lichen planus

Treatment at the Glasgow Dental Hospital (Craig *et al.* 1982) resulted in 83% success rate in the relief of aphthous ulcers of the mouth. After induction the patients were taught self-hypnosis with the following points built in: deep-relaxation, ego-boosting, meditational mantras and the suggestions 'Confidence, Calmness and Courage'. In a random selection of twelve patients, after eight weeks, aphthous ulcers were completely better for five patients, partially better for five patients, and there was no change for two patients. There was no change for four lichen planus patients.

6 Control of bleeding and salivation

Bleeding may present one of two problems: too much, as in haemorrhaging, or too little, as in dry sockets. Both conditions readily respond to the appropriate suggestions under hypnosis. Haemophiliacs present a real problem when faced with the need to extract a tooth or with any other form of surgery, and are commonly in need of transfusions of large amounts of blood or plasma as well as long periods of hospitalization. Lucas *et al.* (1962) reported the extraction of a total of 114 teeth in 24 haemophiliac patients, none of whom experienced abnormal bleeding. Hypnotic suggestions of reduced bleeding were used in combination with protective splints and the critical packing of sockets.

Excessive salivation occasionally causes a problem during routine dentistry. With the use of hypnosis this can be brought under control usually by direct suggestion of symptom alleviation.

7 *Bruxism*

This is a problem of grinding the teeth together when not eating and it may have many different causes. If it is simply the fact that the teeth do not naturally meet together properly, then this can be cured by merely adjusting the occlusion (bite) and a plate may sometimes be worn at night to rest the jaws together in a balanced bite position. If there is an overlay of stress then hypnosis is included in the treatment programme. When these measures fail then referral to a pain specialist is necessary, particularly if there is any form of facial pain or headaches.

8 *Miscellaneous conditions*

Temporomandibular joint (TMJ) symptoms, myofunctional pain dysfunction syndrome (MPDS), and other atypical head, neck and facial pains, as with bruxism, may present as intractable and of a diffuse nature with an unclear aetiology. The treatment pattern consists of first, careful dental investigation followed by referral, if the condition warrants it, to the appropriate specialist.

9 *Special considerations for children*

Prevention is the best cure and in dealing with children at the dentist there is the ideal opportunity to train a child in correct dental behaviour and also the means of controlling physical feelings. It is so rewarding to work with nervous children and see the change which can be brought about by what are after all very simple means. The parents will be only too grateful that the child's dental appointment has been rendered less of a problem.

Hypnopaedodontics (hypnosis in children's dentistry) may be divided into two types:

1 *Informal*, where the patient responds to 'suggestion therapy' and is encouraged to fantasize, just as when listening to bedtime stories and fairy tales. This is ideally used with the younger age-group, and readily combines with relative analgesia. One rather nervous and fidgety young lad I was treating said that he would rather be out riding his new BMX bike when I asked him 'What would you really like to be doing now?' This was the perfect introduction. I suggested he close his eyes and imagine so hard that he really could feel the handlebars in his hands, the transition from wheeling the bike out of the house to feeling both feet on the pedals, hearing the noise of the wheels on the ground, and maybe smelling the new-mown grass in the park. His head nodded gently at each suggestion, so I went on to say that while he was enjoying himself in the park his dental treatment was proceeding comfortably and gently and he could stay in the park until it was time to go home. The filling was satisfactorily

completed and on invitation the lad woke up, feeling good. He commented
that he had had a terrific ride free-wheeling down an enormous hill that he
had always wanted to tackle!

2 The *formal* approach is preferable for children over 9 years old, using those
methods of induction more suitable for adults. Self-hypnosis and self-
relaxation are taught to obviate the possibility of the child's becoming too
dependent on the dentist. Smith (1977) advocated teaching all children hypnoanaesthesia which they can take with them from dentist to dentist.

Recent findings and future developments

In a paper which I presented at the 11th International Congress of Hypnosis and
Psychosomatic Medicine in Leiden, entitled 'Hypnotherapeutic Practices in
Clinical Dentistry' (Nicolaou 1988), I gave the results of a postal survey that I
had conducted. Questionnaires had been sent to dental surgeons who comprised
approximately one-third or so of members of the BSMDH. From the replies I
received from areas as far apart as Stornoway, Cork, Newcastle, Cardiff and the
Home Counties, it is clear that hypnosis is used by dentists as an adjuvant for
many different conditions. These include the relief of pain and anxiety and the
treatment of conditions such as bruxism, TMJ pains, aphthous ulcers and habits
such as nail biting and thumb sucking. Hypnosis also appears to be used in what
may be termed 'prevention': that is, the promotion of comfort and enhanced
toleration of even the most difficult dental procedures with the result that the
whole dental experience becomes more enjoyable and less stressful for both the
dentist and the patient.

In spite of this, in medical and dental schools throughout Britain very little
is being done to present the subject of hypnosis formally or even to provide information about external courses. The attitude to the subject in most universities
is rather conservative (Scott 1978). Happily there is a recommendation in the
1988 Handbook produced by the Postgraduate Medical Federation's Committee
for Vocational Training for dentists that the newly qualified dentist should have
some experience of hypnosis. There are lectures and demonstrations on the use
of hypnosis in dentistry at the Postgraduate Medical Centres, but those dentists
wishing to pursue their interest in hypnosis following graduation usually do so
in their own time and at their own expense by attending the weekend courses
run by the BSMDH and BSECH.

In a paper discussing the use of audiotapes for hypnotic analgesia in dental
practice, Fairfull Smith (1982) describes how a dentist with limited hypnotic skills
can provide a tape for the patients to listen to before and during dental treatment which is found to be effective in reducing pain and distress to the point
where the dental intervention may be painless. Perhaps this could be a way of
introducing dental students and their patients to the advantages of hypnosis.
The patient can benefit from a procedure which reduces dental pain – real or
anticipated – while at the same time the student can experience the delights of
working with a relaxed patient and gain the knowledge of the means to achieve
this bonus.

In a recent report by Edmunds and Rosen (1989) patient anxiety was identified as a significant problem by 66% of the dentists questioned. 'Patient management' and general anaesthesia were the techniques most commonly employed. It is surprising to note that only 55.3% of dentists in general practice had training in any sedative technique. Of the various methods employed, inhalational sedation (relative analgesia) was most often used for the 5–12-year-old age-group, by 9.9% of the dentists. Intravenous sedation was found to be more commonly used for the over-12s (12.8% of the replies). Oral sedation and hypnosis came last on the list. The survey highlights the frequent occurrence of serious patient anxiety encountered by dentists and the eagerness of dentists to seek postgraduate education, as so little is being taught in dental schools on patient management and sedation and even less on hypnosis.

Further studies are being conducted by the newly formed Behavioural Science in Dentistry Group. At a recent meeting at the University of Manchester, Professor Grant, Dean of the Dental School there, said that behavioural science and its relationship to dental care will be of increasing importance in coming years. As the undergraduate course is to be extended to five years, it is to be anticipated that the subject will become an important part of the teaching of the basic dental science. Further qualifications in hypnosis are, however, desirable and the Certificate of Accreditation of the BSMDH is a step in the right direction. The proposed part-time postgraduate Diploma in Clinical Hypnosis at the Medical and Dental School of the University of Sheffield is deservedly attracting a great deal of interest from the dental profession (M. Heap, personal communication).

It is important also to take notice of the fact that the cover given to the dentist by the Defence Union applies to the use of hypnosis in dental treatment only. The *therapy* for which the clinician is adequately trained in dental school is the *dental treatment*. *Hypnosis* comes into the same range as RA and intravenous sedation, in that dentists who have the training and the skill to administer these adjuvants in the course of carrying out their professional day-to-day operative procedures are their own judge as to their own competence in these fields.

The new graduate is inclined to see all problems encountered by the dentist as dental problems. The more experienced practitioner is able to sift out those difficulties which can be solved in general practice and those which have to be referred to a specialist. The dentist–patient interaction is where so many problems of psychogenic origin may be recognized by the dental practitioner with the correct background knowledge and where the patient may be guided to seek further therapy from the appropriate source.

To teach relaxation, confidence building and tension-relieving strategies can do nothing but good in this modern world of drug abuse and antisocial behaviour. Patient selection and professional values are of paramount importance in planning any course of treatment with a patient. The general opinion of dentists using hypnosis (Nicolaou 1988) is that if each one stays within his or her self-imposed limits, then there should be no objection to the holistic approach so long as he or she has an adequate understanding of normal and abnormal psychology.

References

Baker, S.R. and Boaz, D. (1983) The partial reformation of a traumatic memory of a dental phobia during trance – a case study, *International Journal of Clinical and Experimental Hypnosis* 31: 14–18.

Bramwell, M. and Turner, W.A. (1890) Extraction under hypnotism, *British Dental Journal* 11: 153–4.

Chaplin, S. (1988) Prescribing for the anxious patient, *The Dentist*, October, 16–19.

Christian, C. (1989) Bring back the chaperone, *The Dentist*, September, 44.

Clarke, J.R. and Clarke, D.J. (1987) Hysterical blindness during dental anaesthesia, *British Dental Journal* 162: 267.

Conny, D.J. and Tedesco, L.A. (1983a) The gagging problem in prosthodontic treatment. Part I: description and causes, *Journal of Prosthetic Dentistry* 49: 601–6.

—— (1983b) The gagging problem in prosthodontic treatment. Part II: patient management, *Journal of Prosthetic Dentistry* 49: 757–61.

Craig, S., Fairfull Smith, G.W. and Ferguson, M.M. (1982) The treatment of aphthous stomatitis and lichen planus with hypnotherapy, Paper presented at the *Ninth International Congress of Hypnosis and Psychosomatic Medicine*, Glasgow, August.

Edmunds, D.N. and Rosen, M. (1989) Management of anxiety in dental practice in the UK, *British Dental Journal* 165: 253–5.

Fairfull Smith, G.W. (1978) A case of dental phobia combined with didaskleinophobia (scholinophobia), *Proceedings of the British Society of Medical and Dental Hypnosis* 4: 29–38.

—— (1982) The treatment of dental phobia with meditational and behavioural reorientation and self-hypnotherapy, Paper presented at the *Ninth International Congress of Hypnosis and Psychosomatic Medicine*, Glasgow, August.

Feinman, C. (1987) Showing signs of stress, *The Dentist*, September, 20–22.

Goldman, L. (1989) Low retching threshold, *Proceedings of the British Society of Medical and Dental Hypnosis* 6: 24–5.

Graham, G. (1984) First line trauma resulting in dental phobia and its treatment – a pilot study, *Hypnos* 11: 218–21.

—— (1987) Two case histories of ladies who were unable to wear their dentures without feeling sick and retching, *Hypnos* 14: 134–6.

Green, R.M. and Green, A. (1985) Adult attitudes to dentistry among dental attenders in South Wales, *British Dental Journal* 15: 157–60.

Hakeberg, M., Bergren, U. and Carlsson, S.G. (1990) Patient's fear successfully treated, *Scandinavian Journal of Dental Research* 98: 53–9.

Harris, S. (1989) Hypnosis in the mentally handicapped, Paper presented at the Royal Society of Medicine, Hypnosis and Psychosomatic Medicine Section, April, London.

Hobbs, D.A. (1982) Desensitisation by retrograde hypnosis of dental phobic patients, Paper presented to the *Ninth International Congress of Hypnosis and Psychosomatic Medicine*, Glasgow, August.

Kent, G. (1984) Anxiety, pain and type of dental procedure, *Behaviour Research and Therapy* 22: 465–70.

Kleinhauz, M., Eli, T. and Rubinstein, Z. (1986) Treatment of dental and dental-related behavioral dysfunction in a consultative outpatients clinic: a preliminary report, *Hypnos* 13: 77–83.

Litchfield, N.B. (1982) A study of the effectiveness of hypnosis prior to intravenous diazepam in reducing complications of adverse psychological reaction and prolonged recovery, *Australian Journal of Clinical and Experimental Hypnosis* 10: 57–65.

Lindsay, S.J.F., Humphries, G. and Barnaby, G.J. (1987) Expectations and preferences for routine dentistry in anxious adult patients, *British Dental Journal* 163: 120–24.

Lucas, O.N., Finkelman, N. and Tocantins, L.M. (1962) Management of tooth extractions in haemophiliacs by the combined use of hypnotic suggestion, protective splints and packing of sockets, *Journal of Oral Surgery and Anesthetics in Hospital Dental Service* 20: 488–500.

Morcas, B.A. (1984) The treatment of anxiety by reciprocal inhibition under hypnosis, *British Dental Journal* 157: 68.

Morse, D.R. (1984) An exploratory study of the use of meditation alone and in combination with hypnosis in clinical dentistry, *Hypnos* 11: 87–91.

Muir, J.D. and Calvert, E.J. (1988) Vomiting during the taking of dental impressions. Two case reports on the use of psychological techniques, *British Dental Journal* 165: 139–41.

Nicolaou, P.E. (1988) Should professionals stick to their own lasts? One hypnodontist's point of view, *British Journal of Experimental and Clinical Hypnosis* 5: 158–60.

Rowley, D.T. (1986) *Hypnosis and Hypnotherapy*, London: Croom Helm.

Ryder, M. and Wright, P.A. (1988) Dental sedation: a review, *British Dental Journal* 165: 207–16.

Scott, D.L. (1978) University training in medical and dental hypnosis, *Proceedings of the British Society of Medical and Dental Hypnosis* 4: 13–30.

Smith, R. (1977) *A Primer of Hypnosis*, Bristol: Stonebridge Press.

Wardle, J. (1982) Fear of dentistry, *British Journal of Medical Psychology* 55: 119–26.

Wookey, E.E. (1938) Uses and limitations of hypnosis in dental treatment, *British Dental Journal* 562–8.

Woolgrove, J.C., Atkins, J. and Cumberbatch, N.G. (1980) Will it hurt? Pain and fear in the dentist's chair, Paper presented to the British Association for the Advancement of Science.

Zwirn, M. and Vartikovski, R. (1988) Integration of desensitization and indirect hypnotic techniques for the non-cooperative dental patient, *Abstracts of the International Congress of the Israel Society of Hypnosis in Psychotherapy and Psychosomatic Medicine* 25.

10

Hypnotherapy with children

CHRISSI IOANNOU

Introduction

Hypnosis with children has been described as an intense involvement in imagination (Hilgard 1970). Children respond readily to hypnosis because of their imaginative involvement (Erickson 1958, Ambrose 1961, Gardner 1974) and consequently make excellent hypnotic subjects. Imaginative involvement and hypnotizability in children are probably related to several aspects of cognitive and emotional development described by Gardner (1974): (i) A capacity for focused attention, immersion and absorption in the present; (ii) concrete literal thinking; (iii) love of magic, limited reality testing, and readiness to alternate between reality and fantasy; (iv) intensity of feeling states; and (v) openness to new ideas and experiences.

While early uses of hypnotic techniques with children can be found in the Old and New Testaments, modern historical accounts began with Mesmer in the late 18th century. Reviews of paediatric hypnotherapy and bibliographies have been published by Weitzenhoffer (1959) – 86 references from 1886 to 1959 – and by Gardner (1980) – 114 references from 1955 to 1980, mainly in American journals. The latter showed a significant revival of interest in child hypnotherapy in the USA in the 1960s and 1970s. In Britain interest grew from the formation of the British Society of Experimental and Clinical Hypnosis (BSECH) in 1978. Membership was open to clinical and educational psychologists, doctors, dentists, experimental psychologists and a few others. The result of this interest was that hypnotherapy was more available to children with a range of problems and in a range of settings, such as schools, assessment centres, paediatrics, and child psychiatry. This chapter will describe the state of the art in child hypnotherapy, the main hypnotic methods utilized with children, specific applications to some major problems, research, and future developments.

It is widely accepted that children make better hypnotic subjects than adults. Hypnotic responsiveness in children can be measured by the Children's Hypnotic Susceptibility Scale (CHSS) or the Stanford Hypnotic Clinical Scale for Children

(SHCSC). The CHSS (London 1963) consists of 22 items including visual, auditory and sensory hallucinations. The scale's disadvantage is that it requires 45-60 minutes to administer. The SHCSC (Morgan and Hilgard 1979) only requires 20 minutes to administer and is therefore of more practical value to the clinician. The SHCSC includes two forms, one for children aged 6-16 years and a modified form for younger children aged 4-8 years. The modified form includes an active imagination induction, avoiding eye closure which many young children resist, and six test items. The form for older children includes an eye-fixation induction (face on thumb-nail) with relaxation, and the following seven test items: hand lowering, arm rigidity, visual and auditory hallucination, dream, age-regression and post-hypnotic response. This last item is omitted in the modified version. The scale is of value because the child's responses may help the clinician select appropriate methods, it demonstrates to the child how responsive he or she is, and the child's hypnotic responsiveness on the scale can be related to clinical outcome. This helps the clinician assess whether improvements are due to hypnotherapy or to non-specific aspects of treatment (Zeltzer and LeBaron 1986).

The repeated finding of studies on hypnotic responsiveness is of a modest curvilinear relationship with age, with a peak in middle childhood followed by a gradual slight decline into adulthood (London and Cooper 1969, Morgan and Hilgard 1973, 1979). In one study (London 1962), however, of 40 children aged 5-11, children in the middle years were found to be good simulators of hypnosis. London and Cooper (1969) in their standardization sample of 250 children aged 5-16 found large standard deviations for all age-groups, suggesting wide variations in children's responses at all ages. The data did, however, show children to be more responsive to hypnosis than adults. Changes in hypnotic responsiveness with age are explained in terms of a decline in imaginative skills.

Why do children make better hypnotic subjects than adults? Reference has already been made to children's imaginative skills which are easier to access than adults. There are a number of correlates of hypnotic responsiveness in children although a cohesive theory is lacking. The term 'responsiveness' is used rather than 'susceptibility' to show that the capacity to experience hypnosis is a talent of the child and not the therapist (Gardner and Olness 1981). Theories of child development, research, and clinical observations suggest a number of correlates and these are discussed by Gardner and Olness (1981), who draw attention to the following:

1 The relationship between age and hypnotic responsiveness (see earlier).
2 Boys and girls do not differ in hypnotic responsiveness.
3 Children of different ages respond to different induction methods.
4 There is some evidence for a genetic contribution to hypnotizability, although environmental influences and their interaction are also important.
5 There is a positive although modest relationship between intelligence and hypnotizability.
6 EEG studies have found hypnotic responsiveness to be significantly correlated with alpha duration when the child's eyes were open but not closed.
7 Children with high hypnotic susceptibility have been observed to show high

achievement motivation. In this respect children's responsiveness has been related to their desire for mastery and understanding of their environment (Erickson 1958).

8 Children's attitudes to adults may be important; it has been suggested that children are responsive in hypnotherapy because they are predisposed to trust adults, and unlike adults they do not experience anxiety over control (Gardner 1974).

Imaginative involvement seems to be central to hypnosis with children. In adults the positive relationship between imaginative involvement and hypnotizability is well established. J.R. Hilgard (1970) found that highly hypnotizable young adults enjoyed imaginative experiences in childhood and that their parents reinforced fantasy or did not interfere with it. Further support for the relationship between hypnotizability and the development of imaginative involvement in childhood was provided by LeBaron *et al.* (1988). The precursors of hypnotic behaviour are believed to be pretend or make-believe play beginning at age 2 or 3 years, referred to as 'protohypnosis' (Hilgard and LeBaron 1984).

Hypnotherapy may involve any model of therapeutic intervention – for example, behavioural, psychodynamic, or cognitive. It is vital that the therapist is a child-care professional trained in assessment and therapy with children. In other words, he or she should be a therapist trained to work with children first, and a hypnotherapist second. Furthermore, the therapist should be able to apply treatments with or without hypnosis. (The reader not familiar with the range of psychological treatments for childhood disorders should refer to Rutter and Hersov (1985).) The choice of hypnotherapeutic techniques will depend on the child's problem; child characteristics such as age, intelligence and presence of handicaps; the therapist's theoretical orientation; and situational variables. The focus of treatment is an issue which arises at the initial assessment: the therapist must decide on the most effective place to intervene, that is, whether to undertake individual therapy with the child, triadic work with the parents, or family therapy. Of course the decision partly depends on where the therapist construes the problem to be. A child focus would involve psychotherapy which may or may not include hypnotherapy. Hypnotherapy may be the primary therapy or an adjunct to therapy.

Hypnotherapeutic approaches

General principles

Before undertaking hypnotherapy, the therapist must establish rapport with the child and enquire about his or her interests, likes and dislikes, favourite activities, television programmes and fantasies. Misconceptions about hypnosis should be clarified by asking the child what he or she knows about hypnosis. Generally, younger children do not have misconceptions or anxieties and tend to know little or nothing about hypnosis. This didactic session seems more appropriate for adolescents who need to be reassured about being in control. The therapist should have already made a thorough assessment of the presenting problem.

The choice of induction method will depend on the therapist's style and creativity and the child's age and development, likes, interests and hypnotic talent. The therapist must be flexible and be prepared to use a different method if one is not successful. Children enjoy fantasy inductions which capture their imagination and attention. This is the purpose of hypnotic inductions with children. This involvement in fantasy then permits the child to disengage from some aspect of the environment (such as an unpleasant medical procedure) by dissociation. Zeltzer and LeBaron (1986) describe how children respond differently to hypnosis at different age-levels. Pre-school children are not able to internalize imaginative involvement and therefore respond to hypnosis in an active way. Older children can experience hypnosis in an internalized way, focusing their attention on fantasies and images. By adolescence this is enhanced by a greater verbal and cognitive ability. While adolescents will respond to any adult induction method, formal inductions are not necessary with children (Erickson 1958). Pre-school children respond best to active play-oriented inductions. Props are very helpful such as soap bubbles, or toys or puppets, which all require the child's eyes to be open. Children, unlike adults, tend to be fidgety and distractable during hypnosis, and may open and close their eyes or refuse to close them at all. It is their absorption in the images and fantasy which indicates the level of responsiveness. Children's involvement in fantasy can be assessed by enquiring whether an experience felt real or whether they just thought about it. Eye closure is not necessary to induction and has been found the most difficult item for children (London and Cooper 1969). Children can be encouraged to close their eyes by being told that it will be easier to imagine some things with their eyes closed. Gardner and Olness (1981) avoid particular words which may have negative connotations for the young child, such as 'sleepy', 'drowsy' and 'tired'.

Induction techniques have been described in detail by Gardner and Olness (1981). Further methods may be found in Hilgard and LeBaron (1984). Inductions described are permissive and encourage children's active involvement, participation and mastery; authoritarian methods are not recommended with children. Induction methods described are mechanical or ideomotor (e.g. eye fixation or hand levitation) and imagery and fantasy techniques (e.g. riding on a magic blanket). These ideomotor methods are helpful in enhancing imaginative involvement. Focusing the child's attention on sensory details of the experience such as what he or she can see, feel, or hear enhances dissociation further.

Children of different ages prefer different induction methods. Gardner and Olness (1981) list induction methods by age. Methods may be utilized flexibly by the therapist's bearing in mind the child's age and cognitive and social development. The child's sense of adventure, curiosity and challenge may be utilized. For example, an anxious child with sleep disturbance may be asked 'I wonder how Dr Who manages to take a nap with all those Daleks around?' (Gibson and Heap 1990). Hypnotic stages like induction, deepening, treatment and ego strengthening, may sometimes be indistinguishable from one another. Indeed, this is evident in story-telling techniques (to be described later), which form the entire therapeutic procedure. Challenges such as suggestions for not being able to open the eyes should be used cautiously as they may create anxiety (Gibson and Heap 1990).

Progressive relaxation and breathing exercises can be made interesting by accompanied imagery such as blowing soap bubbles, or blowing out candles on a magic cake. Some methods used with adults may be adapted for children, provided that appropriate language and imagery are used. This might include variations of the clenched-fist technique to release tension in anxious children (Gibson and Heap 1990). Therapeutic suggestions may be delivered directly or indirectly by story or metaphor. Karle and Boys (1987) emphasize the importance of the therapist's use of appropriate language. They suggest that an understanding of the language used by the child and family is important, thus avoiding any misunderstanding by the child.

Another important consideration prior to therapy is whether the child requests his or her parent to be present. Young or anxious children usually request their parent to be present. The therapist may make a practice of asking children about their preference. If the parent is present, this can often be utilized by having the child sit on his or her lap or including the parent as co-therapist. Parents are rarely unhelpful when provided with a rationale of the treatment plan (Karle and Boys 1987).

Induction methods

Gardner and Olness (1981) present a sample of hypnotic induction techniques in detail. Any induction method may be used and methods may be combined creatively. Induction methods include visual, auditory and movement imagery, story-telling, ideomotor techniques, progressive relaxation, distraction and utilization methods. Some of the common hypnotic methods will be presented in the following pages. Interested readers should refer to the literature (Gardner and Olness 1981, Hilgard and LeBaron 1984, Karle and Boys 1987, Gibson and Heap 1990) for further ideas on induction methods, and they may also invent their own.

Eye fixation on coin

The child is asked to hold the coin between the thumb and forefinger with the hand elevated at arm's length while suggestions for arm and eye heaviness are given as well as for relaxation and comfort. The child's attention can be heightened by drawing a face on the thumb-nail and asking him or her to look at that or the coin. The therapist can suggest that when the fingers are tired the coin will fall to the floor where the child may find it later. Young children may enjoy having a favourite soft toy hold the coin. Although eye closure has been found to be the most difficult item for children compared to adults (London and Cooper 1969), this can be successful if a foreign coin is used which is unfamiliar to the child (Karle and Boys 1987). The child can be given the special coin to practise self-hypnosis with.

Television fantasy

The therapist may prefer this method which involves children being told to close their eyes and imagine a big television set with good colour and a remote-control switch with which they can choose their favourite programme. They are told that if it is interesting they can take part in it if they want to and that the therapist's voice is like their mum's voice when they are busy watching TV and do not want to be disturbed (Benson 1984a, 1988). Hypnotic or post-hypnotic suggestions may be interspersed, for example, by using the television hero to model or suggest resolution of a problem. Telling the child to close his or her eyes at the beginning overcomes any difficulty with resistance to eye closure at the outset.

Balloon on water
The child is asked to imagine something so vividly that it seems as though it is happening. The child can imagine sitting beside a large tub of water (Karle and Boys 1987) with a balloon floating on top. The child can be asked what colour the balloon might be and to imagine putting his or her hand on top to stop it floating away. Suggestions are given for the balloon to increase in size and push up the child's hand which floats in the air. Further suggestions are given for relaxation and comfort.

Favourite place
A favourite, safe, or happy place may be imagined by the child. The imagery may be intensified by inviting the child to imagine the place so well that it feels like he or she is really there. Suggestions for well-being, relaxation and comfort may be given. The favourite place can provide a valuable dissociative experience for those children undergoing unpleasant medical procedures (Hilgard and LeBaron 1984). It is often included in self-hypnosis for anxiety control or relaxation.

Favourite activity
This is similar to the favourite place except that the child's fantasy is about a favourite activity that he or she likes to do such as cycling, swimming, dancing, a playground activity, or going to the funfair. Active participation is emphasized and the child's attention is drawn to the sensory experiences of the fantasy.

Ideomotor techniques
These techniques require the child to focus on the idea of movement and to *allow* the movement to occur without *making* it happen. A common ideomotor technique is arm levitation. The child imagines a string tied around his or her wrist with a large coloured balloon at the other end floating up in the air. Suggestions for increased lightness in the hand are given. The method is suitable for school-age children although it can be used with younger children. Other examples of this technique include arm heaviness, finger lowering and arm rigidity.

Story techniques in therapy

Young or immature children seem to respond best to story-telling techniques rather than more formal hypnotic methods. A story can be made, incorporating the child's likes, interests and needs. Story-telling can be particularly therapeutic for young children experiencing invasive procedures which may be painful or frightening (Gardner and Olness 1981, Kuttner *et al.* 1988). The story may be original or an adaptation of a favourite story or television programme that the child likes. Therapeutic suggestions for well-being, analgesia, or improvement of the presenting problem can be embedded or interspersed in the story. The technique is more than a distraction. Gardner and Olness (1981) comment on the narrowed focus of attention and alterations in sensation which are also observed in the hypnotic state.

Most children are able to listen to stories by age 4. The story may include indirect suggestions for change such as reduction in itching, anxiety, or pain. Indirect suggestions through personalized fairy-tales have been described by Elkins and Carter (1981) and Levine (1980). The procedure for creating a person-alized fairy-tale involves ascertaining the child's likes and dislikes, particularly favourite fantasy figures, colours, objects and activities. The fairy-tale is then created and it includes the child's likes and fantasy figures who interact with the child in the story. The fantasy figures demonstrate ways of resolving the child's stresses. An audiotape is given to the child to play at bedtime and incorporates suggestions of comfort, relaxation, confidence, and so on.

Crowley and Mills (1985/6) developed story techniques for children utilizing therapeutic metaphor. They elicit object preferences and likes as described above, but also consider the language the child uses as an indicator of his or her 'representational system' (visual, auditory, or kinaesthetic). They believe metaphors are effective because they are processed by the right hemisphere which is presumed to mediate the emotional processes involved in psychogenic sympto-matology. The authors accept, however, that experimental research is required to investigate the elements leading to metaphorical efficacy.

Crowley and Mills (1985/6) reported a case of an 8-year-old boy with secondary enuresis. They used a metaphor about a little elephant called Sammy who had trouble carrying buckets of water at a circus. Indirect suggestions for successful bladder control were given through an old camel who helps Sammy learn to carry water, without spilling, to the right place. The boy had two accidents at one month, and at six-month follow-up the enuresis had ceased.

Callow (1988) has described story techniques with Kathy, a 9-year-old with acute eczema. Four audiotapes of the story were made about a boy who played the flute like an angel. These were posted to Kathy at fortnightly intervals. A piece of music was included on the tape as the 'magic music' to bring about an improvement in her condition. At the end of the story the music is introjected (taken within her) so she no longer needs to hear the music for therapeutic gains to be maintained. Her eczema improved beyond recognition over seven to eight weeks and, although she suffered some relapses over the next twelve months, her skin remained much improved. In addition, she enjoyed improvements in sleep and in her personality.

Fantasy techniques in therapy

The therapist should be prepared to be innovative and creative in using imagina-tive techniques with children. New fantasy techniques can be developed to suit each child's interests. These may include a magic forest, a ride on a roller-coaster at a funfair, or a magic ride on a model aeroplane which the child has made. Other favourites include flying on a magic carpet and travelling in a spaceship (Gibson and Heap 1990). Therapeutic suggestions may be given along with the fantasy.

Tilton (1984) reported on the hypnotic hero technique. After the therapist has ascertained the child's favourite heroes from television, cartoons, books, or imagination, the hero is utilized to help the child with his or her problem while the child is in hypnosis. The therapist delivers suggestions as if they were made by the hero. It has been suggested that young children may follow directions more easily if they appear to come from a revered hero (Gardner 1974). The therapist can increase their effectiveness by also giving the same suggestions in the waking state. Tilton (1984) suggests that this method, which includes self-hypnosis, strengthens the ego, encourages a sense of autonomy, and provides security for the child. A similar method has been used by Jay *et al.* (1985) who used superhero imagery as part of a behavioural package to help children with cancer undergo bone marrow aspirations and lumbar punctures. Although these methods are not referred to as hypnotic, there are elements which are similar to the hypnotic experience such as involvement in imagery. Similar methods have been used to help young children cope with regular blood-testing following renal transplantation (Ioannou 1988).

Benson (1984a) has developed a complete treatment package of hypnotherapy for delinquent and acting-out adolescents. This package is applicable, however, to a wide range of childhood problems. She makes use of symbolic imagery, where hypnotherapy is part of an overall therapeutic strategy which may include extra support in school or environmental changes to reduce external stress. Hypnosis is used for problem solving and strengthening the child's cognitive processes to cope with stress. The method does not use eye fixation or ideomotor techniques such as arm levitation, as adolescents resist authority and control. Benson uses an adaptation of Erickson's method of indirect suggestion (Erickson and Rossi 1979) and guided imagery. Her method begins with a television fantasy induction already described under 'Induction Methods'. Deepening is by a progressive relaxation method, a verbal trigger, and then by counting and imagery of a beach scene. There are four aims to treatment: reduction of anxiety, problem solving, forming goals for the future, and ego-strengthening. An explanation of the sub-conscious is given to the child or adolescent – the subconscious mind being a secret, private part of the mind, where feelings and memories are stored and which also controls habits. The child is reminded that during hypnosis, he or she has control over the subconscious mind and is therefore able to change habits, and learn new ones, such as being calm and relaxed. Self-hypnosis is taught by imagining a television programme and then a descent of twenty steps to a beach. While in hypnosis, the child can focus on habits which need to be changed. Problem solving is carried out by inviting the child to imagine a desk with lots of drawers containing everything to do with his or her life. It requires dusting and tidying; any problems are put to one side and the child signals when this has been done by a finger signal. The child then imagines that the problems are wrapped up in a paper parcel, each problem being labelled on one side, with on the other side ideas as to its resolution. If the child does not know how to resolve the problem, counselling and help are given.

Age-regression may be used if necessary. It is explained to the child that sometimes problems have their roots in the past and were not sorted out at the time, and that it may be necessary to dig up the roots to get rid of the problem. The therapist counts backwards from the child's age and the child indicates when a problem age is reached. The problem is discussed and counselling given as appropriate. Desensitization for anxiety or specific phobias, such as exam nerves or school phobia, may also be given at this point.

The child is encouraged to plan for the future by imagining a crystal ball and getting a clear picture of how he or she would like to be by the age of 20. This picture of the child's future is placed in the middle of a maze – either one with real hedges or a comic maze. The task is to trace a path from the outside to the middle of the maze. The child indicates when this is achieved and lets the therapist know if obstacles are found on the way. These usually symbolize obstacles to treatment and they are explored. The child is helped to reach the goal and further help is given if the obstacles cannot be overcome easily.

Ego-strengthening requires the child to imagine making some very special biscuits, the ingredients being every positive aspect of the child's life: happy memories, all the good times, positive relationships, and every single good thing the child can find out about himself or herself to put in the bowl. The child is told the mixture is what everyone needs to feel confident, calm and relaxed, safe and happy and ready to tackle any problems that come along. When the child eats the biscuits, they produce a confident, warm feeling. Post-hypnotic suggestions for making more biscuits are given because the child is finding out more good things about himself or herself to put in them.

Benson (1988) recently included two more symbolic fantasies: a computer fantasy which the child can use to reprogram habits by cancelling out bad habits and programming good ones, and an overgrown garden full of weeds (which represent stresses) that the child clears away so that new young plants can grow healthily.

The trance is terminated by the child going back up the twenty steps from the beach when satisfied that he or she has everything needed from the session.

Benson comments on the difficulty in evaluating her package. She has used individual case study as her method of evaluation which consists of qualitative rather than quantitative evidence. She found objective evidence of change difficult to identify despite using a standardized treatment script. The difficulties were in setting up adequate control groups and controlling for differences between therapists (Benson 1989). Subjective reports therefore form the basis of evaluations of this method.

Self-hypnosis

Some writers have discussed self-hypnosis in the context of specific paediatric problems. Self-hypnosis is particularly useful when the problem is recurrent, such as migraine headache or nocturnal enuresis. Advantages in teaching a child self-hypnosis include: (1) a sense of control and mastery is experienced and

(2) frequent reinforcement of therapeutic suggestions and imagery exercises occurs (Gardner and Olness 1981). It is wise to add a didactic session on the proper use of self-hypnosis and safeguards as to when and where to practise. Children can use self-hypnosis easily by having a secret password which they say when they are in a safe or private place or by repeating an induction procedure taught by the therapist, such as eye fixation on a coin. An audiotape with a recorded therapy session or personalized fairy-tale may constitute the self-hypnosis to be practised. Children over 5 or 6 should be responsible for their own self-hypnosis. Younger children may need their parents' presence or active involvement in order to assist them in self-hypnosis.

The main difficulty with self-hypnosis with children is that few children continue to practise beyond about six weeks. Children quickly become bored or forget to practise (Kohen *et al.* 1984). Children may be unwilling to use self-hypnosis if they are not sufficiently motivated to resolve the problem, if they are worried that therapy will end when they are 'better', or because of parental interference.

Indications and contraindications

Hypnotherapy may be used to treat a wide range of childhood disorders but this does not mean that hypnosis is a panacea. Hypnotherapy is underutilized with children, often being used as a last resort when traditional treatment methods have failed. It has particular value in the treatment of pain associated with the illness itself or caused by certain medical procedures. Hypnotherapy is found to be enjoyable by children; there are few complications, response to treatment is more rapid and mastery, increased self-confidence and independence are encouraged.

Contraindications are discussed fully elsewhere (Gardner and Olness 1981). The factors which tend to compromise or contraindicate hypnotherapy include: (1) misconceptions about hypnosis; (2) negative attitudes of significant adults such as parents, medical staff and teachers; (3) situational variables such as acute pain or anxiety, which interfere with the child's attention; (4) when a direct medical or surgical approach is indicated; (5) when alternative treatment is indicated; (6) if the child is not significantly motivated to change, for example, because of secondary gain; and (7) if the symptom is masking severe anxiety or depression or psychopathology and to remove the symptom would result in more severe pathology (Gardner 1978, Gardner and Olness 1981).

Specific applications

Hypnotherapeutic methods have been divided into three broad categories:

1 Supportive ego-enhancing methods which increase the child's self-esteem and promote mastery and autonomy.
2 Symptom-orientated methods which focus on removal of specific physical or emotional symptoms.

3   Dynamic insight-orientated methods which aim to provide symptom relief and ego-strengthening.

Supportive and symptom-orientated methods are more commonly used with children although for many a combination may be employed (Gardner and Olness 1981). There are few paediatric problems which cannot be treated with hypnotherapy, though severe handicap is one. Hypnotherapy may comprise the primary therapy for problems such as nocturnal enuresis, undesirable habits, migraine or tension headache, warts, and pain associated with chronic illness or invasive medical procedures. Hypnotherapy may be used as an adjunct in conditions such as asthma, diabetes, malignancies, haemophilia and other chronic conditions requiring frequent hospitalizations and invasive procedures (Olness 1986).

Kohen *et al.* (1984) confirmed the clinical value of hypnotherapy with children in 505 children and adolescents seen over a period of one year and followed up from four months to two years. Problems included acute pain, enuresis, chronic pain, asthma, encopresis, habit disorders, obesity and anxiety. Of these children and adolescents, 51% achieved complete resolution of their problem, 32% improved significantly, 9% had initial or some improvement, and 7% showed no change. Improvements were noted within one or two clinic visits for over half of the children and adolescents, the average number of visits being four. The authors suggested that prediction of responsiveness to treatment was possible within four visits. Further, children as young as 3 were able to effectively apply self-hypnosis in this study.

Ioannou and Hart (see Chapter 6) surveyed the BSECH membership regarding the use of hypnotherapy in Britain with children and pain. The survey suggested hypnotherapy is most often applied in the treatment of anxiety disorders, followed by paediatric medical problems, pain, learning problems, habit disorders, and behavioural and psychogenic disorders. It appears to be applied less in the areas of paediatric surgery and terminal illness.

Sokel *et al.* (1990) describe their hypnotherapy service for children which they have developed since September 1988 at the Hospital for Sick Children, Great Ormond Street, London. Hypnotherapy is used as an adjunct for a variety of childhood problems including asthma, eczema, migraine, pain, and anxiety and nausea associated with invasive procedures. A symptom-management approach is used, often as part of a wider programme which may include family, marital, or individual (non-hypnotic) therapy. Staff training is carried out under live supervision, although it is not clear whether this continues afterwards. Evaluation of 36 children treated with hypnotherapy from a sample of 51 referred to the team over a six-month period, showed 14 (39%) were 'much improved', 15 (42%) were 'improved', and 7 showed no appreciable change. No child showed deterioration in symptoms following hypnotherapy.

Some of the major problems treated by hypnotherapy are presented below with an emphasis on British practice. The reader is recommended to refer to Gardner and Olness (1981) for a comprehensive description of other problems and treatment approaches.

Pain

Hypnosis offers a valuable contribution to the management of acute or chronic pain in children (see also Chapter 6). This field has seen the most exciting and well-designed empirical studies in child hypnotherapy, mostly in the area of paediatric oncology. Gardner and Olness (1981) and Hilgard and LeBaron (1984) provide authoritative and detailed accounts of hypnotic methods and there are a number of other published accounts, all by American authors. The interested reader is recommended to refer to Zeltzer and LeBaron (1986) for an excellent review of hypnosis for children in pain. Children have a better facility than adults to control pain (Wakeman and Kaplan 1978). Hypnotherapy is effective in helping children reduce pain associated with the illness itself, such as cancer and sickle cell anaemia, fractures, and invasive medical procedures such as injections, bone marrow aspirations, lumbar punctures, change of dressings and debridement for burns, with migraine and tension headache and rheumatic pain, for anaesthesia for minor surgical procedures, and for the terminally ill child.

Gardner and Olness (1981) describe several techniques for hypnoanalgesia which can be used in combination, and involve suggested dissociation either directly or indirectly:

1 Direct suggestions for hypnoanaesthesia, for example, 'just imagine painting numbing medicine onto that part of your body'. Imagery of a pain switch-box can be used to show how pain is transmitted by nerves from different parts of the body to the brain, which then sends a pain 'message' back to the body. The child can imagine a switch-box that can turn off incoming nerve signals.
2 Distancing suggestions such as moving the pain away from the self by imagining that the body part does not belong to oneself, transferring the pain to another part, and moving the self away from the pain by imagining, for example, being in the mountains.
3 Suggestions for feelings antithetical to pain such as comfort, laughter, or relaxation.
4 Distraction techniques such as story-telling, focusing on the procedure or injury by asking the child to describe these in detail, and focusing on a less uncomfortable experience such as cold instead of pain.
5 Directing attention to the pain itself. This may be employed for children who cannot be distracted from the pain but for whom subtle suggestions for change can be given.
6 Reinforcement of pain control by self-hypnosis, which may include the use of audiotapes or parents acting as therapeutic coaches.

While there are a few clinicians using hypnosis for pain management in the UK, there are very few systematic controlled studies. Sokel *et al.* (1990) reported the case of Paul, a 14-year-old, with a four-month history of left lower abdominal pain for which no physiological cause was found. Following individual and family therapy, he was readmitted nine weeks later with increased pain. Paul enjoyed building electrical circuits and this was incorporated into his hypnotic fantasy. He was asked to imagine playing tennis in a relaxed and confident, pain-free way and to imagine his brain as a computer with switches to control different functions, and wires connected to different parts of the body. The sensation in his abdomen was adjusted by an imaginary knob. Suggestions for relaxation and pain relief were also given. This session was recorded on audiotape which he was asked to play twice daily. Pain relief was found to be almost immediate. The next day pain was at a comfortable level during a supervised practice. He was discharged and one month later he returned to school. He coped with occasional episodes of pain with self-hypnosis. At eighteen-month follow-up he remained improved with occasional controllable pain.

Sokel *et al*. (1990) also describe the case of Sean, a 6-year-old with multiple medical problems who was phobic of venepunctures. A story about 'Sooty and Sweep' (Sean's favourite television programme) was used by the therapist and later by mother. Sooty says a magic spell to conjure up an arm-length magic glove which has anaesthetizing properties, and which is invisible and can be put on with mother's help. This was successful in helping Sean to cope with his perception of pain.

Karle and Boys (1987) described the use of hypnotherapy with a 16-year-old boy with chronic renal failure, who had intense pain associated with physiotherapy for severe contractures. The boy had two failed kidney transplants and had developed circulatory inadequacy in his limbs and contractures of his arms and legs, as a result of repeated operations. He screamed violently if his legs were touched and passive movement was found painful also. He entered a trance after the first three attempts and was able to use self-hypnosis after five or six sessions with the therapist. He was taught a method of analgesia using imaginary wiring and switches located at the spine. Analgesia involved switching off nerves which transmitted pain from his legs and hips. The boy was able to reduce the pain associated with manipulation of his arms and legs and enjoyed feelings of mastery and pride when he recovered the use of his legs.

There is little work in the UK by way of controlled systematic research on pain. The author is aware of only one or two clinicians conducting such research. Ioannou (in preparation) is currently comparing hypnotherapy with behavioural management methods in helping diabetic children cope with venepunctures. A pilot study for a similar study with children who had kidney transplants has been completed.

Anxiety

Gardner and Olness (1981) believe that anxiety impinges on many paediatric problems, since almost all illness can cause anxiety. Any other problems seen by the clinician will involve some degree of anxiety such as painful medical procedures, problems in learning, and specific fears and phobias. Hypnotherapy will help reduce anxiety associated with chronic illness, dental procedures, surgery, problems in learning, sleep disorders, phobias, and social anxiety. The reader is referred to Gardner and Olness (1981) for a discussion of specific treatment approaches and case examples. Methods for anxiety management often include relaxation, desensitization, cognitive restructuring and various fantasy methods to release anxiety and tension. One such example is the metaphor of steam in the boiler of an old steam engine which may be used to signify the discharge of tension (Karle and Boys 1987).

The use of hypnotherapy in educational settings has been reported by a number of writers in the UK. Macmillan (1988) reported on suggestopaedia with children with learning problems. The method was originally developed by Lozanov (1978) and is believed to be an anxiety-reducing, ego-strengthening technique. The method described by Macmillan (1988) involves rhythmic breathing and relaxation, followed by the lesson material (usually spelling) delivered in short bouts with brief pauses between statements. These suggestopaedia techniques have been used by Macmillan in over eighty pupils in groups and individually; however, only the group results are reported. Pupils who seemed to learn well had the best relaxation responses. Opinion is divided as to whether or not suggestopaedia is a hypnotic technique. For example, Lozanov (1978) does not believe it is hypnosis. Some believe that it enables both halves of the brain to function in an integrated way. Others consider that it shares some aspects of hypnosis such as relaxation and suggestion (Macmillan 1988). There is no evidence, however, of the use of imagery and fantasy so common to the hypnotic experience in children. Some assessment of hypnotic susceptibility would be useful in relation to outcome.

Houghton (1988) presented the case of a 12-year-old girl with achievement anxiety who was anxious about spelling, essay writing and reading aloud in class. Eight hypnotherapy sessions focused on low self-esteem, external locus of control, and fear of failure. She was taught self-hypnosis to control anxiety at night and was able to reduce her anxiety at school and over sleep.

Science-fiction imagery was helpful for a 13-year-old boy with multiple congenital physical abnormalities in reducing anxiety over attending school (Elkins and Carter, 1981). A space-flight metaphor was used where the boy imagined mixing confidently with space travellers.

Habit disorders

Hypnotherapy can be effective in treating a variety of habit disorders (see also Chapter 5). Common habits include nocturnal enuresis, hair pulling, facial tics, nail biting, sleep walking and drug abuse. As with any other problem diagnostic assessment is important. If the habit is maintained by dysfunctional family relationships or related emotional problems, other treatment methods may be indicated such as family therapy. If the habit has lost its original meaning or purpose and there is no secondary gain and if the child is motivated to overcome the habit, hypnotherapy may be helpful.

Many habit disorders such as facial tics and hair pulling function to discharge underlying tension. It is important that the parents do not exacerbate habits by punishment or reinforcement. Hypnotherapeutic treatment aims to extinguish the habit and teach other effective ways of discharging anxiety and tension and coping with stress. The child can be encouraged to feel pride and mastery and positive feelings during treatment. Imagery such as a force field preventing the child from pulling his or her hair (Gardner and Olness 1981) or hands becoming like pieces of steel (Karle and Boys 1987) will help to prevent the habit from being discharged. Allowing the underlying tension to be expressed in an alternative, more acceptable way seems important in treatment and in prevention of symptom substitution. One example would be to send the habit from the face to a little finger.

Hypnosis for nocturnal enuresis works well when other traditional methods such as the pad and buzzer have proved unsuccessful. While it does not offer a better prospect of success, the advantage of hypnotherapy is that the child feels in control of his or her treatment. The goal of hypnotherapy is much the same as with the alarm in that it aims to condition the child to wake to a full bladder. A didactic session about the way the bladder works is instructive for the child, including a statement that he or she is the boss of the bladder muscle. The child may be asked if he or she has a middle name or nickname and is then told that this part stays wide awake while the rest of him or her is asleep. This part is told to be fully awake and respond to the child's bladder sensations by waking the sleeping child to inform him or her of the need to use the toilet (Karle and Boys 1987). Self-hypnosis is important and may be presented on audiotape. It should be a positive experience to outweigh any secondary gain from the habit (Karle and Boys 1987). Finally, it is important that the child sees both the advantages in being dry and the disadvantages in continuing to be wet.

There are no controlled trials comparing hypnotherapy with other methods in the treatment of nocturnal enuresis but the clinical evidence is that it works as well as traditional methods. Olness (1975) reported on a series of 40 children aged 4 to 16 treated by self-hypnosis for nocturnal enuresis. The coin technique was used for induction and then the child was instructed to tell himself or herself to wake up when needing to use the toilet. These children were followed from six to twenty-eight months. Of the 40 children, 31 were cured of bedwetting, 6 improved and 3 did not improve. Of the 31 who stopped bedwetting, 28 did so within the first month of treatment. The data are similar to those obtained with conventional approaches.

Hypnotherapy has also been used to treat solvent abuse. O'Connor (1982) studied in the UK the effectiveness of hypnotherapy versus traditional counselling with no hypnotherapy. There were two matched groups of six adolescents who were long-term chronic abusers with a history of resistance to other forms of treatment but who were motivated to continue to try and give up. Five therapy sessions were given with direct suggestions of gradual weaning from solvent abuse, and an emphasis on positive relaxed feelings. The pilot study showed all 6 in the experimental group stopped attending clinic and were cured at 15-week follow-up. Two of the controls stopped glue-sniffing over the five-week experimental period, 3 reduced their intake and 1 showed no change. Hypnotherapy was found to be an effective therapeutic adjunct. However, larger studies are needed with longer follow-up to determine whether or not hypnotherapy is an effective treatment approach with this population.

Skin disorders

Hypnotherapy can be a useful adjunct in the treatment of eczema, particularly with respect to reducing scratching, itching and discomfort. Images of coolness and wetness are helpful here as well as relaxation and a sense of mastery in controlling its progress. Magical imagery can be helpful for young children (Callow 1988) and this may be presented in story or fantasy form. Karle and Boys (1987) treated a 4-year-old girl who had had severe eczema from one week after birth. She had been on continuous medication (corticosteroids, antibiotics and sedatives) since her first few weeks of life. Despite this she scratched and experienced discomfort and her sleep was disturbed. The girl agreed to learn a way to stop her itching. She was asked to imagine a large red balloon tied to her arm which lifted her to fairyland and when she arrived there she was met by her special fairyland kitten. She was escorted to a clearing in the woods to find a magic pool of water which would make her skin better. The cool fresh water was applied to the itchy skin until the itching stopped. When she was comfortable she floated back to the room and opened her eyes. The child was given a magic key (an Italian coin) to use for self-hypnosis so she could 'go to fairyland and the magic pool' whenever she needed. At the second and third sessions hypnotic suggestions were also given that her hand had acquired some magical properties from the pool and she could soothe her itching in the day when she was not able to 'go to fairyland'. This was very successful and good progress was made. All medication was stopped the following week except emulsifying oil in her bath. She stopped scratching and used her 'magic water' when she itched.

Sokel *et al.* (1990) describe the case of a 7-year-old girl with severe atopic eczema exacerbated by hot sticky weather. She liked bright, sunny and cool days and enjoyed stories with a magical fairy-tale element. After an eye fixation induction using a coin, an image of a garden was used with ten steps leading down to a lower garden with a door in a wall, behind which was a special magical place where she had an adventure to decrease the itching. The girl finds herself with characters from the Mary Poppins film and a beautiful wood in the winter-time with snow on the ground and pine trees. Mary Poppins takes her to the King Pine, a spell makes snow fall from the branches, and the girl is instructed to dip her hands in the special snow and apply it to the affected areas to provide relief. Suggestions for continuing relief are made and for self-hypnosis. The story was beneficial, especially at bedtime, in providing relief.

Research developments

A number of recent American studies have confirmed the ability of children to control physiological processes which were once believed to be only under autonomic control. This voluntary control is easier for children than for adults (Olness 1986). The present section will focus on these research developments.

Research has shown that children can control peripheral blood-flow, auditory evoked potentials, transcutaneous oxygen flow, bronchial dilatation, sphincter responses and cardiac rate (Olness 1986). This ability may be applied clinically in the management of various disorders such as asthma and faecal soiling. It requires more study and has important implications for both diagnosis and treatment. Although the particular mechanisms of voluntary control of autonomic responses by adults and children are yet to be determined, results so far are very encouraging. Dikel and Olness (1980) reported on a study of 48 children aged

5–15 years who were tested for their ability to raise and lower temperature in their index finger with either self-hypnosis or biofeedback or with both combined. All groups showed success at warming and cooling. There were no significant differences between groups, even when compared according to age and sex. Interestingly, the authors found children in the biofeedback-only group spontaneously used imagery similar to that produced by self-hypnosis. The results have implications for the treatment of such conditions as warts, migraine headaches, sickle cell anaemia and Reynaud's syndrome.

Olness *et al.* (1987) undertook a comparison of self-hypnosis and propranolol in the treatment of juvenile migraine in 28 children aged 6–12 years. The study was a double-blind placebo-controlled prospective study with a single cross-over comparison. The children were randomly allocated to propranolol or placebo groups and crossed over for three months. The mean number of headaches per child was 13.3 for three months during the placebo period, 14.9 during the propranolol period, and 5.8 during self-hypnosis. The authors found a significant association between reduction in headache frequency and self-hypnosis. The self-hypnosis was practised twice daily. There were three clinic visits which included standard progressive relaxation, pleasant imagery of the child's choice, a pain regulation method of the child's choice, and practice of pain control by hand anaesthesia.

Olness and Conroy (1985) investigated whether children could voluntarily change tissue oxygen and whether children experienced in self-hypnosis could do so to a greater degree than children not so experienced. They studied 11 children aged 7–17, of whom 8 were previously experienced in self-hypnosis. Children listened to a tape-recording describing oxygen function and its transport to the skin, and after stabilization were asked to attempt to increase oxygen. They listened to a taped hypnotic induction with eyes closed; 9 children were able to increase oxygen significantly, 8 of whom had previous self-hypnosis training.

Olness *et al.* (1989) conducted the first study into children's regulation of immune functions. They found children could significantly increase concentrations of salivary immunoglobulin A by self-hypnosis with appropriate suggestions. They randomly allocated 57 children to one of three groups: self-hypnosis with instructions to increase immune substances in saliva as they chose, self-hypnosis with specific instructions, and a control group with no instructions but who received equal time. Children were assessed on the SHCSC (see earlier). Those who were given specific instructions to regulate salivary immunoglobulin A showed significant increases. No relationship was found between SHCSC scores and immunoglobulin changes. The authors concluded that the children's creativity and thought processes were more important to outcome than hypnotic responsiveness.

Future developments

An increasing number of British psychologists are using hypnotherapy with children, although they are still a minority. From published reports it is evident that very few are engaged in systematic empirical research as compared with their American counterparts. Cultural differences in attitudes to publishing papers have been remarked upon (Benson 1984b). Kazdin (1988) comments on the lack of progress in child psychotherapy research in general and in developing effective treatments for children in particular. While there has been a surge of interest in hypnotherapy with children over recent years, it is clear that more research is required within a scientific framework to evaluate group outcome studies of different therapies. The child hypnosis literature contains a number of single-case studies and anecdotal reports; however, the trend is to report more on series of cases and controlled outcome studies. The clinician often looks to the literature for guidance in choosing effective therapies for children. Research is therefore critical and central to identifying effective treatments for children and adolescents. Kazdin (1988) discusses some myths and half-truths which may prevent therapists from conducting research, namely (1) that therapy is too complex and research would misrepresent or oversimplify it; (2) that research is too difficult to conduct; (3) that therapy is an art beyond scrutiny; and (4) that everyone is an individual and standardizing treatment is inappropriate. Other explanations could include low priority given to research or lack of interest.

In addition, revisions are needed in rating scales. Hilgard and LeBaron (1984) suggest that a scale less detailed than the CHSS (London 1963), and one more detailed than the SCHSC (Morgan and Hilgard 1973) is required. The existing scales do not extend to younger children, however. Scales are required to measure hypnotic responsiveness or 'protohypnosis' (see earlier) in pre-school children. A further difficulty is that of biased scales. Normative studies on the SCHSC and CHSS have used subjects only from the middle socio-economic class. Children from diverse social and cultural backgrounds should be included in the normative samples. Sophisticated research regarding correlates of hypnotic responsiveness is also required including such variables as locus of control, anxiety, and self-concept. Further, more research is needed on the role of imaginative involvement and its relationship to hypnotizability in children. Since children respond differently to different induction procedures it is possible that they respond likewise to different hypnotherapeutic suggestions. Some may benefit from direct and others from indirect suggestion. More work needs to clarify which children benefit most from which methods. Benson (1984a, 1988) found in her work that damaged children and adolescents, who are mistrustful and suspicious, responded well to indirect methods.

Hypnotherapy with children can be a powerful tool to facilitate almost any therapeutic intervention. This is evident particularly in the area of pain management. In Britain it is not common practice to use hypnotic methods in paediatrics and it may in fact be discouraged in some centres (Karle and Boys 1987). As Clinical Psychology moves towards a Health Psychology model, we may see an increase in the application of hypnotherapy to paediatric medical problems, to paediatric surgery, and to the needs of the terminally ill child. The value of hypnotherapy has been demonstrated clinically and experimentally. We can look forward to further studies on children's ability to control physiological functions and its application to life-threatening disorders in particular. In Britain only a

small minority of psychologists are undertaking controlled research and without
critical evaluation the value of hypnosis and hypnotherapy with children will not
be fully recognized.

References

Ambrose, G. (1961) *Hypnotherapy with Children*, 2nd edn, London: Staples.
Benson, G. (1984a) Short-term hypnotherapy with delinquent and acting out adolescents,
   British Journal of Experimental and Clinical Hypnosis 1: 19–27.
—— (1984b) Comments on M. Gibson's review of the literature on hypnosis with children,
   British Journal of Experimental and Clinical Hypnosis 1: 43–5.
—— (1988) Hypnosis with difficult adolescents and children, in M. Heap (ed.) *Hypnosis:
   Current Clinical Experimental and Forensic Practices*, London: Croom Helm.
—— (1989) Hypnosis as a therapeutic technique for use by school psychologists, *School
   Psychology International* 10: 113–19.
Callow, G. (1988) The use of storytelling in a case of childhood eczema, Paper presented
   at the *Fifth Annual Conference of the British Society of Experimental and Clinical Hypnosis,*
   London.
Crowley, R.J. and Mills, J.C. (1985/6) The nature and construction of therapeutic
   metaphors for children, *British Journal of Experimental and Clinical Hypnosis* 3: 69–76.
Dikel, W. and Olness, K. (1980) Self-hypnosis, biofeedback, and voluntary peripheral
   temperature control in children, *Pediatrics* 66: 335–40.
Elkins, G. and Carter, B. (1981) Use of a science fiction-based imagery technique in child
   hypnosis, *American Journal of Clinical Hypnosis* 23: 274–7.
Erickson, M.H. (1958) Pediatric hypnotherapy, *American Journal of Clinical Hypnosis*
   1: 25–9.
Erickson, M.H. and Rossi, E.L. (1979) *Hypnotherapy: An Exploratory Casebook*, New York:
   Irvington.
Gardner, G.G. (1974) Hypnosis with children, *International Journal of Clinical and Experi-
   mental Hypnosis* 22: 20–38.
—— (1978) Hypnotherapy in the management of childhood habit disorders, *Journal of
   Pediatrics* 92: 838–40.
—— (1980) Hypnosis with children: selected readings, *International Journal of Clinical and
   Experimental Hypnosis* 28: 289–93.
Gardner, G.G. and Olness, K. (1981) *Hypnosis and Hypnotherapy with Children*, New York:
   Grune & Stratton.
Gibson, H.B. and Heap, M. (1990) *Hypnosis in Therapy*, London: Lawrence Erlbaum.
Hilgard, J.R. (1970) *Personality and Hypnosis: A Study of Imaginative Involvement*, Chicago:
   University of Chicago Press.
Hilgard, J.R. and LeBaron, S. (1984) *Hypnotherapy of Pain in Children with Cancer*, Los Altos,
   Calif.: William Kaufman.
Houghton, D.M. (1988) Hypnosis with anxious school children, in M. Heap (ed.)
   Hypnosis: Current Clinical, Experimental and Forensic Practices, London: Croom Helm.
Ioannou, C. (1988) Helping young children cope with blood tests following transplanta-
   tion, Paper presented at the *Nineteenth European Conference on the Study of Psycho-Social
   Aspects of Children with Chronic Renal Failure*, Cardiff, August–September.
—— (in preparation) Psychological assessment and intervention of acute pain in
   chronically ill children. Ph.D. thesis, University of Leicester.
Jay, S.M., Elliott, C.H., Ozolins, M., Olson, R.A. and Pruitt, S.D. (1985) Behavioural
   management of children's distress during painful medical procedures, *Behaviour Research
   and Therapy* 23: 513–20.

Karle, H.W.A. and Boys, J.H. (1987) *Hypnotherapy: A Practical Handbook*, London: Free Association Books.

Kazdin, A.E. (1988) *Child Psychotherapy: Developing and Identifying Effective Treatments*, New York: Pergamon Press.

Kohen, D.K., Olness, K., Colwell, S.O. and Heimel, A. (1984) The use of relaxation-mental imagery (self hypnosis) in the management of 505 pediatric behavioural encounters, *Developmental and Behavioural Pediatrics* 5: 21-5.

Kuttner, L., Bowman, M. and Teasdale, M. (1988) Psychological treatment of distress, pain and anxiety for young children with cancer, *Developmental and Behavioural Pediatrics* 9: 374-81.

LeBaron, S., Zeltzer, L. and Fanurik, D. (1988) Imaginative involvement and hypnotizability in childhood, *International Journal of Clinical and Experimental Hypnosis* 36: 284-95.

Levine, E.S. (1980) Indirect suggestions through personalized fairy tales for treatment of childhood insomnia, *American Journal of Clinical Hypnosis* 23: 57-63.

London, P. (1962) Hypnosis in children: an experimental approach, *International Journal of Clinical and Experimental Hypnosis* 10: 79-91.

—— (1963) *Children's Hypnotic Susceptibility Scale,* Palo Alto, Calif.: Consulting Psychologists Press.

London, P. and Cooper, L. (1969) Norms of hypnotic susceptibility in children, *Developmental Psychology* 1: 113-24.

Lozanov, G. (1978) *Suggestology and Outlines of Suggestopaedia*, London: Gordon & Breach.

Macmillan, P.W. (1988) The use of hypnosis and suggestopaedia in children with learning problems, in M. Heap (ed.) *Hypnosis: Current Clinical, Experimental and Forensic Practices*, London: Croom Helm.

Morgan, A.H. and Hilgard, E.R. (1973) Age differences in susceptibility to hypnosis, *International Journal of Clinical and Experimental Hypnosis* 21: 78-85.

Morgan, A.H. and Hilgard, J.R. (1979) Stanford Hypnotic Clinical Scale for Children, *American Journal of Clinical Hypnosis* 21: 155-69.

O'Connor, D. (1982) The use of suggestion techniques with adolescents in the treatment of glue sniffing and solvent abuse, *Human Toxicology* 1: 313-20.

Olness, K. (1975) The use of self-hypnosis in the treatment of childhood nocturnal enuresis: a report on forty patients, *Clinical Pediatrics* 14: 273-9.

—— (1986) Hypnotherapy with children: new approach to solving common pediatric problems, *Postgraduate Medicine* 79: 95-105.

Olness, K. and Conroy, M.M. (1985) A pilot study of voluntary control of transcutaneous PO2 by children: a brief communication, *Pediatrics* 33: 1-5.

Olness, K., Culbert, T. and Uden, D. (1989) Self regulation of salivary immunoglobulin A by children, *Pediatrics* 83: 66-71.

Olness, K., Macdonald, T. and Uden, D.L. (1987) Comparison of self-hypnosis and propranolol in the treatment of juvenile classic migraine, *Pediatrics* 79: 593-7.

Rutter, M. and Hersov, L. (eds) (1985) *Child and Adolescent Psychiatry: Modern Approaches*, London: Blackwell Scientific Publications.

Sokel, B., Lansdown, R. and Kent, A. (1990) The development of a hypnotherapy service for children, *Child Care, Health and Development* 16: 227-33.

Tilton, P. (1984) The hypnotic hero: a technique for hypnosis with children, *International Journal of Clinical and Experimental Hypnosis* 32: 366-75.

Wakeman, R.J. and Kaplan, J.Z. (1978) An experimental study of hypnosis in painful burns, *American Journal of Clinical Hypnosis* 21: 3-12.

Weitzenhoffer, A.M. (1959) A bibliography of hypnotism in pediatrics, *American Journal of Clinical Hypnosis* 2: 92-5.

Zeltzer, L. and LeBaron, S. (1986) The hypnotic treatment of children in pain, *Advances in Developmental Pediatrics* 7: 197-234.

11

Professional and
ethical issues

HELLMUT W.A. KARLE

Introduction

Well over fifty years ago, Hilaire Belloc wrote a verse that he entitled: 'The Microbe'. This concluded with words which are as relevant today as they were then and as trenchantly applicable to the subject of this book as to their original target:

> . . . scientists who ought to know
> Assure us that it must be so.
> Oh, let us never, *never*, doubt
> What nobody is sure about.

The preceding chapters of this volume will have introduced new readers to, and reminded others of, the uncertainty, controversy, and sometimes conflict, concerning the nature – even the existence – of hypnosis. It was much easier for the contemporaries of Mesmer, and even those of the young Freud, to deliberate upon the ethical issues in the use of what was, to them, a well-defined phenomenon – a technique, and a process – than it is for us in the light of our more extensive information and the confusion that this has produced.

If, as some eminent researchers consider, hypnosis is no more than role-play, conscious compliance with instruction, response to social pressure, or some other perfectly ordinary and everyday piece of behaviour, then there can be little or no discussion of ethical problems or issues. If, however, hypnotic techniques actually are inherently powerful means of influencing behaviour (as other, equally eminent, practitioners declare) then there *are* questions to address.

For the purposes of this discussion, I shall assume that hypnosis, hypnotic techniques, and hypnotic phenomena have characteristics which set them apart from 'ordinary' or 'normal' waking states, experiences, behaviour, and processes. I shall also limit this discussion to the clinical field and training for clinical applications of hypnosis. Within that, I shall assume that hypnosis is not itself a treatment but the means by which treatment may be *delivered* or *mediated*. I shall divide the discussion into two areas: one based on alleged dangers in the unskilled use, misuse and abuse of hypnotic techniques in one or other form of therapeutic endeavour, the other on the question of public accountability.

The dangers of hypnosis

A search through the *Cumulated Index Medicus* reveals very few publications on ethical questions, problems and opinions in the field of hypnosis. There is a small number of papers concerning possible dangers or deleterious effects attributed to or possibly consequent on the use of hypnosis in certain situations (e.g. Kleinhautz and Eli 1984, 1987, Judd *et al.* 1985, 1986, Milne 1986, Habermann 1987, Mott 1987). Five case studies are presented in these papers in which hypnotic interventions appeared to be responsible for serious damage to patients, and a further six in which untoward reactions followed some degree of carelessness (e.g. in ending the hypnotic state or removing suggested phenomena). The reviews these authors made of the literature noted rather more numerous instances of deleterious effects of hypnotically mediated treatments, and mention also the incidence (largely anecdotal and sometimes of questionable reliability) of undesirable after-effects of 'stage hypnotism'. In addition, Waxman (1988) reports numerous incidents in which exposure to 'stage hypnosis', that is, participation in hypnotic entertainments and demonstrations in theatres and the like, was followed by undesirable and even dangerous effects. The evidence cited by these authors suggests that there can be dangerous sequelae to hypnotic techniques, and that some form of control of the use of such techniques is as necessary as has been thought to be the case in the practice of medicine and surgery.

The British Medical Association has twice taken steps to investigate the reality and the medical utility of hypnosis, and the related topic of what public control may be desirable in the use of such techniques. Two reports have been published as a result (BMA 1892, 1955). Both reports stated that hypnosis had been found to have real effects, and both predictably declared that hypnosis was a *medical* procedure. The first, based not only on examination of the then extant literature but also on experiments carried out by members of the Committee themselves, acknowledged the objective reality of hypnotic phenomena, and stated that these had significant therapeutic potential. The report concluded by recommending restriction of its use to 'medical men' (*sic*). The second, based largely on a search of the literature and evidence submitted by a variety of specialists, suggested that the use of hypnosis should be restricted to 'persons subscribing to the recognized ethical code which governs the relation of doctor and patient', adding that this 'would not preclude its use by a suitably trained psychologist or medical auxiliary of whose competence the medical practitioner was personally satisfied and who would carry out, under medical direction, the treatment of patients selected by the physician.' (BMA 1955).

In short, the committees set up by the BMA to consider hypnosis as a means of treatment, and which produced these reports, clearly believed that hypnosis had real effects, and that some formal control over the use of such techniques was necessary in the public interest.

The International Society of Hypnosis (ISH) and each of its member societies has promulgated an Ethical Code. The discussion which led to the Code adopted by the British Society of Experimental and Clinical Hypnosis (BSECH), and comments on the ISH Code were published in the Bulletin of that Society (BSECH 1982). Membership of BSECH is permitted only on condition that candidates pledge formal adherence to that Code. Other constituent societies of the ISH have similar codes and regulations.

A few years ago, I wrote two papers on the potential dangers to the public from hypnotic treatments offered by people without qualifications in any of the recognized clinical professions – medicine, dentistry, clinical psychology, and so on. These papers were circulated to organizations and individuals who have an interest in such matters: the BMA, the British Society of Medical and Dental Hypnosis (BSMDH), the BSECH, the British Psychological Society, the Department of Health, various members of Parliament who have taken an interest in related topics, the Consumer Association, and various eminent persons. They also went to the major newspapers. The response, where there was any (apart from BSECH and BSMDH who were positively interested), came in one of two forms: demands that I quote chapter and verse of people who have suffered at the hands of 'hypnotherapists' before any interest would be taken, or accusations (sometimes veiled, and sometimes explicit) that a demand for formal or statutory regulation of hypnotic therapies was simply the desire of psychologists and doctors to establish a 'closed shop' for their own profit.[1]

Dr David Waxman had made comparable efforts a few years earlier, which equally ran into the sand of the Home Office's assertion that no one had complained about the activities of 'hypnotherapists', an assertion which appears to be unmodifiable by evidence other than successful court actions.

It seems, therefore, that despite the published evidence and opinions of members of established professions who use hypnosis, and of the BMA itself, those responsible for the government of the nation do not consider that there is a problem, or that there are any dangers to the public stemming from lack of regulation.

The situation in other countries varies greatly. In Australia, for example, one notes that New South Wales has no legislation whatsoever on the use of hypnosis, while Tasmania, the South Australian State and Western Australia have very strong statutory control under the Psychologists Acts (Australia 1973–85).

Queensland differs from all the other Australian states. There, in contrast to those states where the use of hypnosis is restricted to registered psychologists, medical practitioners and dentists, current legislation extends licence to use hypnosis to others appropriately registered. Such registration depends upon successful application to the Psychologists Board of the state either on the grounds of past successful practice and evidence of 'good fame and character' on the part of the applicant, or by means of the wide generalization indicated in the phrase 'is approved by the Board as a person entitled to practise hypnosis for therapeutic purposes' (Australia 1977). The endeavours of the Australian Society of Hypnosis to obtain more restrictive legislation in this state has effectively been blocked for some years by the small but apparently influential lobby of 'lay hypnotherapists'.[2]

A similar variation, from no legislation at all to rigid and narrowly determined restriction of the use of hypnosis to registered medical or dental practitioners, and psychologists, is to be found internationally.

Hypnosis is used for clinical purposes (that is to say, to treat disorders, distress, malfunction and pathology), in virtually any and all specialties. A brief scan through the *Handbook of Hypnosis and Psychosomatic Medicine* (Burrows and Dennerstein 1980) will reveal references to virtually the whole gamut of human suffering and medical endeavour, and much the same will be seen in any current book on clinical applications of hypnosis. Unless all the eminent writers on this topic throughout the last century are either mistaken or dishonest, then hypnotic techniques can have significant effects on all physical aspects of human functioning, from the arteries to the viscera, and equally, on psychic processes.

If hypnosis can affect these functions therapeutically, then it can do so *pathogenically*. And if that is the case, it is potentially dangerous. The same argument is, of course, equally true of and applicable to other therapeutic models and techniques. It is notorious in the field of allopathic medicine, for example, that any drug which, in proper dosage, has therapeutic effects, will be pathogenic in excess or when otherwise misapplied. The same is true of other therapies. For example, manipulatory therapies such as chiropractic and osteopathy, to the degree to which they may be therapeutically effective, can do harm, or be pathogenic. Homeopathic and herbal treatments, to the degree to which they produce physiological effects, may also be similarly helpful or harmful. If *anything* affects physical or psychological functioning, the effect can be beneficial – or deleterious.

If this is granted, of hypnosis or herbalism indifferently, then the dual potential applies in at least three forms. First, if the *wrong* treatment is applied; secondly, if the treatment is *mismanaged*; thirdly, if it is applied *with malicious intent*.[3]

Misapplication

Misapplication, that is to say, using the wrong treatment, largely stems from a failure to diagnose, or from misdiagnosis. For example, a common request to anyone who employs hypnotic techniques in therapy, is for help with chronic pain. Suppression of pain or increased pain tolerance is readily achieved with a good proportion of people who make such a request (see Chapter 8). The potential then exists for the sufferer to learn to mask the symptom of a disorder which, if progressive and life-threatening, may place him or her in danger – at least of not seeking appropriate diagnosis and treatment until the disorder is further advanced and perhaps even too advanced for successful treatment to be undertaken. If the pain, for example, is due to a carcinoma which has not been detected, pain control obtained through hypnosis is the *wrong* treatment. Judd *et al.* (1985), quoting Rosen (1960) cites also the finding that severe depressive states sometimes present in the disguise of somatic pain. Hypnotic treatment in such cases 'may uncover a severe depression or be followed by a suicide attempt'.

Similarly, an individual complaining of obsessive ruminative thoughts can be aided to mask these, and may develop psychotic disintegration (see also

Kleinhautz and Eli 1987: 156). In such instances, whatever technique is employed through hypnosis, would be the *wrong* treatment.

This is, to be sure, no more than a roundabout way of insisting upon the crucial necessity of a proper diagnosis before treatment is decided upon and carried out. This principle applies to each and every form of therapy, whether conventionally medical, heterodox, or psychological.

The ethical codes of all the societies concerned with hypnosis which restrict their membership to conventionally qualified members of the relevant professions,[4] and indeed the codes of some of the independent groups outside these professions, properly insist that practitioners *should not employ hypnotic techniques outside the confines of their existing professional boundaries*, except with the consent or supervision of a person appropriately qualified to treat the condition concerned.

Thus, for example, a clinical psychologist will not treat a client for pain unless the client's medical practitioner approves of such treatment in the particular case and retains responsibility. It appears, however, from time to time, that a similar restraint is considered to be unnecessary in the case of medical and dental practitioners, whose registration is commonly regarded as justifying their intervention in any field of therapy. Thus one might consider that an obstetrician should not attempt to treat depression by means of what Hartland (1971) calls 'uncovering techniques', Edelstein's 'ego state therapy' (Edelstein, 1981), the ideomotor exploratory approaches of Rossi and Cheek (1988), or any other fundamentally *psychological* technique, yet examples are not difficult to find.[5]

One can argue that remaining within the boundaries of competence of one's profession ensures that one is competent to diagnose – or perhaps that one is competent to diagnose *only* within the boundaries of one's profession. It would follow that such restriction would ensure, for hypnotic techniques as well as all other modes of treatment and treatment delivery, that within the limits of human error, the wrong treatment would not be applied. Similarly, if treatment *outside* those limits is undertaken (such as, for example, if a clinical psychologist treats any physical disorder) only when a diagnosis has been made by a competent person, and hypnotically mediated treatment is prescribed and progress monitored by that person, one would regard such treatment as proper, and indeed, 'safe'.

It is sadly but inevitably true that diagnostic skills in the orthodox professions are not perfect, and it is not uncommon for diagnoses to be changed as treatment progresses and new data emerge. It is not only the initial diagnosis that is important to ensure that treatment is appropriate, but continuous monitoring with appropriate knowledge and diagnostic skills must be maintained if the treatment applied is to avoid error.

A common experience for psychologists is to receive referrals from medical practitioners, both generalists and specialists, when a positive diagnosis apparently cannot be made, and it has been concluded that there is no physical pathology present. This may be correct, for example, in cases such as those noted by Rosen (1960) where pain is the only presenting symptom of an underlying severe depression. However, the absence of a positive diagnosis does not mean there is nothing to diagnose: it need mean no more than that either the condition is as yet not clear enough, not advanced enough, or too masked by other factors, to be diagnosed, or that inadequate, insufficient, or insufficiently skilled investigations have been made. The 'default' diagnosis of 'It must be psychological' is not adequate. Such a diagnosis must, if it is to be meaningful and reliable, be a positive one: the condition must be identified within the context of 'psychological', and 'psychological' *tout court* simply will not do. It is *not* a diagnosis.

Whatever the reasons for the absence of a positive diagnosis, it is crucial that the sufferer should remain under the surveillance of an appropriate professional while treatment for whatever symptoms are manifest is carried out.

Hence it follows that when hypnotically mediated treatment for a condition outside the professional competence of the therapist is carried out at the request or with the consent of a competent practitioner, the latter must remain involved throughout the course of treatment, and beyond.

I believe there can be no real argument about this issue, whether we are dealing with hypertension or hysteria, depression or dysmenorrhoea, abdominal pain or anxiety. It should be expected that adherence to their specific professional ethical codes inhibits conscientious members of any of the recognized health-care professions from exceeding their proper briefs. It should here be noted that several of the 'independent' schools, colleges and societies of hypnotherapy which have emerged in the last decade or so, impose a restriction on their members underlining that treatment for all disorders should be undertaken only with the consent of the patient's general practitioner.

Mismanagement

Mismanagement is more complex. A practitioner may have arrived at or been given an appropriate diagnosis and embarked upon an equally appropriate treatment strategy, but the patient's response or reaction may be beyond the therapist's competence to manage. For example, when a patient suffering from a physical or psychosomatic disorder is being trained to apply hypnotic techniques to increasing tolerance of a symptom, it occasionally happens that the patient experiences a strong, sometimes violent, emotional reaction. This phenomenon is reported in innumerable publications spanning the last four decades or more (see Kleinhautz and Eli 1984, 1987, Judd *et al.* 1985, 1986, Milne 1986, and the numerous references cited by these authors).

This may occur because the patient has recovered the memory of a previously repressed traumatic experience and then abreacts. Inexperienced practitioners, or those without appropriate training in the field of psychotherapy are likely to find themselves out of their depth and unable to manage the situation in such a way as to enable the patient to survive this experience without further distress, and possibly even damage.

There are many reactions that occur in response to hypnotic procedures – and sometimes simply through going into hypnosis – which are unexpected, may not be recognized, or may be beyond the competence of the therapist. One patient with whom I worked for a time became apnoeic (i.e. became unable to breathe) when entering the hypnotic state for the first time, and did so on every subsequent occasion at the same point in the induction, until we were able to discover and deal with the unconscious anxiety which precipitated this reaction. More seriously still, there have been reports[6] of respiratory arrest following deep relaxation through hypnosis in certain cases of asthma (see Chapter 8).

Some psychological and psychiatric reactions may also present severe difficulties. The emergence of a secondary personality, where the condition of multiple personality syndrome had not been diagnosed and probably had not been even suspected as possible, is likely to be highly disturbing to anyone without experience in the management and treatment of such conditions. Uncertainty, hesitancy, or failure to recognize the phenomenon, on the part of the therapist is likely to be highly disturbing to the patient and may be damaging.

A violent abreaction, especially when occurring in the context of a highly regressed state, requires confident and skilled handling by the therapist if the patient is not to remain distressed and disturbed after the session is ended.

Where, then, in respect both of diagnosis and of the management of unexpected reactions, does the graduate of one of the training courses which exist outside all the recognized health-care professions stand? Such persons generally will have no medical training, no background in clinical psychology, or in any relevant discipline and academic foundation, and are therefore not recognizably competent in the diagnosis of physical or mental disorders, or in the management of complex and powerful psychological reactions. The fact that the same is true of herbalists, many osteopaths, and of many other 'natural' healing professions, makes the problem neither less important nor more easily solved.

The need for thorough training in the recognition, identification and management of a very wide range of potential reactions and conditions is clearly mandatory for anyone using hypnosis for whatever purpose and with whatever supervision or support. Without this safeguard, patients or clients treated hypnotically may be significantly endangered.

Malicious intent

Let us turn now to the topic of what I earlier termed *malicious intent*. This is not the exclusive province of 'hypnotherapists', whether professionally orthodox or heterodox, nor has it any specificity concerning the use of hypnosis. Therapists of any kind are in a powerful position *vis-à-vis* patients or clients. Patients – even when questioning, doubtful, or actively resistant – by the very fact of seeking help, are more suggestible than in other situations, and put themselves in a posture of submission to a greater or lesser extent. These factors can be, and on occasion are, exploited by members of any profession or practitioners who are members of none.

Some of the characteristics of the hypnotic state (*pace* the controversy concerning the veridicality of that concept), such as profound relaxation, suspension of reality testing, developmental regression and therefore enhanced dependency and submission to authority, and raised suggestibility, further increase the vulnerability of the subject to abuse and exploitation. The intensified transference reported by authorities from Breuer and Freud onwards is also to be seen as increasing the vulnerability of the patient to suggestion and influence, and therefore to abuse.

This is no fantasy. There is a long history of such abuse on the part of medical practitioners and members of other established and regulated professions, and I doubt if my own experience of clients who had undergone abuse at the hands of 'hypnotherapists' is unique. It might be helpful to describe here one such case, although, to preserve anonymity, some personal details have been changed.[7]

A woman aged 22 was referred to me by a clinical psychologist in another hospital. She had been in psychotherapy with my colleague for some six months, and had become impatient with what she felt to be her slow progress, and therefore referred herself to an individual who advertised his practice of hypnotherapy in the local paper. She claimed to my colleague some time later that she had been sexually abused by the 'hypnotherapist', and that he had been able to rape her without resistance on her part because she was 'in hypnosis' at the time.

My colleague sought my opinion as to whether the patient's judgement and self-determination could have been so effectively suspended by hypnotic procedures, and whether further hypnotic treatment at my hands might serve to reduce the resultant distress.

The patient's presenting problems had been anxiety, excessive shyness, difficulty in making relationships, and a degree of depression of mood. The 'hypnotherapist' had agreed to provide treatment, saying that the patient would require ten treatment sessions. From the woman's description, the initial steps in the treatment she had received sounded like wholly appropriate forms of anxiety management. However, after the first few sessions, the 'hypnotherapist' had changed the patient's appointments to a time when the Natural Health Centre in which he worked had closed at the end of the day, and introduced physical contact into his 'treatment'. This contact became increasingly intimate during successive sessions, and finally blatantly sexual.

After – *after* – one session, in which he had removed all her clothing, the patient (so she reported) had protested that she felt this was wrong. The 'hypnotherapist' had explained that, since her anxiety, shyness, and difficulty in forming relationships stemmed from sexual inhibition, his treatment was properly designed to free her from this underlying cause, and his explanation, as she reported it to me, fitted well with the principles of reciprocal inhibition (Wolpe 1958), whatever I, or anyone else, might think of his actions. The woman had remained uneasy and uncertain as to the helpfulness of this procedure and the explanation, but had kept the next appointment, at which the 'hypnotherapist' carried out full sexual intercourse.

It was only then that the woman told the clinical psychologist that she had been attending this 'hypnotherapist' and what had happened. She was, to be sure, in any case rather immature, naive, very submissive, and passive, and one may speculate as to the psychodynamics of her submission to the 'hypnotherapist'. None the less, it was clear that she herself *believed* that she was incapable of resistance or even protest while 'hypnotized', and her belief was effectual in suspending normal judgement and immobilizing her. She did not resist or protest on any occasion until she had been 'brought round' after the event. (See Milne (1986) for a discussion of the possibility of 'hypnotic coercion'.)

If this 'hypnotherapist' had been a member of a statutorily controlled profession, and the patient proved to be able to satisfy the relevant adjudicatory body of the truth of her allegation, disciplinary action would have been automatic. Sexual use of a patient under any circumstances is expressly forbidden by the rules of all professions, and there would be no question of the relevance of the patient's consent: the patient's consent is irrelevant and non-exculpatory under any ethical code. However, the 'hypnotherapist' in question was not on the Medical Register, nor Chartered by any other profession, and claimed only membership of a certain *soi-disant* International Society. Had this patient complained to that society, and established her plea, no doubt the society (if it really exists other than on paper) could have banished that individual from membership. This result would be unlikely to receive any publicity nor would it have any effect on the practice of the culprit.

Her only recourse would have been through the courts, with suits of either assault or breach of the 'duty of care'. In either case, her apparent consent to the 'hypnotherapist's' actions – betokened *inter alia* by her failure to protest or resist at the time of the alleged assault and by her willingness to return for a further session after substantial sexual assault, even after intercourse had taken place – would have been a serious obstacle to succeeding in her suit.

Public accountability

In practical terms, the public have *no* real protection against abuse on the part of self-styled therapists of any kind, unless those assaulted or improperly treated, protest and defend themselves forcefully, and with witnesses, then or immediately after, or exhibit physical symptoms to serve as some corroboration of the allegation. In a profound hypnotic state, with carefully designed preparation, in the seclusion in which an abusive practitioner is likely to shroud himself, and given the heightened dependence of the patient status, very few people would be able to protest and resist in ways that would be provable in court, even were they willing to expose what had happened, including their seeking out of the therapist (and the reasons for that). They would also run the risk of exposing themselves to what the defendant might bring up in public about them, whether true or not.

Further, the very people who are likely to seek help through hypnosis are, almost by definition, self-selected as the least able to be positive, self-assertive and confident, and the most likely to enter a submissive and dependent posture in treatment, and thereby effectively establish all the defence needed by the accused.

In short, the law does not provide any protection for the most vulnerable section of the population against abuse of this and related kinds – and little enough, and with great difficulty, for those individuals with more self-possession and assertiveness.

If an individual practitioner of any therapy exploits and abuses a client, only an appropriately constituted professional body with statutory backing can apply any *effective* sanctions, in the form of deprivation of membership, cancellation of registration, or removal of some form of accreditation, which actually and in legally enforceable ways removes the offender's right to practice. In the field of clinical hypnosis, none of the relevant bodies have the requisite status, and their ethical codes have no power behind them. For example, it is of course true that breach of the BSECH code on the part of a member of that Society can result in the cancellation of the offender's membership, but apart from removing entitlement to attend conferences, courses, and other meetings of that Society and formal deprivation of the right to claim 'MBSECH' (and even that would be difficult to enforce), such action would have no real consequence or restraining effect on that individual's subsequent ability to continue in practice – unlike, for example, being struck off the Medical Register in the case of a medical practitioner. None of the relevant bodies have any legal status, none of them have legally enforceable powers, and none of them are *necessary* to a practitioner of hypnotic therapies.

This weakness is not confined to the field of hypnosis. The terms 'psychotherapy' and 'psychotherapist' have at present no legal status, and may be employed by anyone who chooses to do so. The only formal control on such an individual is the common law of 'duty of care', and the commercial law. An attempt to prove lack of proper care in court against a self-styled therapist of any kind would be daunting, although in recent years there have been two successful criminal prosecutions, one against a medical practitioner accused of using hypnosis to extract large sums of money from a patient, and one against a (doubtfully registered) physiotherapist who was convicted of rape, while allegedly using hypnosis.

The UK Standing Conference on Psychotherapy – the 'Rugby Conference' – has at long last come to a form of agreement over the definition of 'Psychotherapist', but is a long way as yet from obtaining statutory registration and appropriate legal sanctions.

It follows from all this that the safety of the public in terms of improper or unprofessional behaviour on the part of 'hypnotherapists', psychotherapists, counsellors, and all other kinds of practitioners of psychological therapies (and many physical therapies too) demands some form of statutory registration, and an associated limitation of all forms of therapy to registered practitioners. For such registration to have meaning, the public must be effectively informed of the existence and significance of the register. Removal from the register would then be a real sanction, and in particular, the complainant would not be required, as in a criminal suit, to prove that there was no collusion or consent on their part to the abusive, exploitative, unprofessional, or improper action of which complaint was made. The complainant's motives, actions and reactions would be irrelevant to the question of the culpability of the alleged offender.

My own experience, when presenting this problem in the relevant quarters was, as noted before, that there would be no interest anywhere in introducing such legislation until and unless adequate evidence is offered that abuse does take place and that the public does suffer. It seems, therefore, that members of recognized professions would have to collect and assemble evidence of all incidents of abuse which come to their knowledge, and then present it publicly, if statutory regulation were to be considered seriously.

The problem of definition

We may introduce here another area of difficulty: that of definition. 'What', the Rugby Conference asked itself, '*is* psychotherapy?' Similarly, we may ask: 'What *is* hypnosis?' It will be abundantly clear that, even amongst those professions involved with hypnosis, there is no agreement on an answer to this question. To compound the problem further, we must note that if we assume that hypnosis can be defined as a state or as a process,[8] we shall find that hypnotic states and processes are commonly employed in a variety of situations and by a wide range of people, without any overt statement (or even sometimes recognition) that hypnosis is involved.

For example, a professional musician consulted me some years ago for help with a problem for which I thought hypnotic relaxation would be appropriate. At the end of his first explicit experience of hypnosis, the musician laughed, saying that this had been a wholly familiar experience: he had for many years been in the habit of deliberately entering an identical state before beginning a performance, and in fact taught his pupils to do the same. Many athletes, sportsmen, actors and other performers commonly practise such exercises to prepare themselves for performance.

Indeed, anyone familiar with hypnotic techniques attending an antenatal class conducted by a midwife and witnessing the relaxation techniques taught both for use during pregnancy and during labour, will have recognized the hypnotic characteristics of the processes employed. Erna Wright's 'neuromuscular dis-association' (Wright 1979) is as good an example of hypnotically mediated control of normally automatic or involuntary physical processes as one may see anywhere.

If one were, therefore, to attempt to design formal control over hypnotic practices, how would one proceed? By including all essentially hypnotic techniques? That would bring the 'self-hype' preparations of performing artists, athletes and sportsmen, the relaxation techniques of midwives, other nurses and physiotherapists – all techniques which have some or all of the characteristics of hypnosis – in any and all situations and milieux, under the same code of control as specifically therapeutic applications. That, of course, would be wholly impracticable as well as inappropriate, even nonsensical.

Alternatively, one might attempt to limit legislative control over those activities which are presented explicitly under the label 'hypnosis'. That would have no effective result, since alternative labels could easily be substituted by those wishing to avoid public control. 'Mesmeric' treatment, 'animal magnetism', 'suggestopaedia' and many other terms would be (and are) unmistakable to the public, yet would escape the law.

In a similar area, that of the terms 'Psychology' and 'Psychologist', the British Psychological Society solved the problem presented by the impossibility of restricting the use of words which are in common parlance, in the same way as did Accountants, Surveyors and other groups, by prefixing 'Chartered'. There are legal sanctions available which limit use of the title 'Chartered Psychologist' to such persons as are entered on the Register of the BPS. It seems that the Rugby Conference intends to establish a similar register, and such a solution may offer the only practicable means of establishing public control of practitioners.

We might, therefore, work towards the establishment of a Register of Hypnotherapists (much as is the case in Queensland), with a statutory limitation of the title 'Chartered Hypnotherapist' to persons who were able to satisfy a formally constituted and publicly accountable body of their qualifications for entry. It would still be open to any individual to offer the public their services as 'Hypnotherapists', but not as 'Chartered' unless they were appropriately registered with the controlling body. The use of hypnotic techniques would still be freely accessible to anyone, and the definition of hypnosis and its cognates would be side-stepped. I doubt, however, whether Chartered Clinical Psychologists or Medical Practitioners would care to append that title – but they would not need to do so as long as they were entered on the Register or automatically, and explicitly, entitled to employ hypnotic techniques by their prior qualifications and registration. Such practitioners would be under the constraints of their respective professions' ethical codes to employ only such techniques (whether hypnotic or other) as they were trained and qualified to employ. It would be perfectly practicable for certain publicly validated qualifications, or entry in other relevant Registers (the Medical Register, the BPS Register, etc.) to be considered equivalent to entry in the 'Hypnosis Register' and make entry therein redundant.

Advertisements for training courses

Turning now to another area of public protection and accountability, I would begin by quoting two examples of attempted deception. The *Bulletin of the British Psychological Society* a few years ago carried an advertisement for courses in 'Ericksonian Hypnosis' (*sic*) which claimed that the advertisers provided the *most recognised* training in this field in Europe' (my emphasis). I protested to the BPS that this advertisement made a fraudulent claim, and subsequent insertions were more modest.

Secondly, my attention was drawn at another time to an advertisement in various journals of another private institution which claimed that its courses in hypnosis and psychotherapy were validated by the City and Guilds Institute. Having checked with the latter, and been advised that no such validation had been considered, let alone agreed, I complained to the Advertising Standards Authority (ASA), and subsequent advertisements omitted this claim, although the printed literature of the organization concerned continued to bear it, at least for some time.

The public is protected against false claims in formal advertising, and the ASA does have teeth as far as statements and claims in public advertisements are concerned. However, there is no control of any kind over advertising other than in newspapers, journals, magazines and posters. It is perfectly possible to distribute leaflets or circulate brochures to enquirers which contain the most outrageous claims without control or possible sanctions. Such leaflets appear through letter-boxes throughout the country, many of them making claims which the layman would not know how to question or evaluate.

The point at issue here is that the ethical practitioner of 'hypnotherapy', whether a member of a recognized healing profession or not, will not make exaggerated or false claims, but the practitioner unrestrained by ethical considerations is at liberty to claim whatever he pleases in the search for a profitable practice. The same is true, of course, of any marketable product, but while one has relatively easy means of recourse if a vacuum cleaner does not perform as the salesman claimed, one has no effective remedy if hypnotic treatment for – to take two examples at random from a leaflet in my files – duodenal ulceration or baldness, fails to produce the promised effect. One need only imagine how the eyebrows of a magistrate would rise as the plaintiff explained that he had believed the 'hypnotherapist's' claim to cure his ulcer or to regrow his hair by hypnosis, for the point to be made.

Similarly, the impressive claims of both the good and the doubtful self-styled 'colleges', 'schools' and 'institutes', which offer training in hypnotherapy, are difficult if not impossible to check. One example would be what describes itself as an 'International Institute' which offers anyone, with or without any prior educational achievements or professional training, a six months' training course – by correspondence – in 'hypnoanalysis', successful completion of which entitles the fledgeling 'hypnoanalyst' to append a string of letters after his name to state his qualification, and (on payment of the relevant sums) further letters indicating his membership of the 'International Institute'.

The advertisements published by the individual who runs this training course are impeccable. Every claim made is absolutely and unquestionably true. Graduates of this training are indeed qualified (in so far as anyone can be) to run their own practices as 'hypnoanalysts', can indeed append the letters offered after their names (since they do not mimic any controlled letters), and of course can indeed belong to the 'institute', which apparently exists merely by virtue of being given that name.

And yet the advertisement *is* seriously misleading to the naive. The inexplicit but unmistakable implication that the training and qualification offered, and the 'institute' which successful trainees may join, have some recognizable and recognized status is false. No one except the organizer and the graduates of his course 'recognize' the course, the qualification, or the 'institute'. It has no publicly accountable accreditation or validation, it has no links with any public body, and it is not accepted by any public employer. However, nothing of that kind is claimed, and therefore no case lies.

Further, anyone who undertook this or comparable training and found it unsatisfactory, or, for example, if graduates of such courses found themselves unable to persuade a Health Authority or other agency to accept them for employment as therapists, there would be no recourse available to them. The course promises qualification to practise as a 'hypnoanalyst'. Since that title is not otherwise claimed and has no formal status, a dissatisfied customer cannot complain that he has not 'qualified', whatever his subsequent experience of attempting to use that title may be. The course does not promise qualification for any *employment*, nor is any other claim made. There appears no doubt that the course provides precisely what it offers publicly and expressly. Tacit implications, or what may be *read into* the advertisements, or between the lines of the brochure which is sent to enquirers, are not subject to the law on advertising.

Conclusions

It appears, therefore, that the public has little or no protection against a variety of potential dangers. This is certainly the case in terms of the capacity of self-styled 'hypnotherapists' to fulfil their common law 'duty of care'. There is indeed little enough protection in terms of the validity of the claims of 'hypnotherapists' from unaccredited and non-accountable training institutions, and of those institutions themselves, other than the criminal law and legislation concerning commerce generally, principally misrepresentation or breach of contract.

It will be clear that legislation to provide specific protection is improbable because of lack of interest on the part of the relevant bodies and their members, quite apart from the opposition in some quarters to the establishment of what is seen as 'closed-shop' or protectionist controls. Legislation is even more improbable in the light of the great difficulty of devising effective definitions, and in any case, any such control could be so easily side-stepped by the use of alternative words as to make it a dead letter.

It appears, therefore, that if protection of the public is necessary, or at the very least, desirable, then two things are needed: first, that there be instituted a form of registration, statutorily mandated as in, for example, the Register of the BPS or that of the BMA, so that terms such as 'Chartered Hypnotherapist' would be restricted to persons who had achieved qualifications defined by statute, which made them acceptable to a publicly accountable controlling body; and, second, that public education be undertaken to ensure as far as possible that knowledge of the accreditation process, the registration of practitioners, and the public accountability and disciplinary powers of the controlling body, is widely disseminated.

In essence, the professional and ethical issues in the use of hypnosis are essentially little different from those in the use of all therapeutically applied techniques, skills and knowledge. These issues are generally more complex and less easily defined outside the clearly demarcated boundaries of conventional physical medicine. The use of defined groups of drugs and surgery are both easily recognizable, so that the 'practice of medicine without a licence' can be readily outlawed, but psychological techniques, together with many of the 'complementary' or 'alternative' therapies cannot be so treated.

As suggested at the beginning of this chapter, *if* hypnotic techniques have any therapeutic capabilities or powers, then equally they can be harmful – just as harmful as drugs or surgery when applied without appropriate knowledge and skills. The public therefore requires the same protection *vis-à-vis* the use of hypnosis as it has demanded of the use of medical and surgical practice.

Notes

1 I wrote a further paper incorporating the gist of these two papers, the responses I gained to them, and my further thoughts on the topic. This was read at the BSECH Annual Conference, 1989.

2 Personal communication from Dr J. Rodney, President, Queensland Executive, Australian Society of Hypnosis, 1985.

3 Malicious intent: where treatment is designed to exploit the patient for a personal purpose on the part of the practitioner, such as sexual gratification or inappropriate financial
  gain.
4 In the UK these are the British Society of Experimental and Clinical Hypnosis, the
  British Society of Medical and Dental Hypnosis, and the British Society for the Practice
  of Hypnosis in Speech Therapy.
5 Rossi and Cheek (1988); Cheek *is* an obstetrician.
6 These were presented informally at the 9th International Congress of ISH, 1982.
7 Many practitioners can relate comparable stories. Published accounts include Heap
  (1984) and Hoencamp (1989).
8 In one of the papers I wrote for circulation, I attempted a definition which could form
  the basis of legislation. This read as follows:

> Hypnosis shall be defined as any state or process in which specific psychological,
> mental, emotional, physiological and other states, experiences, reactions and
> behavioural manifestations (detailed below) are deliberately evoked or produced
> in a person or group of persons in order to achieve a purpose that has been expressly
> stated or clearly implied, involving or purporting to involve changes in psycho-
> logical, social, sensory or other physical and physiological functions, states or pro-
> cesses or in behaviour in the person or persons undergoing the procedure. Such
> actions as are designed or intended to produce the effects detailed below, or could
> reasonably be expected to produce those effects, shall be considered to be an
> hypnotic induction and to be intended to produce an hypnotic state or process in
> the person or persons intended to undergo or intending to be the subject of the
> effects of those actions.
>
> Hypnosis is characterized by the following features, which may appear in any
> number and combination:
>
> (1) Physical: general muscular relaxation, slowing of vegetative functions (heart
>   and pulse rates, respiration, metabolic processes etc.); paralysis, catalepsy or
>   *flexibilitas cerea*, in one or more parts of the body; any bodily changes following
>   suggestions made by the person or persons conducting the process.
> (2) Psychological: a sense or subjective feeling of relaxation, detachment from
>   perception of the immediate and wider environment; disorientation in time
>   and/or place; reduced awareness of sensory inputs; an awareness of turning
>   attention and perception away from the environment towards internal,
>   physical, cognitive and/or emotional processes; heightened and narrowed
>   attention to whatever is said or done by the person conducting the process, to
>   the progressive exclusion of other stimuli, thoughts, perceptions, memories and
>   feelings; heightened suggestibility, so that suggestions made to the person or
>   persons undergoing this procedure (whether referring to cognitive, emotional
>   or physical experiences and events), are more readily accepted and produce
>   more direct results than would normally be the case for that individual; the
>   sense of reality or reality testing, and logical thinking, in the person or persons
>   undergoing the procedure, are reduced or altered so that illogical and/or
>   unrealistic suggestions are accepted and may be acted upon without internal
>   conflict and/or without the person or persons concerned necessarily being aware
>   of the unreality or illogicality of the suggestions.

References

Australia (1973) Psychological Practices Act, 1973, State of South Australia.
—— (1976) Psychologists Registration Act, 1976, Tasmania.

—— (1976) Psychologists Registration Act, 1976, Western Australia.

—— (1977) Psychologists Act, 1977, State of Queensland.

—— (1978) Psychologists By-Laws, 1978, State of Queensland.

—— (1979) Psychologists Registration Amendment Act, Tasmania.

—— (1980) Statutory Rules, 1980, No. 217, Psychologists Registration Regulations, Tasmania.

—— (1984) Bill: Psychologists Registration Act, 1984, State of Victoria.

—— (1985) Health Practitioners and Allied Professionals Registration Act, 1985, Northern Territory of Australia.

BMA (1892) Statement by a Committee appointed by the BMA to investigate the phenomena of hypnosis. In sub-appendix A of *Appendix X. Supplement to the British Medical Journal* April 23, 1955, 192.

BMA (1955) Medical use of hypnotism: Report of a sub-committee appointed by the Psychological Medicine Group Committee of the B.M.A. *Appendix X. Supplement to the British Medical Journal* April 23, 1955, 190–93.

BSECH (1982) Comments on the ISH Code of Ethics and Resolution, *Bulletin of the British Society of Experimental and Clinical Hypnosis* 5: 77–9.

Burrows, G.D. and Dennerstein, L. (eds) (1980) *Handbook of Hypnosis and Psychosomatic Medicine*, Amsterdam: Elsevier/North-Holland Biomedical Press.

Edelstein, M.G. (1981) *Trauma, Trance and Transformation*, New York: Brunner/Mazel.

Habermann, M.A. (1987) Complications following hypnosis in a psychotic patient with sexual dysfunction treated by a lay hypnotist, *American Journal of Clinical Hypnosis* 29: 166–70.

Hartland, J. (1971) *Medical and Dental Hypnosis and its Clinical Applications*, London: Baillière Tindall.

Heap, M. (1984) Four Victims, *British Journal of Experimental and Clinical Hypnosis* 2: 60–62.

Hoencamp, E., (1989) Sexual coercion and the role of hypnosis in the abused therapeutic relationship, in D. Waxman, D. Pedersen, I. Wilkie and P. Mellett, (eds) *Hypnosis: The Fourth European Congress at Oxford*, London: Whurr Publishers.

Judd, F.K., Burrows, G.D. and Dennerstein, L. (1985) The dangers of hypnosis: a review, *Australian Journal of Clinical and Experimental Hypnosis* 13: 1–15.

—— (1986) Clinicians' perceptions of the adverse effects of hypnosis: a preliminary survey, *Australian Journal of Clinical and Experimental Hypnosis* 13: 49–60.

Kleinhautz, M. and Eli, I. (1984) Misuse of hypnosis: a factor in psychopathology, *American Journal of Clinical Hypnosis* 26: 283–90.

—— (1987) Potential deleterious effects of hypnosis in the clinic, *American Journal of Clinical Hypnosis* 29: 155–9.

Milne, G. (1986) Hypnotic compliance and other hazards, *Australian Journal of Clinical and Experimental Hypnosis* 14: 15–29.

Mott, T., Jr (1987) Adverse reactions in the use of hypnosis, *Australian Journal of Clinical and Experimental Hypnosis* 14: 147–8.

Rosen, H. (1960) Hypnosis: application and misapplication, *Journal of the American Medical Association* 172: 683–7.

Rossi, E.L. and Cheek, D.B. (1988) *Mind–Body Therapy: Methods of Ideodynamic Healing and Hypnosis*, New York: Norton.

Waxman, D. (1988) The problem with stage hypnotism, in M. Heap (ed.) *Hypnosis: Current Clinical, Experimental and Forensic Practices*, London: Croom Helm.

Wolpe, J. (1958) *Psychotherapy by Reciprocal Inhibition*, Stanford, Calif.: Stanford University Press.

Wright, E. (1979) *The New Childbirth*, London: Spar Books.

Name index

Subject index